BLACK FAMILIES IN THERAPY
A Multisystems Approach

BLACK FAMILIES IN THERAPY
A Multisystems Approach

NANCY BOYD-FRANKLIN, Ph.D.

*Department of Psychiatry of the University of Medicine
and Dentistry of New Jersey—New Jersey Medical School*

Foreword by Monica McGoldrick, M.S.W.,
and Paulette Moore Hines, Ph.D.

THE GUILFORD PRESS
New York   London

© 1989 Nancy Boyd-Franklin
Published by The Guilford Press
A Division of Guilford Publications, Inc.
72 Spring Street, New York, NY 10012

Printed in the United States of America

Last digit is print number: 9 8 7

Library of Congress Cataloging-in-Publication Data

Boyd-Franklin, Nancy.
Black families in therapy
Bibliography: p.
Includes index.
1. Afro-Americans families—Mental health. 2. Afro-
Americans—Social conditions. 3. Family psychotherapy.
I. Title.
RC451.5.N4B69   1989   616.89'156'08996073   88-24416
ISBN 0-89862-735-4

To A. J.

*for all of his love and support
and for his belief in me and in this project.*

Foreword

MONICA MCGOLDRICK AND PAULETTE MOORE HINES

Here is the book we've all needed—the essential text for everyone working with Black families—Black as well as White, experienced as well as beginning practitioners. *Black Families in Therapy* has been a long time in coming but it has been well worth the wait. Since the development of the family therapy field we have needed a manual that would provide practical and informed help to clinicians trying to understand the complex and special problems of Black families. Articles and books have appeared here and there but nothing has filled the need for a comprehensive, theoretically clear framework with specific guidelines to help us in working with Black families. Dr. Boyd-Franklin has drawn on her extensive background in teaching and clinical practice to offer us this basic tool in an extraordinarily clear, well-written form.

Dr. Boyd-Franklin demonstrates a remarkable ability to combine theory and practical application. She avoids the pitfalls of over-simplification, on the one hand, and overly academic complexity, which has made other texts impractical and difficult to read, on the other. Black families represent a distinct cultural group, which has at the same time great diversity. Dr. Boyd-Franklin's personal life experience and background, which combines both southern Black and West Indian roots, qualifies her well for the task of suggesting basic patterns and yet reminding us of the importance of the variations in the experiences of different Black families.

Dr. Boyd-Franklin also does an excellent job in dispelling the perjorative myths which have abounded regarding the "deficits" of Black families. She emphasizes the strengths of Black families without covering up their vulnerabilities. She does not avoid the difficult political and societal issues of racism, slavery, and the "victim system," which are essential to any discussion of the Black experience in the United States. She aims to help clinicians to empower Black families to appreciate their strengths; to cope with the institutions of our society, which remain basically racist; and to increase their connectedness with the variety of resources available within their families and culture. She delves into the soul of complex and sensitive issues such as racial identity, skin color, and spirituality. Issues commonly faced by Black couples and single parent and middle-class Black families are discussed along with the implications for therapy.

Black Families in Therapy is replete with useful information and ideas rooted clearly in a historical context which helps us understand the traditional and evolving values of Black families. For example, we learn that religion, which plays a significant role in Black family life, is such an integral part of many African cultures that there is no separate word for it. This fact is especially interesting when we think of the extraordinarily secular nature of the family therapy movement. No wonder there has for so long been such a misfit between most of the leading family therapy models and Black families. So often this has led to the idea of Black families being "bad therapy cases."

Dr. Boyd-Franklin takes us a long way in bridging the gap—the multisystems model that she has developed extends beyond but draws on what is relevant in our clinical training and illustrates through numerous, vivid case examples how we can work effectively with Black families whom we have served so poorly until now. The author emphasizes that the relational aspects of the therapeutic process are paramount for Black families; in so doing, she highlights the need for heightened attention to "use of self" in the training and supervision process.

In one section, Dr. Boyd-Franklin shares a quote from a client of Parnell and Vanderkloot (1989) who describes his sentiments about his therapists as follows: "All the other people were nice and helpful, but it is as if I were out in a canoe in rough water. Everyone else was standing on the shore calling out directions. You dove into the water, swam out, got into the canoe, and showed me a new way to shore" (p. 461). Similarly, readers of this book will find that the author has not just thrown out a life jacket; she is explicit, practical, and as sensitive to the issues of practitioners as she is to the families she describes with such genuine respect. This book is a major contribution to the family therapy field and should be required reading for every family therapist, program administrator, family researcher, and human service professional who works with Black families.

Preface

This book has provided a unique and special opportunity to bring together the scholarly work and research available on Black families with ideas developed from my own clinical experience and practice. It has proved to be both a very exciting and a difficult one to write: exciting to share years of work with Black families, but difficult to struggle with the need to present complex clinical material without replacing old stereotypes with new ones. The cultural and clinical examples presented in this book are intended to widen the lens through which Black families are viewed and to provide the clinician with a series of hypotheses that can be explored and tested out with the families they treat. In this context, the knowledge of the culture of a particular ethnic group expands our view as clinicians rather than limiting it with stereotypical perceptions. Each family can thus be approached as a unique entity. The clinician must test cultural hypotheses and accept or discard them according to his or her experience of the family. Knowledge about culture is a flexible hypothesis and not a rigidly held thesis.

I am particularly aware of the ethnic and cultural diversity that can exist in families because I grew up in a Black family with both Afro-American and Caribbean roots. I was born in Harlem in New York City and raised in the Bronx. My paternal family has southern Black roots and moved to New Jersey and New York from North and South Carolina. My maternal family has its roots in Jamaica in the West Indies.

This book is based on my clinical experiences with Black families over a 14-year period. For eight of those years, I have been a teacher and a supervisor of family therapy cases in the Department of Psychiatry and the Community Mental Health Center of the University of Medicine and Dentistry of New Jersey–New Jersey Medical School (UMDNJ). We serve a predominantly Black population in Newark, New Jersey. I also see a number of Black and White families, couples, and individuals and run therapeutic support groups for Black women in my practice in Brooklyn, New York.

One of the key elements in the treatment of Black families which this book addresses is the therapist's use of self. It is ultimately the therapist's ability to use himself or herself and to connect on a human level with Black families that will make all of the difference in treatment outcome. Therefore, I have chosen to depart from the tradition of many scholarly, research, and clinical publications and to use the first person at appropriate times in this book. Many clinicians are trained to assume a detached, "objective" and somewhat distant clinical posture with their patients. In my experience, this can be counterproductive with Black families and can cause them to leave treatment before therapeutic work can begin. I hope that this book can demonstrate to clinicians that they need not sacrifice professionalism or "therapeutic objectivity" when they extend their humanity to others.

The cases presented in this book are taken from a variety of sources. In some of them, I was the therapist. In the majority of the cases, however, I was the supervisor in our training programs for psychology interns, psychiatry residents, child psychiatry fellows, social work trainees, and clinical staff. A small number of other case examples have been provided by other therapists and colleagues in the field. *All of the names, and in some cases the identifying details, have been changed in order to protect the confidentiality of both the client families and the therapists involved.*

Acknowledgments

I have been very fortunate in the course of writing this book to have had the help and support of many wonderful people along the way. The first of these is my husband, Dr. A. J. Franklin, who gave freely of his love, help, support, and clinical expertise throughout the process. He has brought the concept of role flexibility to a new level. I have also been aided by two very special editors, Beverly Martin who assisted with the early conceptual stages of the book, and Nancy Worman whose careful and thoughtful editing has brought the book to its conclusion. To my typist, Hazel Staloff, I would like to give special thanks for the typing and word processing of many drafts and for her encouragement throughout this project.

During the writing process I have learned the real meaning of "extended family" and have had the encouragement and help of numerous people in my personal and professional support system. Many of these individuals willingly shared their knowledge, read drafts of the manuscript, gave interviews, and provided ongoing support. These special people include: my mother, Regina Boyd; my brother and sister-in-law, Randy and Dawn Boyd; Rozetta Wilmore-Schaeffer, A.C.S.W.; Rosemary Allwood, C.S.W.; Dr. Sandra Lewis; Dr. Cheryl Thompson; Dr. Joy Dryer; Myrtle Parnell, C.S.W.; Jo Vanderkloot, C.S.W.; Dr. Paulette Hines; Monica McGoldrick, M.S.W., and her entire study group at UMDNJ-Piscataway; Frank Dillon, A.C.S.W.; Dr. Diane Shrier; Dr. Gloria Steiner; Dr. Linwood Bulluck; Dr. Charles E. Smith; Dr. Elizabeth Hill; Bertina Baer, M.S.W.; Dr. Ellen Wachtel; and Dr. Vera Paster. In addition to the individuals already mentioned, there are a number of members of our Advanced Family Seminar in Newark who have challenged me to expand my beliefs. These include Dr. Susan Cook, Christopher McVey, A.C.S.W., Julia Alemán, M.S.W., Susan Kunkel, A.C.S.W., Dr. Phyllis Kresch, and Dr. Sharon Boyd. I would also like to acknowledge the continued support of all my friends and colleagues in the Association of Black Psychologists, who have provided mentorship throughout the years.

For their administrative support, I would like to thank Mr. Gary Lamson, Vice President of Mental Health Services and Dr. Sheldon Miller, the Chairman of the Department of Psychiatry of the University of Medicine and Dentistry of New Jersey—New Jersey Medical School in Newark. Finally, I am deeply indebted to all of the families, staff, and trainees at our own Community Mental Health Center who contributed to the cases presented in this book.

Contents

I

BLACK, AFRO-AMERICAN FAMILIES: THE CULTURAL CONTEXT

CHAPTER 1

Black, Afro-American Families in Therapy: An Overview

During my training as a family therapist and as a psychologist, I searched for a clinical reference book that would bring together current cultural
knowledge about Black families and the clinical experience of family
therapists. While the period from 1965 to 1980 saw a proliferation of
literature addressing the cultural context of Black families, it was dis-
persed throughout journals and books from a wide range of disciplines,
running the gamut from psychology, psychiatry, and psychiatric social
work to education, anthropology, sociology, and history. To further
compound the problem, the student or professional seeking information
on the cultural background of Black families is now faced with the
widespread unavailability of these publications, many of which had
only one printing and so are obtainable only from universities with
special archives on the topic. Over the past 16 years, I have been
repeatedly surprised to discover that many clinicians are totally unaware
of the work of some of the preeminent researchers in this area. With this
in mind, I shall take the liberty of both citing and quoting extensively
from important scholars whose work may now be difficult to obtain.
Many of the theories mentioned in this book have greatly influenced not
only treatment approaches but also national decision making and policy
that has affected the lives of Black people (Hill, 1972, 1977; Moynihan,
1965; Wilson, 1980, 1987).

Thus, this book has been written with the intent of forging this link
between the cultural history of Black families and the clinical experiences of family therapists who have worked with these families. The
attempt to provide a linkage between family therapy and ethnic and
cultural issues is not a new one. Foley (1975), Minuchin, Montalvo,
Guerney, Rosman, and Schumer (1967), and Sager and Brayboy (1970)
were some of the early family therapists who explored treatment issues
involved in therapy with Black families. In 1982, Monica McGoldrick,

John Pearce, and Joe Giordano edited *Ethnicity and Family Therapy*, establishing the importance of ethnicity in the family therapy field. Their book represents a very significant beginning, but further work is needed to elaborate on the distinct needs and issues of each cultural and racial group. Today, an increasing number of Black families are being referred to clinics and community mental health centers in large numbers. These families bring to therapy many issues specific to their race, cultural background, history, and response to mental health services that must be addressed. This volume is intended to provide a forum for new clinicians and for therapists already involved in the field who are beginning to include an understanding of ethnicity in their work with Black families. It is also intended to serve as a comprehensive text for the training of family therapists in these issues.

Black Afro-American families represent a distinct cultural group, within which there is a tremendous amount of diversity. This book will focus on these families exclusively. Clearly, there are many areas of similarity with other cultures. For example, there is no question that many other ethnic groups (e.g., Hispanic, Italian, Chinese) have strong extended family and kinship ties, and thus may have some structural formations that correspond to those of Black families. A detailed analysis of these areas of similarity and difference, however, is beyond the scope of this book.

Given the necessary consideration of ethnic comparison, there is a potential in any of the ethnicity literature for stereotyping. This is a particularly sensitive issue in writing a book of this kind, and I have sought to avoid the process of simply replacing old biases with new ones.

McGoldrick et al. (1982) have addressed this dilemma:

> There are those who argue that . . . ethnic generalizations do more harm than good. In our view, developing a relatively simple paradigm is the only realistic way to expand our knowledge. But it is only a start. The danger of training anyone in the details of a particular ethnic group is that it will ultimately squeeze people into unreal categories and reify their culture, as we have rigidified diagnoses. We think the solution to the problem lies in maintaining openness to new experience, once we have a framework, rather than in avoiding a framework because it is not altogether accurate or complete. We hope readers will move past stereotypes, using them as starting points from which to learn more. (p. xvi)

It is my hope that this book will expand the knowledge of the cultural variables in Black families, while at the same time increasing the sensitivity of clinicians to the diversity and the nuances of those families. As a family therapist, I view this cultural material as providing the beginning hypotheses that clinicians can use as a framework in their work with Black families. I hope that these hypotheses are not rigidly viewed as applying to all Black families, but are carefully assessed with each new family that enters treatment. Throughout the book, the importance of recognizing individual differences and the unique qualities of each family will be stressed.

THE RATIONALE FOR THIS BOOK

Beyond the stated need to continue and supplement work on the articulation of the Black cultural context, one might ask why a book on Black families in therapy is necessary. Black families are being referred to our clinics, hospitals, and mental health centers in record numbers. Many clinicians, however, are feeling frustrated when working with this population, indicating a need in the family therapy field for a more comprehensive volume on this racial and ethnic group. The fundamental premises of this book can be enumerated as follows:

1. There is a great deal of cultural diversity among Black families that is often overlooked or misunderstood.
2. Black Afro-American culture represents a distinct ethnic and racial experience that is unique for a number of reasons, including: history; the African legacy; the experience of slavery, racism, and discrimination; and the victim system.
3. The illusion of color blindness or the "class not race" myth needs to be challenged as both misguided and counterproductive.
4. There are many myths about Black families in the social science literature that have painted a pejorative, deficit picture of Black family functioning.
5. There is a need to clarify and understand the strengths of Black families, which can serve as a foundation for therapeutic work.
6. The reasons for the fact that many Black families are resistant to traditional forms of treatment and often do not follow through on referrals to community mental health centers and clinics must be explored if such resistance is to be overcome.
7. It is necessary to differentiate between what is functional and what is dysfunctional in the Black families we treat as family therapists in order to construct an accurate framework for the process of restructuring in family therapy.
8. There is a need in the family therapy literature in general and in the work with Black families in particular to focus on the concept of empowerment as a central part of any treatment plan.

This chapter will present an overview of each of the above issues, which are central themes for this book. It will also provide a background against which clinicians can view both the clinical and the cultural material presented here.

CULTURAL DIVERSITY: THERE IS NO SUCH THING AS *THE* BLACK FAMILY

First, it must be clarified that there is tremendous cultural diversity within and between Black communities in the United States. In an earlier work, a colleague and I (Hines & Boyd-Franklin, 1982) discussed these sociological variations, emphasizing the purpose of our work as sensitizing "clinicians to the cultural context in which Black people have lived and continue to live in the United States" (p. 84). This sensitization is an ongoing challenge. The tendency of policymakers and clinicians alike has been to categorize racial and cultural groups along stereotypical lines, a tendency particularly prevalent with regard to Black families. Given the heterogeneity of cultural variables that are present in Black families and communities, it ought to be patently clear that there is no such entity as *the* Black family. The great diversity of values, characteristics, and life-styles that arises from such elements as geographic origins, level of acculturation, socioeconomic status, education, religious background, and age reveals such categorization to be inaccurate and ultimately unproductive as an assessment tool.

Although in writing a book about Black families one must acknowledge a certain level of cultural similarity, it is possible to highlight group tendencies for exploration without reducing the group in question to a simple paradigmatic formation. There is a need for a constant verification of the reality of individual differences within any cultural group. For example, a large number of Black families in the South live in close communities in which they have lived for generations. During the years from 1940 to 1950, over 1.5 million Blacks migrated to the North, Midwest, and the West Coast (Hines & Boyd-Franklin, 1982). In recent years, many Black families have returned to the South and ventured to the Southwest and the West. The move from the South to more urban areas of the country created many stressors for Black families and drew heavily on the "survival skills" developed during the years of slavery and in its aftermath. It is important for the therapist working with these families to recognize the relevance of this background and to validate these skills without indulging in stereotyping vis-à-vis either the background itself or the personal characteristics to which it has given rise in a particular family.

Black people in this country are not a monolithic group. There are differences between Black families from the North and those from the

South. There are also important urban versus rural differences. The case examples reported here were drawn primarily from a Northern, urban sample of poor as well as middle class families. In-depth geographical comparisons are beyond the scope of this book, and further work is needed by therapists in different parts of the country in order to clarify these differences.

In addition to the Black Afro-American families discussed above, there have been a number of waves of immigration from the West Indies in the last century. Brice (1982) describes these migration patterns in detail. There is tremendous diversity among these families as well. The West Indies were colonized by the French, the British, the Spanish, and the Dutch, who also brought Blacks as slaves from Africa. The history of Black West Indians and their immigration patterns to the United States is an area worthy of careful study in the research and clinical literature, but one beyond the scope of this book. There are also many Black families who have come to this country within the last 40 years from the countries of Africa. There has been very little clinical literature addressing the needs of this group. The focus in this book, however, is primarily on Black Afro-American families whose ancestors were originally brought to this country from Africa as slaves.

BLACK AFRO-AMERICAN PEOPLE: A DISTINCT RACIAL AND CULTURAL EXPERIENCE

While it is necessary to emphasize the heterogeneity of Black families, of equal importance is the consideration of how Black Afro-American families differ from other ethnic groups. The four main areas in which the experience of Black people in this country has been unique from other ethnic groups are the African legacy, the history of slavery, racism and discrimination, and the victim system.

The African Legacy

Long before Black people were brought to this country as slaves, they belonged to tribes descended from ancient civilizations on the continent of Africa. This legacy is so rich in custom and mythology that the task of capturing its complexity is far beyond the contextual range of this book. A number of historians, sociologists, anthropologists, and psychologists have documented this heritage in great detail (e.g., Bohannan, 1964; Herskovits, 1958; Jahn, 1961; Mbiti, 1969; Nobles, 1980). In the exploration of the cultural context of Black Afro-American families, however, I shall focus primarily on the concept of family kinship and collective unity (Nobles, 1980) and on the role of religion and the African philosophy of life (Mbiti, 1969; Nobles, 1980).

Kinship ties make up what is perhaps one of the most enduring and important aspects of the Black African heritage. Nobles (1980) and Mbiti (1969) have stressed the emphasis in African culture on the "survival of the tribe." This sense of family survival has persisted through the centuries and these survival skills are some of the most lasting strengths of Black Afro-American families today. The emphasis in African culture was on the survival of the tribe rather than the individual, the nuclear family, or even the extended family. As Nobles (1980) stated, "In traditional life, the individual did not and could not exist alone" (p. 29). It is often difficult for those raised within a purely Western philosophical and familial system—a system focused on the individual and the nuclear family—to conceive of and then attempt to understand a world view that places the well-being of the social whole before that of its members. Mbiti (1969) states the essential tenet of the traditional African's view of her- or himself as "I am because we are; and because we are, therefore, I am" (p. 108).

As the reader explores the chapters in this book addressing the issues of Black extended families and the multisystems approach to treatment, it is important to bear in mind that for some of the Black families that we treat, this group-oriented philosophy may still be very much in effect. The concepts so central to Western therapy of differentiation, clearly defined boundaries, separation, and individuation are often very new ideas to such families.

The other aspect of the African legacy that must be recognized and accounted for by anyone who works with Black Afro-American families today relates to the central role of religion and spiritual beliefs in many Black families. The first observation is that religion or spirituality

> permeated every aspect of the African's life. It was, in a very real sense, not something for the betterment of the individual, but rather something for the community of which the individual was an integral part. For the traditional African, to be human was to belong to the whole community. (Nobles, 1980, p. 25)

Nobles (1980) describes the essential nature of African religious experience, noting the extent of the unified quality of the African spiritual sensibility:

> Curiously enough, many African languages did not have a word for religion as such. Religion was such an integral part of man's existence that it and he were inseparable. Religion accompanied the individual from conception to long after his physical death. (p. 25)

The legacy of this belief system has survived years of slavery and has influenced both the strong sense of "family" (i.e., the extended family group) and the very strong religious or spiritual orientation of many Black Afro-American families today. In relation to these two areas of exploration, Chapter 3 explores in detail the role of the extended family, and Chapter 5 elaborates on the role of religion in the lives of many Black people today.

The Impact of Slavery

From African tribal communities, Black people were captured and transported to this country as slaves. The impact of this process on the lives of the slaves has been most recently described by Hines and Boyd-Franklin (1982), Rose (1982), and Giddings (1984). The institution of slavery was disruptive by nature: Slave masters attempted to destroy the kinship bonds and the cultural system of Black Africans. This institution attempted to rob the African people of their homeland as well as their human traits. Slave masters utilized a dehumanizing process that attempted to deprive the African men and women of their traditions— including family ties, language, customs, food, and spiritual rituals (Kinney, 1971). African people were brought to this country to be bought and sold, according to each individual slave's market value, to his or her suitability for a particular region and/or task. Slaves thus often lost family members to the expanding market or to early death. Since slave masters were only required to provide slaves with the barest essentials for survival, life expectancies were low (Ernst & Hugg, 1976) and mortality was high (Pinkney, 1975; Rose, 1982).

Other attempts were made to destroy the traditional concepts of family. Traditional tribal marriages were not allowed, but nor were slaves allowed to marry according to European practices. Since men and women could not legalize their marriages, every child born to a slave was thus not a legally recognized family member. Mothers, father, and children could be sold away from each other, disrupting any semblance of family security or stability. Both Black women and Black men were abused sexually—men as breeders to increase the labor supply and women as sexual objects for White slave masters (Giddings, 1984; Pinkney, 1975; Rose, 1982).

Despite the attempts to deprive them of any form of human rights and of their own culture, Black people sought to maintain family tribal customs and spiritual rituals. There are many examples of this survival of human dignity in the face of enforced degradation. Black people created their own marriage rituals such as "jumping the broom," which acknowledged a union between a man and a woman. The process of informal adoption (discussed in Chapter 3) had its origins in African tribal traditions and in the "taking in" of children by other slave families when their parents were sold or killed. Spirituality survived in many forms, most saliently in an African belief in famlial and tribal reunion in the afterlife. It is not accidental that the "Negro spirituals" often contained hidden messages of escape, liberation, and rebellion. Songs such as "Wade in the Water" were used to signal an escape—Black women as well as men taking an active role in the attempts at liberation (Giddings, 1984). The African heritage of loyalty to tribe and culture can still be found in Black Americans' strong orientation toward and dependence on a kinship network. As a colleague and I (Hines & Boyd-Franklin, 1982) have noted, "[this] kinship network, not necessary drawn along blood lines, remains a major mode for coping with the pressures of an oppressive society" (p. 87).

The Impact of Racism and Discrimination

It is difficult to convey fully to someone who has not experienced it the insidious, pervasive, and constant impact that racism and discrimination have on the lives of Black people in America today. Both affect a Black person from birth until death and have an impact on every aspect of family life, from child-rearing practices, courtship, and marriage, to male–female roles, self-esteem, and cultural and racial identification. They also influence the way in which Black people relate to each other and to the outside world.

Slavery set the tone for Black people to be treated as inferior. Skin color was and is a badge of difference. The process of discrimination is evident at all levels of society from theories about genetic inferiority (Jensen, 1969) and cultural pathology (Moynihan, 1965) to segregation that existed blatantly in the South until the Civil Rights era in the 1960s and still occurs in subtler forms today. There are continued inequities in the United States of the 1980s that are manifested by the disproportionate numbers of Black people who are poor, homeless, living in substandard housing, unemployed, and school dropouts.

This process of discrimination is evident at all class levels. It does not disappear or lessen with advances in economic status, education, the neighborhood in which one lives, career, or job level. Chapter 12 on Black middle-class families reveals that Black middle- and upper-class families continue to experience different forms of discrimination despite the advances brought about by the 1960s and 1970s.

The Victim System

Pinderhughes (1982) gives a very clear formulation of the ways in which this history of slavery and oppression have combined with racism and exclusion to produce the "victim system." She defines it as follows:

> A victim system is a circular feedback process that exhibits properties such as stability, predictability and identity that are common to all systems. This particular system threatens self-esteem and reinforces problematic responses in communities, families and individuals. The feedback works as follows: Barriers to opportunity and education limit the chance for achievement, employment, and attainment of skills. This limitation can, in turn, lead to poverty or stress in relationships, which interferes with adequate performance of family roles. Strains in family roles cause problems in individual growth and development and limit the opportunities of families to meet their own needs or to organize to improve their communities. Communities limited in resources (jobs, education, housing, etc.) are unable to support families properly and the community all too often becomes itself an active disorganizing influence, a breeder of crime and other pathology, and a cause of even more powerlessness. (p. 109)

Pinderhughes (1982) likens this formulation of the victim system of racism and oppression to Bowen's (1978) concept of the societal and familial projection process. This process is so extensive in American society that it has had a pervasive effect on Black Afro-Americans irrespective of class, education, income, employment, section of the country, or life-style. This societal projection process might take the form of viewing poor Black families as "lazy" and having caused their own poverty. By the same process, many Black middle-class professionals often experience a societal projection process where they are made to feel inferior by the implication that they have attained their status purely as a result of affirmative action concessions.

Multigenerational experiences with this system of racism and oppression and the special aspects of the Black Afro-American cultural heritage have combined to produce features that are unique and different from any other group in American history. Throughout this book, a continual question will be raised for the reader as to the relative similarities and differences between Black Afro-Americans and other cultural groups. Although many similarities will be noted, there are nevertheless some striking differences, arising from the effects of forced immigration as an enslaved population. Most ethnic groups have experienced some degree of discrimination, particularly in the first generations of their immigration to the United States. But for Black Afro-Americans of all class levels, a markedly virulent strain of discrimination has persisted in a variety of forms for multiple generations over a period of 400 years. While I recognize fully the extent to which this point of view has been debated and comparisons made to other groups, it is helpful for clinicians to understand that many Black people in America hold this view and that it permeates their experiences.

Attempts to Build Positive Black Identity

The 1960s were years of rapid change and increasing assertiveness for Black people. Black Afro-Americans sought to reclaim their African cultural heritage and to understand more clearly the evolution of their culture in America. The phrase "Black pride" characterized the many manifestations of this growing assertiveness, such as the wearing of Afro hairstyles and the attempts to trace one's family history and cultural heritage in order to return in some sense to one's ancestral roots (e.g., A. Haley, 1977). Personal exploration also became an important aspect of the black individual's move toward a sense of self-worth.

For a percentage of the Black population, this period opened the doors to educational, vocational, and professional opportunities that had heretofore been closed to them, a change that had a profound effect on Black families. It was an attempt to reverse the effects of the victim system, and as such was the first widespread move to restructure the very foundations of racial inequality in the United States.

THE ILLUSION OF COLOR BLINDNESS OR THE "CLASS NOT RACE" MYTH

One prevalent myth in the mental health field is that all the differences seen in Black families are essentially class issues rather than racial or cultural ones. Clearly, class and socioeconomic issues play a major part in the life experiences of many Black families in this country. This is particularly true of poor Black families. In recent years, however, Wilson, in his book *The Declining Significance of Race* (1980) and more recently *The Truly Disadvantaged* (1987), has argued that race has become less important than class in affecting the lives of Black people. He contends that while racism was clearly a factor in the past in creating the impoverishment of many Black families, now many Black people have benefited from the advances of the 1960s and 1970s. He states, however, that the benefits of these advantages have been felt largely by Black middle-class families. He has used the term Black "underclass" to describe the Black families who are trapped in poverty and who experience little relief or upward mobility. Wilson points out the class and income discrepancies between these poor Black families and Black middle-class families. He discusses the move of many Black middle-class and even working-class families from traditional Black inner-city neighborhoods, which has contributed to their decline. On the one hand, Wilson is absolutely correct in pointing out that a large number of Black people in this country have been deprived of the benefits of increasing job opportunities. However, he therefore concludes that the issues now are not racial but class issues. In my opinion, it is a serious error to separate these issues in this way and to minimize the significance of race. Throughout this book, attempts will be made to look at both class and racial issues and their impact on Black families. Those who separate the two or ignore one or the other oversimplify a very complex issue. Thomas and Hughes (1986) have pointed out, in their analysis of Wilson's work, that rather than a "declining significance of race" they see a "continuing significance of race" in determining the psychological well-being of Black people. In Chapter 9, the issues facing poor Black families are addressed. Chapter 12 discusses the issues facing middle-class Black families. A key point in all of these chapters is that for many Black families, racism and its impact continues to be experienced, particularly on a psychological level, even as they move into a more middle-class socioeconomic level. It will also explore the disillusionment and insecurity that many Black families feel in terms of the gains. As Thomas and Hughes (1986) have demonstrated,

> Social and economic changes over the years in the status of black Americans may have created a climate of rising expectations in the black community. To the extent that these heightened expectations have not been fulfilled, the psychological benefit of the real social and economic changes which have occurred may have been negated. (pp. 839–840)

This comment is particularly important for therapists to consider given that we are addressing the impact of these psychological factors that are influenced by the political, social, and economic reality. In the final analysis, while technically there have been socioeconomic gains for some Blacks, there are serious questions as to whether many Black people feel psychologically secure in their ability to maintain these gains.

While it has been well documented that class and socioeconomic issues play an important role in treatment (Hollingshead & Reddick, 1958; Riessman, Cohen, & Pearl, 1964), the impact of racial difference on the therapeutic process cannot be denied (Grier & Cobbs, 1968). In an earlier study (Boyd, 1977), a significant number of White clinicians interviewed saw the differences between Black and White families as related solely to class and not to racial differences. Thomas and Sillen (1974) point out that for some therapists, it is easier and more comfortable to deny that racial differences exist and to see problems only in class or economic terms. Such a belief is unfounded and thus counterproductive, leading to what Thomas and Sillen (1974) have referred to as "the illusion of color blindness." This phrase refers to the tendency on the part of many members of the mental health field to deny the impact of color differences in therapy. As Thomas and Sillen explain,

"Color Blindness" is no virtue if it means denial of differences in experience, culture, and psychology of black Americans and other Americans. These differences are not genetic, nor do they represent a hierarchy of "superior" and "inferior" qualities, but to ignore the formative influence of substantial differences in history and social existence is a monumental error. (p. 58).

Mayfield (1972) stresses the importance of recognizing the issue of being Black and poor in American society, pointing out the easier access of poor White people into the labor market due to the lack of color boundaries. It cannot be emphasized enough that "Mental health professionals must recognize that there are differences between poor communities and poor predominantly black communities" (p. 106).

Although Mayfield focuses on the poor Black populations, it is important to note that these differences apply for Blacks at all levels (Billingsley, 1968; Scanzoni, 1971). The effects of long-term racism are not effaced by the climb up the economic ladder, causing "blacks at all class levels . . . [to react] by seeking to establish themselves as a recognized and viable ethnic group, with their own sense of identity and racial pride" (Scanzoni, 1971, p. 13). This book addresses the issues of racial difference and discrimination at all class levels.

THE PREVALENCE OF THE DEFICIT VIEW
OF BLACK FAMILIES

Many early studies of Black families have characterized them as "disorganized, deprived, disadvantaged" (Moynihan, 1965; Frazier, 1950, 1966). Other researchers, such as Deutsch and Brown (1964), also characterized Black families as disorganized with many children coming from broken homes. This view was shared by Pettigrew (1964), who perceived a supposed relationship between "the black matriarchy," fatherless homes, and juvenile delinquency. During the 1960s the predominant position was to see Black families as "disadvantaged," one of the most widely read advocates of this viewpoint being Moynihan (1965).

Moynihan published a report for the U.S. Department of Labor in which he painted a devastating picture of Black families:

At the heart of the deterioration of the fabric of Negro society is the deterioration of the Negro Family. . . . It is the fundamental source of the weakness of the Negro Community at present. (p. 15)

Moynihan saw Black families as highly unstable and approaching complete breakdown, and the continual expansion of welfare programs as a measure of the "steady disintegration of the Negro family structure over the past generation" (p. 6). The Black family he termed a "tangle of pathology." One of the central targets of his analysis was the Black woman, whom he viewed as perpetuating a matriarchal culture—a culture that was in turn viewed as perpetuating pathology due to its noncomformity to the "normal" family structures of the dominant culture. By extension, then, the Black family structure could itself be categorized as nonconformist and fundamentally pathological.

Moynihan drew support for his arguments from the works of other deficit theorists, both Black and White. Frazier (1950; 1966) is considered to have established the "pejorative tradition" in the study of Black families in general and low-income Black families in particular (Hill, 1972, p. 1).

THE STRENGTHS OF BLACK FAMILIES

In the last 20 years, a number of researchers have challenged the deficit views of Black family life (Billingsley, 1968; Hill, 1972; Jones, 1980; Staples, 1971; White, 1972, 1984). During the late 1960s and early 1970s researchers and scholars challenged the preoccupation with pathology that so many American social scientists had displayed. More recently, researchers have explored the strengths in well-functioning Black families (Gary, Beatty, Berry, & Price, 1983; Hines & Boyd-Franklin, 1982; Lewis & Looney, 1983; McAdoo, 1981; McAdoo & McAdoo, 1985; Royse & Turner, 1980).

Authors such as White (1972) called upon scholars and researchers to restructure the study of Black culture from a more positive perspective. His view pointed out that when traditional theories, which were developed for White populations, were applied to Black people, the result was often the development of theories based on "weakness-dominated" or "inferiority-oriented" conclusions (p. 43).

White (1972), Hill (1972), and McAdoo (1981) challenged Moynihan's (1965) characterization of Black families as "matriarchal." White (1972) points out that many Black families are viewed from a middle-class frame of reference, which makes the assumption that a "psychologically healthy" family must consist of two parents. Since, as White states, Black men are often not "consistently visible to the white observer" erroneous conclusions about matriarchy are often drawn. It should be noted as well that the characterization of matriarchal structures as inherently deficient is itself a product of the traditional patriarchal bias. Today many Black families are headed by single mothers. While this is a reality, it would be a serious error to view such family structures—and

thus a considerable proportion of Black families—as inherently pathological. Lindblad-Goldberg & Dukes (1985) have demonstrated that a
healthy single parent and a sufficient extended family and/or community support system can lead to healthy family functioning.

The focus on strengths in terms of Black family life-styles began in the
late 1960s. Hill (1972) cites strong kinship bonds, strong work orientation, adaptability of family roles, high achievement orientation, and
strong religious orientation as important strengths of the Black families
he studied. It is important to note here that such strengths should not be
read comparatively (i.e., as perceived to be stronger than in other ethnic
groups/cultures) but merely as inherent within the Black cultural
framework.

The first strength that has been repeatedly recognized in Black families is that of strong kinship bonds and extended family relationships.
Black families have historically taken in other children and the elderly,
and "doubling up" has been a common practice among these families
since the days of slavery (Hill, 1972, 1977; McAdoo, 1981; Royse &
Turner, 1980).

Hill (1972) describes this kinship-oriented informal adoption process
in detail:

> Since formal adoption agencies have historically not catered to non-whites,
> blacks have had to develop their own network for informal adoption of
> children. This informal adoption network among black families has func-
> tioned to tighten kinship bonds since many black women are reluctant to
> put their children up for adoption. (p. 6)

As was emphasized earlier, the strengths of these bonds is also attribut-
able to the African tribal heritage of Black people, as well as to the
importance of maintaining family and community cohesion in the face of
the adversities connected with slavery and its residue. The attention to
cohesion has had positive effects on the lives of Black people: "[The]
tight kinship network within black families has proven itself to be an
effective mechanism for providing extra emotional and economic support in the lives of thousands of children" (Hill, 1972, p. 6).

As a result of these strong kinship bonds, many Black families have
become extended families in which relatives of a variety of blood ties
have been absorbed into a coherent network of mutual emotional and
economic support. This is one of the most important facts that many
deficit theorists have overlooked in their statements about "Black matriarchy."

Much of the role flexibility in Black families probably developed as a
response to economic necessities. Hill (1972) points out that the high
percentage of women and adolescents who have had to work to help

support the family has forced the typical Black family to be unusually versatile in the assuming and fulfilling of family roles. Older children stand in as parents and caretakers; mothers fill the shoes of both parents or trade traditional roles with fathers, and so on. Hill believes that "such role flexibility helps to stabilize the family" (p. 17). If the roles in a particular family are flexible, then that family is more likely to be able to cope with changes in circumstances. Family members are apt to be more generally capable when not restricted to what is usually a sex-stereotyped, narrowly defined role. This should be viewed as a strength.

Hill's work stressed the importance of not viewing differences as pathological, and the importance of aiding the many different family structures to function as healthily as possible. He warned against "pre-judging [a family's] adequacy on the basis of moral judgments" (p. 22).

Work orientation among Black families is another area of consideration that many have thought to be misrepresented by social scientists. Unemployment statistics and welfare rolls are often cited as examples of the lack of a strong work orientation in Black families. Little consideration has been given to the ways in which the structure of the welfare system and the reality of job discrimination have contributed to this process. Labeling Black people as "chronically unemployed" or "un-motivated" is a way of blaming the victims for the very economic and social situation that has created their victimization. In response to this approach, a number of researchers have discussed the strong emphasis on work and ambition in Black families (Hill, 1972; Lewis & Looney, 1983). These studies have pointed out that the literature has tended to overlook the stable Black families in which hard work is definitely an important attribute. It was quite common for women to work in Black families long before this became the norm in the American population as a whole (Billingsley, 1968; Hill, 1972; McAdoo, 1981). More recently, researchers have begun to compare working and nonworking Black single-parent mothers and have explored values including the hard work and survival strategies of this group (Lindblad-Goldberg & Dukes, 1985). Willie (1974) in his article entitled "The Black Family and Social Class" described the "heroic effort" on the part of many Black families to promote family survival with their hard work.

The issue of strong achievement orientation in Black families is often confusing to Whites of different cultures who do not see this enacted according to their own cultural expectations. Lewis and Looney (1983) in their study of well-functioning working-class Black families discuss the messages these families gave their children that they could "make it" in spite of discrimination. Education is seen as the way out of poverty for many Black families as it is for many other ethnic groups. For some Black families, however, although the value and the belief in education are very strong, the ability to translate this in terms of the schooling of their children has not been accomplished. This is particularly true of some inner-city Black families who feel powerless to change their schools and who have been made to feel unwelcome in these institutions. One of the key themes of this book is the process of empowering these families through therapeutic interventions to make a difference in the lives of their children and in their education. The therapist can thus utilize the cultural strength and belief in the education of Black children to help mobilize them to produce change. This strong belief in the value of education can also be utilized to engage Black families who may at first be resistant to the treatment process.

One final strength that is frequently overlooked in the literature is that of religious orientation. Black people have been using spirituality and religion as a survival mechanism for generations. Many researchers and scholars have discussed this process (Hill, 1972; McAdoo, 1981; Pipes, 1981). Lewis and Looney (1983) found that a strong religious orientation was an extremely important value in the well-functioning working-class Black families that they studied. Because of its central cultural importance, the psychosocial support system of religion and the innate sense of "spirituality" in the lives of Blacks will be discussed in detail in Chapter 5.

In summary, it is the above body of literature—representing both the deficit and strength positions—that has most strongly influenced the professional and personal perceptions of psychologists and social workers, psychiatrists, nurses, ministers, teachers, and educators. This book focuses on the utilization of the strengths of Black families in the treatment process of family therapy, seeking to move beyond categorization to the situation-specific consideration of the functioning of Black families.

BLACK FAMILIES' RESPONSES TO THERAPY: THE ISSUE OF "RESISTANCE"

The response of many Black families to the treatment process is one of the central concerns of this book. "Resistance" to therapy is a common reaction of Black families and often very frustrating to clinicians working with them (Boyd, 1977). The presence of "resistance" and its related issues needs to be considered in relation to the timing of different relevant interventions. Not only can these issues influence the process of joining with all family members who enter treatment, but the therapist must also be sensitive to the fact that some interventions actually evoke "resistance" to treatment.

The traditional sources of help for Black families have been extended family members, very close family friends, and ministers or church leaders. For many Black families, the idea of going for treatment is a very new one, and often the questions asked by therapists can be perceived as intrusive. Thus, therapeutic approaches that focus on an initial extensive history intake may increase hesitancy and suspicion rather than facilitate the process of joining. These issues will be discussed in more detail throughout this book as they relate to different models of family therapy. Many Black families perceive therapy to be the process of labeling them as "crazy," often fearing the reaction of their extended family members, friends, and community. This is compounded by the fact that Black families are often not self-referred, but are sent for treatment by schools, courts, hospitals, or social welfare agencies, often under considerable threat or pressure. This can contribute to their resistance in approaching and utilizing treatment. In addition, as is fairly common in many ethnic groups, parents often place a high value on privacy, teaching their children from very early ages to "keep family business within the family," or not to "air dirty laundry in public." It is often difficult for many family therapists to comprehend the extent to which therapy is considered "public" in Black communities.

The type of resistance and suspicion often manifested by Black families should not be summarily categorized as pathological or as a contraindication for successful treatment. Grier and Cobbs (1968) have labeled this suspicion of intent as "healthy cultural paranoia" that many Black families have developed over generations in response to racism, oppression, and discrimination. Often it takes the form of a refusal to identify with and trust persons differing from themselves in color, life-style, class values, and so on. Hines and Boyd-Franklin (1982) point out that this suspiciousness is frequently a direct learned survival response that Black children are socialized to adopt from an early age. This extends particularly to "White institutions," as most clinics and mental health centers are perceived to be in Black communities. Chapter 7 discusses the ways in which this sense of suspicion can also be heightened by premature use of paradoxical prescriptions and by some of the common training techniques employed in the field, such as one-way mirrors where sessions can be observed, and the use of videotape equipment.

There are two other major areas that contribute to the resistance of Black families to treatment and to their tendency to discontinue therapy if they perceive the therapist as "prying into their business," particularly before trust has been established: (1) the negative history that many Black families have with the welfare system and other social institutions and agencies; and (2) the fear of exposing secrets or myths or particularly toxic unresolved family issues.

Experience with Welfare and Other Systems

One of the issues that has led to the resistance of Black families toward mental health services has come from confusion about the relationship between mental health clinics and other agencies (e.g., welfare, courts, schools) (Hines & Boyd-Franklin, 1982). Many Black families have a history of experience with agencies such as those of the welfare system and have experienced the intrusive and prying manner in which these agencies tend to handle their cases. The welfare system has had the power to discontinue the family's financial security if the father of the children (or another man) is proven to be living in or contributing to the household. As has been noted elsewhere, "many families have experienced the intrusion of social service workers into their private domains, sometimes to the extent of having such workers define what they 'should' or 'should not' be able to afford (e.g., television, phone), etc." (p. 101). If there is "evidence" of a man's presence, the family is then in serious economic jeopardy.

Often if the father of a child was able to contribute a small amount, even if the parents were not living together, this could compromise the family's financial allotment from welfare. This, coupled with the tragic unemployment rates for Black men and the last hired, first fired policies in this country, has contributed to the breakup of many Black families and the fragile nature of some family units.

Given the legacy discussed above, it is not surprising that many Black families are very hesitant to approach our clinics, hospitals, and mental health centers, since all are clearly perceived as White institutions and as extensions of these social service agencies. Black therapists are often surprised to discover that they are viewed by Black families as part of these institutions, and thus are not trusted initially. Chapter 8 discusses ways in which therapists can join with Black families to overcome this resistance. Chapter 6 explores the therapist's use of self in this process.

Family Secrets

Another area that contributes to the resistance of Black families to treatment has to do with the perception by many families that therapists will pry into family secrets. There are two forms of secrets: (1) those that are kept from "outsiders" but are known by most family members and

(2) those that are kept from other family members. It is helpful to discuss each of these separately.

Clearly, families of all cultures have secrets. However, because of the legacy of mistrust discussed above, there are many personal issues that Black families have learned to label as "nobody's business but our own." Some of these have been mentioned in the first section. For example, it is not unusual for a Black family entering treatment to present as a single-parent family to the intake worker when in fact the mother has had a live-in boyfriend for over 5 years, and this person has served as a stepfather to her children. Often this will not be revealed until a high degree of trust is established. This person is frequently an important actor in family interaction and true structural change can not occur until he is involved.

Black families are often concerned about the judgments imposed on them by outside agencies and may therefore be sensitive about discussing with an outsider such issues as the fact that children may have different fathers. Since so much of the early social science literature (e.g., Moynihan, 1965) referred to single-parent Black families on welfare as pathological, Black people are well aware of and sensitive to this bias.

The type of secret that is kept from certain members within the family is the more toxic and difficult to explore. Often these secrets are multigenerational (Bowen, 1976) and have been passed down over generations. They are often unconscious, obscure, or nebulous. It is not unusual to discover that there is awareness on the part of family members that there are secrets or loaded issues that are never discussed. These secrets take many forms and often do not surface until one is very far along in the treatment process. The issue of secrecy has serious clinical implications. The following are some of the most common: (1) informal adoption and secrets about true parentage; (2) fatherhood; (3) unwed pregnancy; (4) a parent who had "trouble" at an earlier age; (5) an ancestor who was mentally ill, alcoholic, or a drug abuser; (6) ancestors (particularly White); (7) skin color issues. These may be secrets from other family members, particularly the younger generations or they may be toxic or loaded areas in the present family system that are never discussed.

FUNCTIONAL AND DYSFUNCTIONAL BLACK FAMILIES

As has been described above, a tendency has arisen based on the pejorative literature to view the standard of White nuclear families as ideal and to view the variety of family structures in the Black community as pathological. One purpose of this book and a theme throughout is to help clinicians recognize the strengths in Black families and to establish models for functional extended families and single-parent families. It will also help the clinician to distinguish what is functional and what is dysfunctional in the families they treat. It would be ludicrous to assume that the extended family always functions as a strength in all Black families. It is only when we as therapists can clearly make these distinctions that we can effectively restructure families within their cultural context, and thus produce change. Chapter 3 will focus on these issues in terms of extended family functioning.

THE CONCEPT OF EMPOWERMENT AS A TREATMENT GOAL

Empowerment and therapeutic change are important treatment goals with a family regardless of ethnicity or cultural background. However, given the legacy of slavery and the history of racism experienced by Black people in this country, they become essential components of any treatment plan for this cultural group. One of the most devastating outcomes of the legacy of slavery and oppression is the feeling of powerlessness and rage that many Black people experience (Grier & Cobbs, 1968).

Empowerment as used in this context is defined as the process whereby the therapist restructures the family to facilitate the appropriate designation and use of power within the family system and to mobilize the family's ability to successfully interact with external systems. Solomon (1976) and Weaver (1982) have explored this concept of the empowerment of Black people through the use of social work strategies.

Throughout this book, the concept of empowering Black families is emphasized and incorporated into the treatment process. It is important to give this concept consideration because it is central to the initiation of effective therapeutic change when treating Black families. Many of these families have a multigenerational history of victimization by poverty and racism. Unlike other cultural or ethnic groups who can "blend in" or become part of the "melting pot," Black people by virtue of skin color are visible reminders of the inequities of society. Empowerment therefore consists of helping people to gain the ability to make and implement basic life decisions in their own lives and the lives of their children. Empowerment often involves helping parents to take back the control of their own families and feel that they can effect important changes for themselves. This is very threatening to many family therapists because it often requires them to take a stand vis-à-vis a decision made by another agency, thus forcing them to abandon their stances of "neutrality" in therapy. As many of the chapters of this book will demonstrate, therapy with families in general, and with Black families in particular, is an *active therapy* that forces the therapist to examine his or her own values and political, cultural, and religious beliefs and biases, and to intervene accordingly. It is through this examination and the therapist's ability to convey respect for the families she or he treats that the therapist creates an atmosphere in which empowerment can occur. The final chapter of the book explores the ways in which therapists can empower themselves through training in these cultural and clinical issues.

OVERVIEW OF THE BOOK

With these themes in mind, this book is divided into four main sections. The first explores the cultural context of Black Afro-American families. It is intended to provide the clinician with a comprehensive cultural background in such areas as racism, racial identification, and skin color issues (Chapter 2); extended family patterns and informal adoption (Chapter 3); role flexibility and boundary confusion in Black families (Chapter 4); and religion and spirituality (Chapter 5).

The second section of the book provides the therapist with the clinical tools necessary to join effectively with Black families, evaluate the "real" family system, and restructure and produce change. Chapter 6, a detailed discussion of the therapeutic use of self, functions as a frame of reference for the presentation of theories and techniques of family therapy that are important as guidelines for effective work with Black families. Chapter 7 presents a review of the contributions of the major theorists in the field of family therapy to the treatment of Black families. Chapter 8 details a multisystems model that seeks to provide therapists with an effective approach to treating these families. Chapter 9 expands that multisystems approach to the treatment of poor Black families and discusses intervention in the systems that intrude on their lives. Chapter 10 provides a case example describing this approach and combining material from both the cultural and clinical sections.

The purpose of the third section is to explore different presentations of Black families in terms of structure (single-parent families, Chapter 11); class and socioeconomic differences (Black middle-class families, Chapter 12); and couple issues (Chapter 13).

The final section and chapter is devoted to the development and training of the clinicians who work with Black families. Chapter 14 will present a training model that incorporates the cultural framework with the development of self in the process of training and empowering clinicians to work effectively with Black families. Chapter 15 summarizes the major themes of the book and discusses directions for future clinical and research work.

CHAPTER 2

Racism, Racial Identification, and Skin Color Issues

INTRODUCTION

Racism has had its effect at all levels of society. It can be external to the family and experienced as discrimination or internalized in a sense of shame about oneself. This chapter explores first the external experiences of racism and discrimination, and the dilemma of Black parents in helping children cope with these issues. It also explores the impact of the legacy of slavery on Black families today. One very important area in which this legacy is still felt in many Black families is the issue of skin color and its relationship to family dynamics and toxic family secrets. These issues, although experienced to some degree by "people of color" throughout the world, have a particular significance for Black Afro-American families. It is these experiences that make this racial and cultural group distinct and unique. These issues, in both their external and internal manifestations, complicate the task of parenting for many Black families. To illustrate the clinical implications of such issues, examples will be given throughout this chapter.

EDUCATING BLACK CHILDREN TO THE REALITIES OF RACISM

There are a number of issues related to growing up Black in this country that cause concern for many Black parents. One of the most difficult tasks for all Black families, irrespective of socioeconomic level, is that of educating their children about the realities of racism in this country, while concomitantly teaching them to strive to "be all that they can be." The task is not an easy one. A parent must help a child to develop a sense of self and of his or her "Blackness." At the same time, children must be given enough information about the realities of the world so that they are prepared without becoming immobilized or so bitter that they are unable to function. Many Black parents make a great effort to instill in their children an awareness of their heritage and the struggles of the Civil Rights movement.

Socioeconomic factors are very relevant to the consideration of the race issue. Although racism and discrimination are present in American society at all levels, they may be experienced differently depending on the family's socioeconomic circumstances. This is true for the Black child who grows up in a predominantly Black, inner-city community or a sparsely integrated suburb.

For poor, urban Black families, the task is to help motivate children to achieve and believe in themselves despite the blatant evidence of discrimination that they view every day. For example, young children may see many of the older teenagers in their community unemployed and the evidence of the last hired, first fired policies of the labor market in the widespread unemployment of both teenagers and adults. Many wonder why they should bother to study and go to school if they will end up in similarly hopeless situations. Such negative examples give rise to tremendous struggles for Black families who are trying to raise motivated children. One frequently hears in Black homes, "You have to set an example for your younger brothers and sisters." It is often very difficult for parents to continue working to motivate younger children when an older child succumbs to drugs, truancy, and/or other destructive activities.

In his speech before the Democratic National Convention on July 19, 1988, Jesse Jackson, the Black presidential candidate, repeatedly stated that a part of his mission was to "keep hope alive." He phrased very eloquently the task of all Black parents who, in the last 400 years, have had to "keep hope alive" for their children and families despite the realities of slavery, racism, discrimination, etc. This ability to keep on believing in the future is one of the strengths and most powerful survival skills of Black people. As stated earlier, many Black parents struggle to strike the precarious balance between helping their children learn to reality test what is in fact related to racism in their world. The philosophy of hope and the belief in a better future for their children has empowered many Black parents to tell their children that they can be anything they choose to be. Sometimes this takes the form of a very deeply ingrained spiritual belief system (see Chapter 5), which has sustained these families through generations. Some of the families who come to our clinic, particularly those who are burdened by the oppressive realities of poverty, feel powerless and hopeless. Empowering parents to change their interaction with a school system and to be effective with their children begins to reverse this feeling of hopelessness. As Jesse Jackson has often said in his speeches, it can convey to all family members that they can make a difference. His message to Black school children is clear and unequivocal "You are somebody" and "You can be somebody."

The inequities of unemployment and job discrimination can have a tremendous impact on family life and on the issue of motivating children. A Black child who grows up seeing his father and older relatives struggling to work but having difficulty maintaining employment gets a message more powerful than words. The disproportionate numbers of Black men and women who are unemployed often experience blows to their self-esteem that affects their functioning as parents. The following family is an example:

The Davis family was a Black, inner-city family that came for treatment when Johnny (age 12) had an incident in which he "threw a desk at a teacher in school." When asked about this Johnny reported that she was "prejudiced."

His mother initially came for family sessions with Johnny and his two younger siblings, aged 10 and 8. When the therapist asked when the problems began, Mrs. Davis reported that her husband had lost his job as a construction worker in November and there was no "winter work." She stated that he had been "cheated out" of his unemployment benefits. Mrs. Davis worked in a local luncheonette but it wasn't enough to support the family.

The therapist asked Mr. Davis to attend a family session. It was very difficult getting him to attend. He finally agreed to come in alone to see the therapist while the kids were at school and his wife was at work. Mr. Davis was a proud tall Black man who told the therapist that he had never been unemployed in his life and was embarrassed about his status. He reported that the construction business was always slower this time of year but he felt that he had been discriminated against because he and a number of other Black men had been laid off while a number of white workers had been kept on.

The therapist understood his pain and joined with him on how furious he must be feeling. She asked him if he knew that his son was dealing with a very similar situation in school. He had not seen the similarities. The therapist asked the father if he would attend a family session and help talk to his son about how to handle racism and still hold onto his belief in himself. Mr. Davis came to the following family session with his wife and three children. With the therapist's encouragement he talked to Johnny about his experience at school and drew parallels with his own situation. He got very involved and told his son that there were other ways to "fight back" besides throwing a desk, such as being the best he could be in his work. His son pointed out that his father "still got burnt." His father was able to tell his son that he was furious but that he was fighting back by going out every day to look for work and by his determination.

In subsequent months, Mr. Davis attended a number of family sessions. He was given the task of teaching his son about life as a Black man. Paradoxically, both father and son benefited. Mr. Davis became more determined to show his son that he was not giving up, and he eventually found a job. His son learned how to continue to "fight back" by doing his best at school.

Discrimination can also affect Blacks at higher socioeconomic levels. Black professional families living in predominantly white suburbs are often faced with subtle and overt forms of racism. The following example illustrates a very overt manifestation of racism and its effects on a family.

Mr. and Mrs. Simpson moved into a small suburban town that had very few Black families. They have three children, all girls, ages 5, 7, and 10. Two days after moving in a cross was burnt on their front lawn. They came to seek the help of a family therapist when their two younger children began to experience a number of phobic symptoms including nightmares and fears of leaving the house. The 7-year-old child became school phobic.

In the first session, the whole family appeared. The entire family was very depressed in the first session. Although it had been 3 months since the incident, the mother stated that they all were still traumatized by the event.

The therapist first legitimized the fears and the anger that the family was experiencing as a normal reaction to a very traumatic situation. The 7-year-old had become the focus of the family's concern. The therapist was able to relabel this as a family problem and focus on their need to support each other through this crisis.

In a later session, it became clear that one of the factors that had prevented the family from "pulling together" to support each other was that the decision to move to this town had been very rushed and problematic. Mr. Simpson had been transferred by his company, which had a branch in a nearby town and the parents had not had time to fully research the area. Mrs. Simpson was very angry at her husband for making this move. The therapist told the parents that they would have to talk this out if they were going to get past it and help their family through this crisis. A number of sessions were held alone with the parents to discuss the stress this had created on their marriage.

In a family session during this time, Mr. Simpson was asked to discuss with his 7-year-old daughter her fears of going to school. Both parents agreed to support their daughter by taking her to school until she felt more comfortable. With the therapist's encouragement the parents arranged a meeting with their girls and the school principal to discuss their fears. In a future session, the therapist asked Mr. and Mrs. Simpson to teach their daughters about racism so that they could understand it and ask them questions. They explained prejudice to their daughters for the first time. Mr. Davis explained sadly that he had never felt it was necessary before.

In the final months of treatment, the therapist proposed that Mr. and Mrs. Simpson had felt rushed into moving and into making decisions, over which they felt no control. She encouraged them to "do their homework" about other communities in their area and know that they had a choice about whether or not to remain. As the school semester drew to a close, both of the older girls strongly stated their desire to move. The parents ultimately made the difficult decision to move to a more integrated community some miles away.

This family experienced more blatant discrimination. It is particularly significant that this occurred in a predominantly white, Northern suburb in 1987, not in the deep South in 1940. There are more subtle forms as illustrated in the following example.

Ms. Jones was a hard-working Black single parent with high aspirations for her two children, Melanie, age 9 and Brian, age 7. She was a paraprofessional in the public school system and had a great deal of knowledge about schools in her area. The family lived in a predominantly Black area in New York City. Both of her children were in their neighborhood schools for the kindergarten and first grade. Her oldest child had been there for the the the second grade. Ms. Jones became increasingly dissatisfied with the quality of their education. She heard about a program that arranged scholarships for minority children at predominantly white prep schools. Both of her children were accepted at a very prestigious school. Melanie began to experience difficulty by December of her first year. She seemed to have given up and stopped working. Ms. Jones was furious. She had worked so hard to give her kids this opportunity, and now Melanie was "blowing it." In a family session, the therapist asked Ms. Jones to talk with Melanie about what it had been like for her going to this new school.

Melanie burst into tears. She told her mother that she had never felt so alone. She was used to having lots of friends at her other school. Here she was the only Black child in her class. None of the other kids ever invited her to do things with them. They all came in with designer clothes which she didn't have. A child in her class in an angry verbal interchange had told her she was "too black to be her friend." Ms. Jones was shocked. She asked Melanie why she had not told her before. Melanie stated that she had tried but her mother was so angry at her for not doing well that she was afraid.

The therapist normalized Melanie's struggle as very common for Black children who enter private schools on scholarship. She relabeled Ms. Jones' anger as her intense desire for her kids to have a good education. She then helped Ms. Jones and Melanie and Brian to "brainstorm" on ways to deal with this. Ms. Jones shared with her children what she often felt like being one of the few Black paraprofessionals in her school. These discussions continued over many weeks. With the therapist's encouragement, Ms. Jones offered to go with Melanie to her school and talk with her teacher. She obtained the phone numbers of some of the parents Melanie wanted to establish friendships with and made phone calls to arrange playtime outside of school. The therapist then stated that Ms. Jones shared something in common with her daughter in having to deal with being "different." The therapist asked the mother how she had dealt with this. Ms. Jones stated that she had always had her own friends, who had known her "all her life." She then asked Melanie if she missed her neighborhood friends. Melanie responded, yes, tearfully. Her mother made a commitment to both children to help them maintain their own social networks outside of school.

Black parents often find themselves faced with helping to build bicultural networks for their children so that they have the support of other Black children and families when they encounter discrimination in other parts of their lives. The family therapist who can validate this struggle and normalize it can be a great help to Black children as well as their parents.

BUILDING SELF-ESTEEM AND POSITIVE RACIAL IDENTIFICATION

One of the greatest concerns of Black parents raising children in America today is the process of encouraging the development of self-esteem and positive racial identification. This is not an easy task, since children are often exposed to negative images or caricatures of Black people on television and in other types of media. Since the 1960s many Black parents have been sensitized to the need for helping their children to learn about their history and develop positive role models.

Many Black inner-city parents, particularly single mothers, struggle with the problem of identifying positive Black role models for their children. In the course of family therapy, these mothers often express the need for supports in this area. In these situations, it is crucial that the therapist discuss both the "traditional supports" (i.e., extended family and church) and the community resources (e.g., Big Brothers, Boys' Club, Police Athletic League, community groups, etc.) that can provide these supports. The case that follows illustrates this difficulty.

Darryl Brown (age 10) was a Black child who was referred for treatment by his school. He was described by his teacher as bright but unmotivated. He had recently been picked up by the police for vandalizing school propery with a group of other boys. His mother was a very overwhelmed single parent. She was 25 years old and had three younger children (aged 7, 2, and 1). Her boyfriend had left her at the time, and she was managing alone. Her mother, who had been her main support, had died 2 years earlier. Things had begun to "fall apart" at home after that. Her mother had helped her "control" Darryl and she didn't feel that she could do it alone. The therapist joined with her around the issue of how difficult it was to provide a child with all his or her needs. She talked with her about "getting some help."

The therapist encouraged the mother to call a local Black social worker who had started an after-school program for boys in their area. He helped them with homework and organized basketball games for them. Ms. Brown went to meet with him and agreed to get Darryl there every day.

In a family session Ms. Brown discussed this with Darryl, and told him that she would go with him to help plan out his activities after school. Ms. Brown was greatly relieved at having an option. She began to take charge. The therapist encouraged her to monitor his progress and "stay in touch" with the worker and with Darryl's school. The worker became a very important role model for Darryl.

Ms. Brown expressed concerns about the weekend when Darryl was "out on the streets." In a family discussion about this, the therapist asked if they had ever belonged to a church. Ms. Brown explained that she had belonged many years ago but had not in recent years. The therapist explored whether this had been a support for her. Ms. Brown replied that it had. The therapist suggested that it might be a help for her in raising the kids and in finding activities and positive Black role models for the kids. Ms. Brown and Darryl agreed to "try it." In the next few months, Ms. Brown became increasingly more active and less depressed and Darryl became more engaged in youth activities. His acting-out behavior had stopped.

In May, Ms. Brown was in a panic. School was ending soon and the after-school program would stop for the summer. The therapist carefully explored options with her in a family session with the children. Although Ms. Brown had repeatedly stated that she had "no family left," the therapist decided to reopen this issue. She asked her where her family came from originally and learned that she still had an aunt and an uncle in South Carolina. With the therapist's encouragement, she called them to ask if they would "take Darryl for a little time." To her surprise, they invited the whole family for the summer.

This family's situation illustrates the process whereby family therapists can help support families in identifying positive Black role models for their children and in providing them with constructive alternatives to "the streets." This often requires, however, that therapists be aware of both traditional networks and important community resources. In many Black communities there are caring Black adults who have started activities for children. The therapist who is working with poor and isolated Black families in particular must find a way to discover these resource people. One should also keep in mind the tradition of "sending children South," which has been an important part of the socialization of Black children for generations. It reconnects them with their family roots and often reinforces positive identification by providing alternative familial role models.

SKIN COLOR ISSUES AND THE STRUGGLE FOR POSITIVE RACIAL IDENTIFICATION

Clark and Clark (1939) in their classic studies of racial and skin color identification found that Black children of that generation often evaluated the color black and Black people less positively than the color white and White people. This discovery has caused considerable concern for Black parents for many generations. Black parents who feel proud of their racial identity often find that their young children also struggle with this issue, especially since the push for integrated school systems. Many Black parents have reported the often upsetting experience of having a child say "I wish I were White." Such statements are understandably a source of much anxiety for these parents.

Comer and Poussaint (1975) in their guide to child-care issues for Black parents offer a number of vignettes and examples that can be very useful to therapists in helping families cope with this issue. Their suggestions serve a particularly helpful purpose by providing a number of ways of reframing and normalizing the experience. The authors report a frequent question from Black parents: "The first time my four year old raised a question about race, he said 'I'm white.' Does this mean that he doesn't like being black?" (p. 68). This is not necessarily the case. For some Black children, who are raised in a predominantly White neighborhood or school, this is not an uncommon response. The parents' response to this statement can make all the difference. A simple "No you are black . . . like Daddy and Mommy" (Comer & Poussaint, 1975, p. 68) is clear and can help to reinforce positive racial identification.

If the parent is clearly proud of her or his own blackness this will be conveyed to the child. Many Black parents from the 1960s to the present day take very seriously the task of developing this sense of positive racial identification, a focus captured by the words of a familiar 1960s song by James Brown "I'm Black and I'm proud." This process is a continual struggle for Black parents particularly because skin color is such a loaded, toxic issue in many Black families, often determining the nature of family interaction, as is discussed below.

SKIN COLOR AND FAMILY DYNAMICS

The Historical Perspective: The Role of Slavery and Racism

Historically skin color differences began to influence the lives of Black people in this country early in the slavery era. Grier and Cobbs (1968) argue that the mark of slavery has never fully disappeared for Black people in this country, that the feelings and assumptions that formed the psychological underpinnings of the slaveholding structure have yet to be purged from the national psyche. Thus both Black and White people have been profoundly affected by this legacy. They further assert:

> The culture of slavery was never undone for either master or slave. The civilization that tolerated slavery dropped its slaveholding cloak but the inner feelings remained. The "peculiar institution" continues to exert its evil influence over the nation. The practice of slavery stopped over a hundred years ago but the minds of our citizens have never been freed. (p. 20)

Sexual exploitation on the part of White slave masters resulted in many "mulatto" or light-skinned children, who were often raised in the master's house and became house servants. These individuals were given many privileges within the plantation system. Unlike the African sense of beauty that admires a deep, dark, black skin color and values and reveres Black hair and skin features, in this country the White standard of beauty was imposed through slavery and other institutions. After the Civil War, the Southern Reconstruction continued this tradition of favoritism of light-skinned Blacks by the White South. Many of these individuals continued the tradition of racism and oppression against dark-skinned Blacks. Throughout the generations it was often easier for light-skinned individuals to get an education, a job, and so on. A class system was thus created in many Black communities based on skin color.

Before the days of integration the "Jim Crow" laws of segregation were pervasive throughout the South. Black people were blatantly discriminated against and given separate facilities ranging from parts of restaurants and lunch counters to separate restrooms. The school system was totally segregated prior to the change in legislation that resulted from the Brown vs. the Board of Education case in 1954. With the Black consciousness raising in the 1960s, attempts were made to change all of this. The Civil Rights movement led to integration and desegregation of public facilities and schools. Via slogans such as "Black is beautiful," the appearance of Afro hairstyles, and the reconnection with their African heritage, attempts were made by Black people to promote positive Black identity and to change the stereotypes of the past.

In Chapter 1 the concept of a "victim system" (Pinderhughes, 1982) was explored. One of the consequences of this system and the historical legacy discussed above has been that some Black families have identified with the dominant culture and incorporated some of the prejudices of the majority White culture. Within some Black families an intrafamilial color prejudice developed, which Allen (1982) describes as "the color schisms that divide the Black race" (p. 68). As this chapter will demonstrate, these schisms can sometimes divide families as well. Some whites referred to Black people with derogatory terms such as "nigger," "darkie," "coon," and so on, which emphasized the difference created by this badge of skin color. The following is an example:

Marcus King, a 68-year-old dark-skinned Black man who was raised in Alabama, described the following incident, which occurred when he was 7 years old. Although it had happened over 60 years ago, he felt that it was engrained forever in his memory. He and his father, a local handyman, were walking home when a crowd of four White men approached them. They were obviously drunk. One of the men held him while the others began taunting his father, calling him "nigga" and asking what he had in his bag. They forced him down on the ground, held a knife to Marcus' neck and threatened to cut Marcus' throat if his father did not eat dirt from the road. After some resistance his father began to eat dirt. Marcus still recalls the rage he felt and the immense sadness when the men finally left and his own father was too embarrassed to look him in the eye.

This kind of behavior was not unusual in the South in the early 20th century, and is a painful reminder of the rage that many Black people still feel and experience. This type of degradation of the honor and manhood of a Black man in front of his family has left scars that are not easily repaired.

Color has many different levels of symbolism for Black Afro-Americans. Many Black people view their color proudly, as a badge of pride and honor. Others are negative or at best ambivalent and view their blackness as a "mark of oppression" (Kardiner & Ovessey, 1951). At the other end of the spectrum there have been light-skinned Blacks in each generation who have denied their blackness and have "passed" for White.

All Black people, irrespective of their color, shade, darkness, or lightness are aware from a very early age that their blackness makes them different from mainstream White America. It sets them apart from White immigrant groups who were not brought here as slaves and who have thus had a different experience in becoming assimilated into mainstream American culture. The struggle for a strong positive racial identity for young Black Afro-American children is clearly made more difficult by the realities of color prejudice. Black writers such as Alice Walker (1982) express concerns about the divisions that skin color issues have created in Black families and Black communities:

> The matter of color, quiet as it is kept, is still an issue among us. Color still affects our thoughts, attitudes and perceptions about beauty and intelligence, about worth and self-esteem. Yet if we are to stand together and survive as a people, we cannot allow color to become the wedge that . . . destroys us. (p. 66)

Skin Color and the Projection Process in Black Families

Bowen (1976, 1978) has described a family projection process whereby a family ascribes or projects roles, expectations, and acceptance onto an individual, as well as the multigenerational transmission process whereby these roles and expectations are passed to the next generation. All families project characteristics onto their children based on appearance. However, in Black families, since skin color, hair texture and facial features are such toxic issues in our culture, a child's skin color can help to explain why that child has been singled out for the family projection process. The darkest or lightest child in the family may be seen as different and therefore targeted as the family scapegoat at an early age.

Because of the class system that evolved from the slave system, one can find a number of different responses to skin color in different Black families. In some families light skin color is prized and regarded as something special, while in other Black families, dark-skinned members are preferred and light skin color is seen as a constant reminder of the abuse of Black women by White men. In these situations, there can be considerable shame and guilt attached to this issue.

Because of the laws of genetics, variations in skin color within a Black family are quite common. Allen (1982) describes such a variance:

> The only real law of nature is that when Black folks' genes get together, all things and all colors are possible. . . .
>
> None of my parents' children came out with even remotely similar skin colors or hair textures, so conceivably we could have created our own intraracial discrimination right in the privacy of our own home. In many Black families that's where it really does all start: parents favoring the lighter ones, telling them they're pretty, giving them a stronger sense of self worth. When the experience of the darker person in this family encompasses trauma and personal rejection, it's easy to see why the position of light-skinned folks in the universal Black family is considered a favorable one. (p. 128)*

Children of different fathers may be identified as looking like their fathers and the personality characteristics attributed to those individuals may be projected onto their children. For example, it is not unusual to hear, "He looks just like his daddy, and he's no good just like him too." Children of the same mother and father can often vary considerably in appearance and skin color, which can intensify sibling rivalry. A child can sometimes be significantly lighter or darker than both parents, perhaps resembling an ancestor. This can occur simply because the laws of genetics can yield different skin color among children of the same parents. It is in fact quite common in Black families. In some Black families, however, if the relationship between the parents is unstable, this may lead to questions from an early age about the paternity of a child. Since these questions are often "secrets" and are rarely addressed directly, they are even more toxic in the family.

Examples of Skin Color Issues

The following section will attempt to capture through vignettes the deeply painful issue that skin color can represent for some Black individuals and families. There are numerous examples of dark-skinned Black people who can remember painful experiences as children and as adults in which they felt rejection by family members, peers, and members of their communities. Alexis de Veaux (1982) makes a number of references to this hurt and pain. In describing her interactions with her aunt when she was growing up, she states:

> Red, you instructed me, was a color I should never wear. I was absolutely "too dark" you said. "Whose little black child are you?" you'd tease. "Who knows who you belong to." Did you know then that your teasing mirrored my own apprehension? Who did I belong to? Who does a dark-skinned child belong to in a family where lighter skin is predominant? (p. 67)

The following example of a Black woman seen in therapy also illustrates this point:

Carla, a 40-year-old Black woman painfully revealed her experience of having grown up in a family in which she was openly "put down" because she was darker skinned than her mother. Her mother told her that she was too dark and that she had been "born bad," implying a connection between the two. Carla had spent much of her life in a rage at her mother. Her brother, who had a lighter complexion and "curly hair," was doted on by her mother and could do no wrong. Carla described a painful memory in which her mother openly criticized her hair but refused to cut her brother's hair until he was almost 3 years old. At the time of that haircut, her mother cried openly, carefully collected his hair, and put it away in a special box, which she would frequently take out to admire in later years.

Children can sometimes be very cruel to each other and hurtful about skin color differences. Sometimes these insults come from white youngsters:

William, a dark-skinned Black man, aged 20, reported an experience in his childhood years in which he was chased home from school in a suburban, all-White neighborhood by a group of White children, calling him a "Black nigger" and daring him to fight back. Ever since those early days William had attempted to "blend in and not make waves." He wore glasses (even though they were not needed), dressed in the most nondescript fashion and tried hard to avoid recognition at all costs.

The following example articulates another little girl's inner struggle with a situation in which the name calling came from her Black peers:

> Blackie ain't my name, I want to say. It hurts. It's painful. It's embarrassing, Momma. Livia is dark as me. Why everything black got to be evil, everything dark got to be ugly? I say nothing. I learn the bravado of strike back. Incorporate the language of segregation: "inkspot," "your Momma come from blackest Africa," "tar baby, tar baby," "black nigga." I say it in [great]

anger to others on the block. This is a skill. It is a way to hurt another deeply. We all practice it. . . . (de Veaux, 1982, p. 68)

This form of fighting back and sometimes disguised self-hatred can often be seen in the process of "ranking out" and "playing the dozens" in which many Black inner-city children express their feelings toward each other within the protection of a "game."

Being light-skinned in certain Black families can lead to certain privileges. However, it can also lead to its own peculiar problems and feelings of rejection. The need for identification and a sense of belonging is an important emotional issue for everyone. For many light-skinned Black people, the dilemma of not being identified as Black can cause pain and discomfort, as in the case below:

Jean, a 20-year-old fair-skinned Black woman, reported a number of experiences in the course of her life in which people did not know she was Black. She told of periods in her early growing up years in Bedford-Stuyvesant, a predominantly Black section of Brooklyn, in which she was frequently called "whitey" or "oreo" by other children on the block. She reported an experience in therapy with a White therapist in which after 2 years of treatment, she brought in pictures of her family to show her therapist. Her therapist was stunned when she realized for the first time that Jean was Black. Jean was angry and was able for the first time to talk about her feelings of not belonging and feeling different. Her own ambivalence had kept her from openly clarifying her racial identity earlier.

Mary, another light-skinned Black woman in her 40s, had been a member of an interracial work group for many years. She was furious and hurt when a White co-worker, upon learning that she was Black, said, feeling that she was giving a compliment, "Oh, I never would have known you were Black." Mary described this experience as "feeling as if a knife had been driven in her heart."

In family situations, the child who is different may receive special privileges or they may be scapegoated or ostracized. Ironically, both of these situations can sometimes occur simultaneously.

Sam, age 14, was a light-skinned Black adolescent who was the third child in a family of six. Although there was a range of skin colors in his family, he was the lightest. From the adults in his family and extended family, he often received many special privileges and comments about how handsome he was. This special attention created an intense sibling rivalry between Sam and his brothers and sisters, who frequently scapegoated him and excluded him from their games. Sam grew up very unsure of himself and very threatened when anyone acknowledged his appearance.

In the 1960s, with the emergence of the Black power movement, and the call for "Black pride," many light-skinned Black people found themselves the object of years of collective anger by their darker peers.

As has been seen, this process of denigration can be especially painful when it occurs within a family. Since Black families often have a range of skin pigmentation represented within the immediate and/or extended family, it is quite possible for a number of children of the same parents to range in skin color from very fair to very dark. Black people are acutely aware of these ranges of color, many of which are not seen or experienced by those from other ethnic groups. All of these issues and the ways in which they are handled are specific to the given family and that family's attitude toward color. The paradox remains such that a light-brown-skinned woman may be considered "dark" if she were born into a very light-skinned family or "light" if her family members had darker complexions.

Secrets About Skin Color Issues and Its Treatment Implications

Any area as toxic as this one is fertile ground for the development of family myths and secrets. This is compounded by the fact that these issues are rarely discussed openly in many Black families. Given the many family "secrets" about birth, paternity, and informal adoption discussed above, a child who looks very different from the rest of his family or household members may have a very difficult time while growing up. Children may be favored or rejected because of lighter skin color. A child may be scapegoated as the darkest member of the family or favored because he resembles an ancestor. This is such a toxic issue for many Black families that it is often denied; such families will often resist discussion of it in the initial stages of treatment. Alternatively, many times children experience teasing not within their families but in their peer group and in the community. The following example illustrates this point:

The Kent family was a Black single-family unit composed of Martha Kent and her three children: Glenn (13), Martha Lee (10), and Ronald (8). Ms. Kent came to our clinic seeking help for her youngest child, Ronald. He had become withdrawn, isolated, depressed, and had begun to act oppositional toward her. When the entire family was seen, Glenn and Martha Lee reported that Ronald was often teased by other children in the neighborhood because he was very light skinned. (His mother, brother, and sister all had dark complexions.) Glenn stated that he had had to defend his brother for years from kids who called him "White boy" and "oreo," but now Glenn had entered junior high school and Ronald felt he had lost his protector.

It became clear that Glenn had served as a parent figure as well as the protector in the family. Ms. Kent presented as a very depressed woman who was "trying to go back to school" and who was supporting her children on welfare. When the therapist asked her if she was aware that this had been occurring, she shrugged her shoulders, looked very sad, and stated that she had so many burdens she really had "tuned out" Ronald's problems. The therapist helped her to speak directly with her son about his concerns and about the teasing by other kids.

Ronald, who had never known his father, was able to ask some questions about him, which his mother answered honestly. She told him that his father had not been White but had been a light-skinned Black man like him. The therapist encouraged her to ask him what she could do to help. He was clear that she should get the principal to talk to the children who were bothering him.

In subsequent sessions Ms. Kent reported that she had gone to the school with Ronald and "stood up for him." She was also able to mobilize his older sister and brother to help him learn how to defend himself. Glenn agreed to "stop by the school" periodically to make his presence felt, and Martha had offered to walk him to and from school as long as he needed that support.

In other families, the issues are within the family and are far more subtle, unconscious, and entrenched. The following case provides an example:

Karen was a 25-year-old Black woman who was treated at an inpatient unit in the Bronx following an acute psychotic break. She had become extremely paranoid and felt that family members were out to get her. In the course of her inpatient treatment, she had reported to her therapist that she had always been treated as a second-class citizen in her family because she was the darkest member. As time for discharge approached, she became increasingly agitated. Family sessions were arranged.

Karen's family consisted of her father Mr. Morris (age 45), her mother, Mrs. Morris (age 44), and her older sisters, Beatrice (27) and Gladys (26). In the family session, Mr. Morris was peripheral to the other members. Mrs. Morris, Beatrice, and Gladys were close together and Karen sat on the other side of the room. Karen resembled her father most in complexion and features, while Beatrice and Gladys had inherited their mother's light-brown complexion. Mrs. Morris, who acted as the family spokesperson reported that Karen had always "given her trouble" and been a "bad seed." Her sisters reinforced this view. Mr. Morris was visibly uncomfortable and turned away and became more sullen. The therapist asked Mr. Morris if he shared their view. He said "things have always been hard on Karen." The therapist asked him to switch seats with Gladys and discuss this issue with his wife.

Mr. and Mrs. Morris were very rigid. Their body posture was turned away from each other, and there was a charged air of hostility between them. Karen became very uncomfortable when they were asked to speak to each other, and blurted out "You have always hated me because I look like him." The therapist intervened and asked the parents what Karen meant by that. Mrs. Morris stated that her husband had never "done right by the family" and she never should have married him. When this was explored, it emerged that Mr. and Mrs. Morris had first met in their hometown in North Carolina. Mrs. Morris' father had owned a store. Mr. Morris had been from a poor family and had been unemployed. Her parents had objected and her mother had been very critical of this and of the fact that he was dark skinned.

Mrs. Morris had become pregnant with Beatrice and had been "forced" to marry Mr. Morris. They moved North and Mr. Morris had had many difficult years supporting the family. When Karen was born, Mrs. Morris had transferred her anger, frustration, and disappointment onto this child. Mr. Morris had withdrawn and become more and more peripheral.

The therapist asked Mr. and Mrs. Morris if they thought there was any way to get past this history, and make a home for Karen. The parents talked openly for the first time about their disappointment in and anger at each other.

Mrs. Morris was helped to discuss these issues openly with Karen. She acknowledged her feelings of resentment but shared with her daughter how frustrated and overwhelmed she had felt having had three babies in 3 years. Karen was able to share with her mother how she bitterly resented the preferential treatment her sisters had received.

The channels for communication were opened. Mr. and Mrs. Morris were asked to discuss with Karen what would have to change in order for her to return home. They set rules about her return to her job and continuing in outpatient treatment. A contract was made in which the family would be seen also for outpatient family therapy after her release.

Thompson (1987), in her excellent case example, reports the following experience from her psychoanalytic treatment of a Black female patient:

Ms. B., the oldest of three children, lived most of her childhood with her divorced mother, her grandmother, her aunt, and two siblings. She came from an essentially middle-class family where skin color was part of the attribution of middle-class status. Ms. B. described herself as a favored child by her aunt and her grandmother. However, she described herself as falling from grace once she began to make friends with the neighborhood children. The following two vignettes helped us begin to understand and disentangle the morass of rejection and isolation. At about age 7, Ms. B. was playing with a neighborhood child when her aunt came outside and sent the child away, yelling at the patient that she was not to play with that child because she was too dark skinned.

Ms. B. needed to deny the perception that the child rejected by her caretakers was more like her mother in appearance than anyone else in the family. To protect herself and to preserve the idealizations of her mother, she accepted the rejection to be of herself, rather than her mother. Self-rejection further served to shield her from her mother's pain. When the patient became angry with her mother and devalued her, she raged with her for not protecting her from the aunt and grandmother. She was unable to see that her mother could not protect her because she too was a victim of the same rejection.

At about age 20, Ms. B. spent the summer in a theater company where she became friends with a young White man. She invited him to her home to meet her family. After the family visit, Ms. B. stopped being friendly with him because she felt the young man did not accept her more obviously black mother. These vignettes allowed the patient to understand the reversal and ambivalence that characterized her relationship with her mother. She began to allow the deeply denied pain of her mother's existence to come to consciousness. During this process Ms. B. became able to understand her mother's idealization of her. Also, she was able to acknowledge the mother's wish that Ms. B. would become a vehicle for her acceptance within her own family. With the development of some empathy, the patient was able to talk with her mother and allow the mother to share information that, up until then Ms. B. had not known. Her mother had been adopted and had never felt accepted by the aunt or grandmother. It was never a legal adoption, but one in which she was delivered to this woman in early childhood. Ms. B.'s mother could not explain why she was "adopted." It was a family secret, but she hypothesized that she was the product of some extended family member's indiscretion. (pp. 400–401)

Such sensitive topics as skin color and racism present problems for Black parents in terms of fostering a sense of pride, self-esteem, and positive racial identification in their children. The next chapter will explore other aspects of family organization, particularly vis-à-vis the extended family and kinship system.

CHAPTER 3

Black Extended Family Patterns and Informal Adoption

INTRODUCTION

The extended family is so essential to an understanding of the lives of many Black families that it is presented here in detail. We as family therapists must expand the field of our vision from the focus on a nuclear family model to the incorporation of an extended family and multisystems model if we are to treat Black families effectively. This forces us to expand our techniques to include more complex interactions and requires a very special sensitivity to the strengths of this type of family organization, as well as to the distinct problems that it can present.

A number of scholars and researchers have now documented the strength that extended kinship relationships provide in many Black families (Billingsley, 1968; Hill, 1972; McAdoo, 1981; McAdoo & Mc-Adoo, 1985; Stack, 1974; White, 1972, 1984). As clinicians and family therapists, however, it is imperative that we understand the complex interrelationships that can exist, and that we develop some cultural and clinical guidelines as to the characteristics of well-functioning extended families. This will greatly aid us in the process of assessment and treatment planning for this population. It is my belief that understanding the cultural norms for well-functioning extended families will help us to delineate problems clearly when they exist. Although the extended family has been a major source of strength for Black people, it would be a serious error to assume that it always functions as a support within a given family. As Hill (1977) has stated: "Our emphasis on the strengths or the positive functions of the extended family is not intended to obscure the fact that the extended family network may also have some negative or dysfunctional consequences" (p. 38). This chapter will explore the positive and disruptive issues related to effective assessment of extended family networks in Black families. In order to accomplish this, the chapter is divided into three sections: (1) a comprehensive description of Black extended family networks, including a discussion of reciprocity in Black families, nuclear family households within an extended family culture, and an exploration of the different forms of extended family constellations; (2) an exploration of the differences between functional and dysfunctional patterns in Black extended families; (3) a discussion of informal adoption in many Black families, which focuses on the benefits of this process as well as the problems, secrets, and clinical implications.

BLACK EXTENDED FAMILIES AND KINSHIP NETWORKS

Many Black families function as extended families in which relatives with a variety of blood ties have been absorbed into a coherent network of mutual emotional and economic support. White (1972) has pointed to "the numbers of uncles, aunties, big mamas, boyfriends, older brothers, and sisters, deacons, preachers and others who operate in and out of the Black home" (p. 45). He adds that when Black families are viewed from this perspective, one can recognize the extent to which:

> a variety of adults and older children participate in the rearing of any one
> Black child. Furthermore, in the process of childrearing, these several adults
> plus older brothers and sisters make up a kind of extended family who
> interchange roles, jobs, and family functions in such a way that the child
> does not learn an extremely rigid distinction of male and female roles. (p.
> 45)

White further emphasizes that this use of an extended family model can help family theorists and therapists formulate ways to employ family strengths, thus lessening the negative impact of a deficit view of Black family structure.

RECIPROCITY AND THE EXTENDED FAMILY NETWORK

For many Black extended families, reciprocity—or the process of helping each other and exchanging and sharing support as well as goods and services—is a very central part of their lives. It has been one of the most important survival mechanisms. Stack (1974) has given, from an anthropological point of view, some of the most indepth descriptions of the way in which exchange and reciprocity networks operate in many Black communities. She describes a number of different levels at which

family members interact, including "kinship, jural, affectional and economic" factors. This reciprocity might take many different forms, from
lending money to taking out "kin insurance" by taking care of a relative's child, with the understanding that the same help will be returned
when needed. It also takes the form of emotional support, knowing that
a relative can be counted on to "share the burden" in times of trouble,
and that one will offer such emotional support in return (Stack, 1974).

An important problem in the reciprocity system in some Black families
is the imbalance that can sometimes result in the overburdening of one
or more individuals. Therapists need to be especially aware of this
potential imbalance since it is not uncommon for an individual or individuals to come to occupy an overly central and depended-upon
position in the family network, such as a member who functions as the
family "switchboard" through which all messages are conveyed. In
these families the extended family may exist in structure, but the exchange of support is imbalanced to the extent that one member may
become "burnt out." Thus it is essential that the therapist explore not
only the question of whether the extended family support system exists,
but also whether it functions in a supportive, reciprocal way.

NUCLEAR FAMILY HOUSEHOLDS WITHIN
AN EXTENDED FAMILY CULTURE

It would be conveying a common misconception to represent most Black
families as living continually with extended family members. In fact, a
large number of Black families function along nuclear lines—as independent single-family households with either a mother, father, and
children, or a single parent with children.

These individuals and families, of course, vary in their degree of
contact, reciprocity, and involvement. This can depend on a number of
factors, including geographic proximity and connectedness versus emotional cutoff. These independent nuclear family households often participate actively in the process of reciprocity described previously and
are active in their extended families.

For many Black families who live far apart geographically, it is a
common practice for one or more family members to serve the role of
family connector who writes, talks, or corresponds regularly with different extended family members. Independent nuclear households, even
in different parts of the country, are thus kept in contact and updated
about births, deaths, marriages, divorces, significant events, and family
gossip.

There are clearly some Black families who function largely as nuclear families and see very little of their extended kin. Some have established or recreated new networks through friends or by joining a church in their community. Given, however, that the cultural norm for most Black families is at least some regular involvement with extended family members, it is important for the therapist to explore the hypothesis of "emotional cutoff" (Bowen, 1976) with a family who appears to be very isolated. Emotional cutoff can occur when a family or individual severs its relationship with extended family members. It is very rare for this to appear as the "presenting problem" in Black families. Sometimes the acting out or withdrawal of a particular child may initially bring a family into treatment and it is only later that the therapist becomes aware of significant losses or cutoffs from the family of origin. This sometimes occurs as some individuals and families move up the class, educational, and economic status structure. Chapter 12 on Black middle-class families discusses this in detail.

DIFFERENT BLACK EXTENDED FAMILY MODELS

Black extended families exist in many different forms and structures. These are not rigid or static and may undergo considerable change over time. It would be reasonable to assume that any one Black person may have participated in various family forms at different times in his or her lifetime. Living arrangements are extremely varied and often extremely changeable in Black extended families, manifesting what Minuchin (1974) has described as "permeable boundaries." For example, a relative may live with the extended family during times of trouble and move out again when he (or she) is "back on his feet." Therapists must recognize this permeability if they are to understand the true nature of the interactions in these families. The examples delineated at the end of the following paragraph are intended to give the reader a sense of the diversity of family combinations.

Many therapists have now been exposed to the concept of an extended family among Blacks. It is significant, however, that just as many express considerable confusion about the various types of extended families. Billingsley (1968), Hill (1977), McAdoo (1981), and White (1984) have explored many different combinations of kinship relationships. Billingsley's (1968) distinctions help to clarify some of this diversity. He divides Black extended families into four major types: (1) subfamilies; (2) families with secondary members; (3) augmented families; and (4) "nonblood" relatives.

Subfamilies

Billingsley (1968) viewed subfamilies as consisting of at least two or more related individuals. Hill (1977) summarizes these as follows:

(a) The "incipient" extended family, which consists of a husband–wife subfamily with no children of their own living in the household of relatives;
(b) the "simple nuclear" extended family, which consists of a husband–wife subfamily with one or more own children living in the household of a relative's family;
(c) the "attenuated" extended family, which consists of a parent and child subfamily living in the house of a relative. (p. 33)

Because of the economic realities facing many Black families, the involvement of subfamilies is extremely common. This type of extended family often confuses clinicians because they sometimes become constrained by their narrow definition of "home" or "household." It is very common for this type of extended family to be spread over many households that are all next door, in the same building, or very close by.

The first example given by Hill (1977) is a very common structure in the initial young adult phase of the life cycle and during the courtship period. A young couple (who may or may not be legally married) may live in the home of the man or woman's family of origin until they can "be on their own" financially. This is particularly common in situations in which a young woman or teenager becomes pregnant.

Over time, this can extend to a whole nuclear family unit living within a larger extended family household. Often there is more than one subfamily within the broader household. The case of the Colt family illustrates this pattern.

Mr. and Mrs. Colt had married very young and had two daughters Angie (35) and Alice (40). Alice had become pregnant at age 17 and her son Clarence had been raised as part of the Colt family. They had always lived within the extended family household.

The younger daughter, Angie, had left home at age 20 at the time of her first marriage. When she was divorced 3 years later, she returned "home" to her mother's house. Three years later, she began dating Manny. They married a year later and were given a floor in her mother's house. At present, Angie, Manny and their two children (ages 5 and 2) are part of this large extended family household.

It is extremely important to ask Black families where they are living and ask them to describe the living arrangements. Many poor Black families often find that economic circumstances have forced them to double up in situations that create overcrowding and lack of privacy. Therefore, the defining of any boundaries around the spouse subsystem (Minuchin, 1974) or the subfamily becomes very difficult. The following case provides an example:

Carl Brown (aged 12) was referred to our clinic for acting-out behavior in school, truancy, and fighting with other children.

Mary Brown and Earl Stetson had been living together with Ms. Brown's two young children (aged 12 and 5) for 3 years. After a fire in their apartment, they were forced to move in with Ms. Brown's mother and her two adolescent children (aged 18 and 17). This apartment had two bedrooms, a living room, a kitchen, and a bathroom. Ms. Brown and Mr. Stetson were given a small bedroom that they shared with her two children forcing the two teenagers to sleep in the living room.

Both Ms. Brown and Mr. Stetson described the living arrangement as a nightmare in which they had no privacy. They could not discipline their children or raise them in terms of their own lifestyle. There was a constant bottleneck in the kitchen and the bathroom.

Carl and the other children were all furious with each other because of the disruption in their lives. When the family was asked what the problems were, they all focused immediately on their living situation.

Secondary Members

Hill (1977) has identified a group of extended families who take in different relatives or "secondary members": (1) "minor relatives" (e.g., nieces, nephews, cousins, grandchildren, siblings under 18); (2) "peers of the primary parents" (e.g., cousins, siblings close in age to primary parents); (3) "elders of the primary parents" (e.g., aunts, uncles); (4) "parents of the primary family" (p. 34). Hill (1977) further points out that many of the dependent secondary members in Black families are grand-children and great grandchildren.

There are endless examples of Black extended families containing "secondary members" (Hill, 1977). The vast majority of these family members are children. These situations are discussed in more detail in the section of this chapter on informal adoption. Here, the focus instead is on adult "secondary members," who fall most commonly into the following three categories: (1) peers of the primary parents; (2) elders of the primary parents; and (3) parents of the primary parents. An example of this arrangement is provided by the case below:

Jo Ann was 18 when her mother died. She was the youngest of three children. Her older siblings Anna (28) and Calvin (30) lived with their own families. Anna felt that Jo Ann was too young to "live on her own" so Jo Ann came to live with Anna, her live-in boyfriend, and her two children (aged 5 and 3).

Some adults move in with extended family when they are "between jobs" or "between relationships." Because of the problems of job discrimination, chronic unemployment, and cost of housing, this is a common occurrence in some families.

Jimmy (35) was a divorced man who had had a history of long periods of unemployment. He had worked as a dishwasher, as a hospital porter, and in a grocery store but had been laid off whenever times were bad. During these times, Jimmy moved in with his sister Janice and her two teenage children. The children had long known that Uncle Jimmy was likely to show up at any time and stay with them for an indefinite period of time.

Black families are far more likely than some other ethnic groups to take in elderly family members; nursing home care is usually considered only as a last resort. This is particularly true for elderly parents and grandparents, partly because of the long parenting role Black grandparents play in family systems. Leisurely retirement is rare; Black elderly must be really physically incapacitated to warrant hospital rather than home care. What often happens is illustrated by the following case example:

Ellie (age 75) was living in Harlem on the top floor of the home of a friend. She had lived on her block for many years. Her daughter and her family had moved to the South and repeatedly begged her to join them. Ellie insisted on staying in her own home with her friends and in the neighborhood where she had lived for 50 years.

During a visit to her daughter, Ellie suffered a stroke. Her daughter took in Ellie and she became a part of their household.

Augmented Families

A smaller but significant number of Black children are being raised in households in which they are not even related to the heads of these households. Hill (1977) states that "about 100,000 (6%) of the Black children living in families without either parent are not relatives." It is also very interesting to note that a large proportion of nonrelated individuals living with Black families are adults, including roomers, boarders, lodgers, or other long-term guests. Hill (1977) states that "over half a million (522,000) Black persons live with families with whom they are not related by marriage, ancestry or adoption" (p. 36). This is a very important piece of information for a therapist who is attempting to build or contact a network for an adult Black patient who may have been discharged from a psychiatric hospital or be homeless. This "taking in" of adults has been a way that Black families have augmented their incomes and shared limited living space.

Nonblood Relatives

One distinction between Black families and some other cultures that share the extended family pattern is the presence and importance of individuals who are not related by blood ties but who are part of the "family" in terms of involvement and function. Stack (1974) refers to these family members as "fictive kin." These "fictive kin" might include play "mamas," "aunts," or "uncles," godmothers and godfathers, babysitters, or neighbors.

I remember that as a child in my own family, I was not allowed to call adults by their first names without the prefix of "aunt" or "uncle." My parents' close friends were treated as part of the family. It was not until I was about 6 or 7 that I began to make clear distinctions between these "aunts" and "uncles" and my blood relatives. Godparents are often very important in Black families. My own godmother had been my mother's best friend since childhood, and she was extremely close to our family and a very special part of our growing up years. She provided the little extras, special gifts that my parents could not afford.

In addition, the large proportion of nonrelated individuals living with Black families that was mentioned under the heading "Augmented Families"—roomers, boarders, lodgers, or other long-term guests—should be included in this section, with the distinction that while some of these relationships are transient, many of these individuals live with a family for many years and are accepted as part of the family. My paternal grandmother, whose family came from North Carolina and Southern New Jersey, moved to Harlem and over the years frequently took in boarders. Many of these were young women from her hometown who were new to the "big city." These women became a close part of her extended family and would often come back to visit her with their children for many years after.

Neighbors, close friends, babysitters, and former babysitters are also important extended family members in many Black families. These individuals often become play "mamas" or "aunts" to children.

THE ROLE OF FAMILY REUNIONS IN MANY BLACK EXTENDED FAMILIES

Family reunions have long served a function of bringing together extended kin who may not see each other regularly. There has been a resurgence of interest in this time-honored family ritual since the publication of Alex Haley's book *Roots* (1977). Some families have constructed a "family tree" that includes special pictures and memories. Some have interviewed older "family historians" who know the background and generational connections of the family.

As in many other cultures, family reunions can take many forms and serve many different functions for Black families. Weddings and funerals provide impromptu reunions in which connections are renewed and maintained, while once a year or every few years, some families gather in a central, convenient location or return to their hometowns in the South. Often for children raised in Northern or Western cities, this is a rare glimpse of the growing-up experiences of their parents and their grandparents. Although family reunions vary considerably according to family style and traditions, there are some common experiences. One is the central and unifying role of food. Everyone participates in the cooking, and platters of turkey, ham, fried chicken, candied yams, potato salad, collard greens and ham hocks, black-eyed peas and rice, and so on abound. Some families with strong religious background will focus a part of their reunion around reconnecting with their home church or "spiritual roots." Attempts are made to bring everybody home, and often money is pooled to help transport those who could not otherwise attend.

In some Black families, these reunions do not begin until the death of a very central family member who may have served as the family's switchboard or connector. Often families will then perceive a vacuum for which the ritual of the reunion begins to compensate.

In any case, these reunions are often special, joyous occasions that provide a very welcome emotional and spiritual refueling for all generations. They bring together the young, middle, and older generations and give all a sense of roots and continuity.

It is important for therapists to be aware of this ritual in Black families. In some families where geographic distance has created isolation, the ritual of a reunion can sometimes be prescribed or recommended.

THE QUESTION OF FUNCTIONAL VS. DYSFUNCTIONAL EXTENDED FAMILIES

As has been established above, the presentations of Black extended families may vary considerably. We have seen that although it was the tendency in the sociological literature prior to 1968 to view difference as pathological, the extended family system can clearly be a source of strength and support in many Black families. As family therapists, however, we must be able to distinguish between functional and dysfunctional Black extended families.

Just as there is considerable diversity among Black nuclear families, there are many different types of extended family structures. It is important for therapists to understand how these structures and roles interplay when they are functional and how they become problematic and dysfunctional when they are confused or unclear. It would be a great disservice to the Black families we treat if we so glorified the "strengths" that we could not recognize problems when they appear. Once we have a model of what is functional, we have the beginning of a strategy for therapeutic change and restructuring.

Minuchin (1974) has used the terms *enmeshed* and *disengaged* to describe a continuum of family functioning, with enmeshed being the overinvolved end of the continuum and disengaged the extreme of being cut off. Extended families also present along this continuum. In some Black families, the extended network is so enmeshed that extended members are constantly intruding in the family's functioning, role relationships, and boundaries (Minuchin, 1974), or at the least rules of participation become blurred. In other families who present with dysfunctional patterns at our clinic, extended family members are structurally present but don't get involved or interact in a supportive way. These families are more disengaged and it often takes a great deal of acting out by the identified patient to bring them in for treatment. Still other dysfunctional families are cut off entirely from extended family contacts, an isolation that often contributes significantly to the presenting problems.

The Functional Extended Family: Clear Boundaries

As illustrated by the review of the literature previously, the extended family model found among the Black population was perceived as somehow aberrant and dysfunctional. The strengths and positive aspects of such familial systems were lost in the shadow of the "normal" nuclear family model. However, there has been growing evidence that extended families are, indeed, functional family models (Billingsley, 1968; Hill, 1972; McAdoo, 1981; McAdoo & McAdoo, 1985; White, 1984).

The following example highlights the basic components that distinguishes a functional extended family system from one that is having difficulties.

Joyce, a 25-year-old Black female, grew up within an extended family system that consisted of her maternal grandparents, a maternal aunt and uncle who were married, two nephews, and a younger uncle who was unmarried. Each of the married family members had their own living space within the house. Joyce's parents moved into a very large room on the second floor of the home that had a bath. They shared the kitchen with the grandparents who lived on the first and second floors. Off the kitchen on the first floor was a small room that was occupied by "Aunt" Joan, a close friend of the grandmother, who boarded with the family. She had a job as a live-in domestic with a family during the week and stayed with Joyce's family on the weekends.

The family was able to have "private" places for each subfamily unit; children had free reign of the house and interacted and were cared for by different adults, but it was also very clear as to who the parents were. Although there were kitchens in the top two apartments, the grandparents' kitchen was the hub of the house. The family table could seat 16 and often did, especially on Sundays and holidays. Joyce often played on the floor of the kitchen with her siblings and cousins while the adults were cooking.

When Joyce was 2, her mother returned to work and the grandmother took care of her and other children in the household. There was an interchange of babysitting, children's clothes, maternity clothing, cribs, baby carriages, and so on between the different families.

This combination of separate, private subfamilies in one extended family household and easy sharing and interchange clearly outlines the elements that make an extended family system function well. First, the boundaries were flexible but also very clear (Minuchin, 1974; Minuchin et al., 1967). Secondly, there was no confusion with regard to who were the parents or executive figures and, thus, parental authority was not undermined. The meeting of emotional needs and the availability of a support system for both children and parents are also components important for the functioning of this model. Another important pattern in many Black families is that of informal adoption.

Informal Adoption Among Black Families

The term "informal adoption" (Hill, 1977) or "childkeeping" (Stack, 1974) refers to an informal social service network that has been an integral part of the Black community since the days of slavery. It began as, and still is, a process whereby adult relatives or friends of the family "took in" children and cared for them when their parents were unable to provide for their needs. This might have been for medical, emotional, financial, housing, or other circumstantial reasons. As Hill (1977) points out, "during slavery, for example, thousands of children of slave parents, who had been sold as chattel, were often reared by elderly relatives who served as a major source of stability and fortitude for many Black families" (p. 1). This informal adoption network still serves many vital functions for Black families, such as "income maintenance and day care, services to out-of-wedlock children and unwed mothers, foster care and adoption" (p. 3).

In their classic study Billingsley and Giovanni (1970) explored U.S. child welfare policies and their impact on Black children. Hill (1977) questions the effectiveness of the child welfare system in providing for the needs of Black children. He states that "although lip service is often given to the belief that the first priority should be on maintaining children in their own homes or with relatives and that foster care should only be a last resort, actual agency practice is the reverse" (p. 19). Social service policies have changed somewhat in the last 10 years since Hill's report, but unfortunately, although many states' child welfare agencies explore extended family members as possibilities for placement, they often do not know enough about Black cultural patterns to go far enough in searching for blood and nonblood supports. As a result, as Hill (1977) has shown, "Black children are disproportionately over-represented in foster care homes and facilities" (p. 20).

Billingsley and Giovanni (1970) point out that the original adoption agencies were not designed to meet the needs of Black children. Therefore, the informal adoption process provided an unofficial social service network for Black families and children, which was totally unrelated to the child welfare system.

There are many different reasons why an "informal" adoption might occur in a Black family. Children born out-of-wedlock are often informally adopted by an older female relative. This is particularly true in situations such as teenage pregnancy where a mother is too young to care for a child alone. Her female relatives will assume some of the responsibility for raising the child. In some circumstances, where the mother is extremely young, Stack (1974) points out that she "may give the child to someone who wants the child, for example, to the child's father, a childless couple or to close friends" (pp. 65–66).

The literature provides a number of useful examples. Hill (1977), Frazier (1966), and C. Johnson (1967) have all emphasized the importance of parental divorce or separation as a factor leading to informal adoption among Blacks. Stack (1974) gives some examples of such situations, all of which illustrate the notable flexibility of the Black extended family to cope with a variety of family structures. This kind of structural flexibility is in response to the changes in familial arrangements due to the breakup of marriage or "consensual union" (Stack, 1974). Children are frequently divided among various immediate and/or extended family members until the custodial parent (usually the mother) is able to take actual custody of them again.

The following is a description of a slightly different situation:

> Soon after Flats resident Henrietta Davis returned to the Flats to take care of her own children, she told me, "My old man wanted me to leave town with him and get married. But he didn't want to take my three children. I stayed with him for about two years and my children stayed in town with my mother. Then she told me to come back and get them. I came back and stayed." (Stack, 1974, p. 65)

Hill (1977) states that the death, illness, or hospitalization of one or more of the child's parents is another factor often leading to informal adoption. Instead of orphaned children becoming state wards, a relative or close friend of the family will "adopt" the children.

Mattie Cornwell had inherited from her mother and grandmother the job of being the switchboard and caretaker of her extended family. When she was in her 70s her two young great nieces (aged 4 and 6) were orphaned. As their great aunt and the oldest female in the family, she took the children and raised them with her husband.

Short-Term Adoptions

The circumstances discussed above are more likely to lead to long-term informal adoption arrangements. There are, however, a number of short-term arrangements that often arise out of economic necessities, crisis situations, or child-care needs. In situations in which the parent is involved in a new relationship or marriage, the children are sometimes left with grandparents or other relatives until their mother can establish her new home (Stack, 1974).

A mother may request or require kin to keep one of her children. An offer to keep the child of a kinsman has a variety of implications for child givers and receivers. It may be that the mother has come upon hard times and desperately wants her close kin to temporarily assume responsibility for her children. Kin rarely refuse such requests to keep one another's children; likewise they recognize the right of kin to request that children be raised away from their own parents (Stack, 1974). Individuals allow kin to create alliances and obligations toward one another, obligations that may be called upon in the future.

Hill (1977) points out that "many children are often taken in by relatives simply because they wanted a child to raise" (p. 49). Sometimes this is prompted by a fear of being alone in old age. Other individuals and families are unable to have children and may want to adopt a child. Often a teenage pregnancy or the addition of another child to a financially overburdened family may prompt an informal adoption:

Bessie (40) and her husband Howard (42) had been married for 12 years. They had been trying to have a child for many years and had gone through extensive infertility testing. They were considering adoption when they received a call from a cousin in Georgia telling them that a younger cousin was pregnant. Both of her parents worked and were unable to care for the child and they were concerned that having a baby so young would drastically alter their daughter's life. Bessie and Howard offered to adopt the child right after birth. They traveled to Georgia, picked up the child, and raised her as their own.

Short-term informal adoption can also become an extension of already existing day-care services provided by Black extended family members in order to permit a parent to go to work, school, or a training program (Hill, 1977; Stack, 1974). A similar common scenario is the result of the strong educational orientation of most Black families (Hill, 1972; Mc-Adoo, 1981; McAdoo & McAdoo, 1985). Tremendous sacrifices are often made to permit a child to go to or be closer to a good school. In some circumstances, a child will live with relatives closer to the desired school during the week and return home on the weekends.

Problems Presented by Informal Adoptions

There are a number of levels on which informal adoptions can present problems in some Black families. The last part of this chapter will discuss the secrets that can arise in Black families surrounding issues often related to informal adoptions. These secrets can be very harmful to family relationships and can persist for many generations.

Another level of conflict has to do with the perceptions by different family members of the duration of the informal adoption. For example, as stated above, children are sometimes placed with a family member after a death, a hospitalization, a separation, or a divorce. Often the family member who takes in the child does so with the belief that the adoption will be permanent, or the process of adoption is left ambiguous. If, at a later point, the natural parent reclaims the child, this can present heart-wrenching problems. The following example illustrates this common dilemma.

Karima (aged 12) was referred for treatment by her guidance counselor. She had been a good student until this school year when her grades began to deteriorate rapidly and she seemed very preoccupied. Mrs. Bond, her grandmother, brought her for therapy at the school's request.

The following history emerged. Karima's mother had died when she was 3 years old. Her father, Mark Bond, who worked as a teacher and had an active social life felt that she would be cared for best by his mother, Mrs. Bond. In the last year Mark Bond has remarried, his new wife was pregnant and at her urging, he was beginning to try to "bring his family together" by taking Karima to live with him. Mrs. Bond began to panic. She lived alone, loved her granddaughter, and was very threatened by her loss. Karima felt caught. Her loyalty was torn. She became sad and depressed and reported that she loved both her father and her grandmother.

The therapist asked for a session with Karima, her grandmother, and her father. Both Mark Bond and Mrs. Bond seemed very angry with each other and tense. They each engaged in a process of trying to get the therapist on "their side." Karima, sitting in the middle, burst into tears. The therapist asked her to come out of the middle and sit next to her. She asked the father and grandmother to talk with each other about the issue of where Karima should live and what was best for Karima. They found it very difficult to focus on this issue and continued to insult each other. Mrs. Bond accused her son of "dumping his daughter on her" when he needed to and now he was "tearing her heart out" by taking her away. Mr. Bond accused his mother of stealing his daughter's love and turning her against him.

The therapist persisted and pointed out that this battle was "tearing Karima apart" and asked if they could put their own issues aside long enough to decide what might be best for her. A number of sessions were necessary before they could successfully negotiate an arrangement in which Karima would continue to live with her grandmother during the week and go to her same school. She would visit her father on the weekends.

This case has much in common with custody battles between divorcing parents, in which the angry issues between the couple are acted out over the issue of custody of the child. In "informal" adoption situations it is more complex because the biological or natural parent often has legal guardianship in the eyes of the law. It is a very recent notion in the eyes of the court to establish the question of "psychological bonding" in these complex situations.

Often family therapists can find themselves in the middle of complex custody battles surrounding informal adoption in Black families. This is often complicated by child welfare agencies who are attempting to clarify or formalize this process. In the following case example, the therapist was asked by the state child welfare agency to make a recommendation regarding custody. He found himself faced with an impossible, Solomon-like problem.

The Elison family were referred by their state child welfare agency for evaluation. Rashan, aged 5, had been raised since the age of 1 by his grandmother, Fanny Elison (aged 45). She had taken in her grandchild at that point because her daughter Clessy Elison (aged 25) had been neglecting him. Clessy had been a heroin addict and had often neglected the care of her child as her craving for drugs increased. She had entered a drug treatment program and claimed to be "drug free." Clessy had been involved with Rashan inconsistently for many years. In the last 6 months, however, she had been taking him each weekend. Fanny Elison reported that her daughter frequently returned Rashan to her dirty and disheveled after these weekend visits. She also claimed that Clessy's live-in boyfriend was a drug dealer who had gotten Clessy "hooked on cocaine." Clessy Elison denied this and accused her mother of trying to take her son from her.

The therapist, in the course of Rashan's evaluation, met with many different subsystems in the family. He interviewed Rashan, Clessy Elison and Rashan, and Fanny Elison and Rashan and determined that the child was fond of both "parents" and got along well with both.

A number of sessions were scheduled with Fanny and Clessy Elison to discuss the issue further. Each managed to cancel repeatedly. Finally, with the intervention of the child welfare agency a session was scheduled at which both appeared.

The therapist and his supervisor met with both family members. Both Fanny and Clessy Elison were obviously angry but very "cold" toward each other. They each chose seats as far from each other as they could in a small room.

Initially the grandmother accused her daughter of being on cocaine and neglecting her son. They had a number of angry arguments about her life-style. The therapist pushed them to talk together about Rashan and observed that in his separate sessions it was clear that they both loved him very much. Fanny Elison told her daughter in a very emotional way that she did not want to "keep her from her son" but that she was very worried about his safety and care. Clessy was able to answer that she never felt that her mother would let her "make up" for past mistakes.

They agreed to work together to try to establish the best living arrangement for Rashan. The grandmother offered to try to help Clessy regain custody by working with her on parenting skills.

In an ideal world, the treatment might have ended on that note. However, approximately 2 weeks later, Fanny Elison appeared very angry when she arrived for the session. She raged at Clessy and told her that Rashan had reported to her that he had seen his mother take drugs in her home. Clessy angrily denied it. Fanny demanded that her daughter leave her "drug-dealing boyfriend" immediately. Clessy refused.

The therapist, who was also becoming very concerned about the presence of drugs in Clessy's life, proposed a compromise. He asked Clessy if she were willing to go into a drug counseling program. She agreed. Fanny Elison agreed that if her daughter gave up drugs she would work with her to share the parenting responsibilities. Clessy went for one meeting with her counselor but dropped the program when she learned that she would have to be tested regularly for the presence of drugs in her system.

She dropped out of treatment. Fanny Elison continued to come for family sessions with her grandson for a number of weeks and was helped to work out a series of visitation agreements with her daughter and grandson, in the grandmother's home, that did not put his well-being in jeopardy.

This case was a very problematic one for the therapist on a number of levels. First, it forced him to face his own value issues regarding the "best interest of the child," particularly regarding the question of drugs. Second, his ideal resolution—that is, a gradual return of custody to the mother with the grandmother helping her daughter to assume appropriate parenting responsibilities—did not occur. Third, the therapist felt pressured by the child welfare agency, the court, the grandmother, and the mother to make a recommendation. He was thus torn between his goal of keeping the child in touch with both parental figures as sources of love and caring and the desire not to place him in a situation that was detrimental to him.

With his supervisor's help, the therapist was able to extricate himself from these complex demands and place the responsibility for the decision on the family. Attempts to negotiate a solution failed and the mother made her choice to withdraw. Ultimately the court made the decision to award custody to the grandmother but to allow the mother to continue to visit her son regularly.

The therapist in such situations must work to avoid the temptation that results from the varying pulls of the family system and the child welfare or legal system to "play God." Ultimately the responsibility must be placed on the family members to set clear limits for each other and to renegotiate complex custody arrangements which may have begun as informal adoptions.

SECRETS ABOUT INFORMAL ADOPTION AND PARENTAGE: CLINICAL IMPLICATIONS

As a result of the informal adoption process, a member of the extended family may have raised a child whose parents were unable to do so. In some cases, this is known by all family members and the children often see their natural parents while they are growing up. In these families although the child may have been told who his or her real parent is, there may be many secrets as to the real reason why the child was given up or "taken in," or there may be secrets as to the parent's present life-style. The following case is an example of this:

Mrs. Gifford, a 65-year-old maternal grandmother, sought treatment for her 11-year-old grandson. In the last year, Kasim had become increasingly depressed, sad, and withdrawn. Finally, his school had suggested that she seek treatment for him. Kasim had lived with his grandmother since he was a year old. Prior to that time, he had lived with his mother. Mrs. Gifford had become concerned when she had visited and found that her daughter was neglecting Kasim. Since his father had never been a part of his life and Mrs. Gifford was his closest relative, she took Kasim in and raised him herself. His mother, Ayana, had been in and out of his life over the years and lived in the same city but on the "other side of town."

In the last year, Mrs. Gifford reported that Kasim had begun to ask why he was not living with his mother and why she had left him. He wondered if he was to blame or if there had been something wrong with him. With careful inquiries by the therapist, he was able to share with his grandmother that other kids often teased him about his mother. Mrs. Gifford became visibly anxious when this was discussed. The therapist finally arranged to see her alone and discovered that there was a "family secret" that she was afraid to share with Kasim: His mother had been a drug addict since her teenage years and had also engaged in prostitution to support her habit. Mrs. Gifford had not wanted Kasim to think badly of his mother and so she had never told him about her life. The therapist helped Mrs. Gifford to see that Kasim was at an age when a child naturally begins to inquire about his roots. She also discussed with the grandmother the fact that the "grapevine" in their part of the city was very strong, and Kasim probably knew a great deal from the other children.

She agreed to have a session with Kasim and the therapist to discuss this further. In the family session, the therapist encouraged Mrs. Gifford to find out what Kasim had heard from the other children and what they teased him about. She was shocked to discover that other children had called his mother a "hooker" and a "drug addict" and that Kasim had kept this inside for some time. Both family members were carrying the burden of this secret. She was then able to ask Kasim if he had questions for her. He immediately asked why his mother had left him. Mrs. Gifford explained the circumstances and was able to help Kasim to understand that he was not with his mother because of her life-style and not because of any flaw in him.

In a subsequent session, the therapist asked that Kasim's mother attend together with Kasim and his grandmother. In this session, the therapist learned that in the last year Kasim's mother had begun to feel guilty about leaving him for so long and had started to see him more often. She had become anxious when Kasim had asked why he couldn't live with her and had been making vague promises to him that he could join her at some point in the future.

The therapist clarified the situation by demonstrating that this "mixed message" was harmful to Kasim. She encouraged Mrs. Gifford and Ayana to discuss the realities of her life situation and work out a regular visitation schedule for Kasim. Ayana shared her guilt with her mother openly for the first time and acknowledged that Kasim could not live with her. They agreed that he would continue to live with his grandmother but that Ayana would visit him regularly every Saturday. Ayana was then asked to discuss this openly with Kasim who had been observing this discussion. Tearfully she told him that she loved him but that she was confusing him by telling him that he would live with her. She discussed with him the decision that he would live with his grandmother but that she would visit him very week.

Kasim cried also but appeared visibly relieved. In subsequent months, his depression lifted and he began to re-engage his friends.

This type of secret, which is in fact "known" by all the parties (and by the community), can be particularly toxic because of the energy that is involved in protecting the family members from this knowledge. The "grapevine" or informal communication network in Black communities is very strong. The following is another example of a complicated family secret concerning an "informal adoption."

George Kent was a 7-year-old Black boy who had been informally adopted by his aunt when he was 6 months old. His mother had "dropped him on her doorstep" one day and never returned. Olivia Kent, his aunt, had raised him along with her three children, Carol (20), Ivy (15), and Althea (12) and Carol's son, Billy (age 5). There had never been any formal discussion in the family as to George's real relationship to the other family members. George had begun to act out and fight at school and at home shortly after the family had been visited by a representative of the local child welfare department. George's mother, an alcoholic, had died in a local hospital and prior to her death had told her social worker about Olivia Kent and George. The child welfare worker informed Ms. Kent that George was now under the guardianship of her agency and a decision must be made as to whether he would remain with Ms. Kent.

This caused a major disruption in the family. Ms. Kent petitioned formally to adopt George but his acting-out behavior had raised questions as to the suitability of his placement in her home.

At the point at which Ms. Kent arrived with George for her first session at our clinic, it was clear that both of them were very frightened and angry about these developments. The therapist helped Ms. Kent to talk about the circumstances that had led up to this dilemma and helped her to discuss this openly with George. George then told her that he had always wondered why he looked different from her other children (he was darker skinned) and that Billy had often teased him about this. He shared that he was very frightened of having to leave.

Mrs. Kent arranged a meeting of all the members of her household with the therapist to discuss the situation. She told them the "secrets" in George's history and asked their support for keeping him. All of the family members were surprised to hear that there was any question of his remaining in their family. A meeting was arranged by the therapist with the child welfare worker and the family to clarify their desire to formally adopt George. He beamed throughout this session. The therapist subsequently wrote a number of letters for the family documenting the "bonding" that had occurred between George and his "family."

Ms. Kent was then able to discuss openly with George the fact that she could not tolerate his acting out at home or in school. He had been "spoiled" by the family and allowed to "get away with" a great deal. She set clear rules for him at home and enlisted the aid of his older "sisters" to enforce these rules. His behavior at home and in school dramatically improved.

Secrets Regarding Fatherhood

There are many issues concerning fatherhood that may become secrets in Black families. For example, in the following case example, a child was raised by a stepfather and was never told the "secret" of his true paternity.

The Brown family was referred for treatment because their son Michael, aged 13, had been acting out, was aggressive with peers in school, often talked back to his mother and father, and broke his curfew. The Brown family consisted of Mr.

Brown, aged 40, Mrs. Brown, aged 30, Michael, and two younger siblings, Milton, aged 9 and Karen, aged 5. Mr. and Mrs. Brown reported that Michael had always respected them until the last year. He had been "running wild," "talking back" to them, fighting at school, and so on. They felt helpless to control him. In the family sessions, Mrs. Brown was the family spokesman and the person who sat closest to Michael. Mr. Brown seemed to alternate between being peripheral and becoming involved in an angry, intrusive way with Michael. The parents clearly disagreed with each other about discipline or limits. The mother was overindulgent of Michael and overinvolved with him. Therefore, the therapist decided to put the father in charge of Michael. The family resisted this process for a number of weeks. Finally, the therapist confronted the parents about this resistance. They became uncomfortable and Mrs. Brown actually looked alarmed. The therapist, sensing that this was an issue between the parents drew a boundary and asked the children to leave the room. Tearfully, Mrs. Brown explained that she had become pregnant with Michael as an unwed teenager at the age of 17. Her family had been embarrassed and angry at her because they had wanted her to go to college. They had hidden the "secret" of Michael's birth and had never discussed it. Shortly after his birth, Mrs. Brown met and married her current husband, who had raised Michael as his own. The other two children were his.

Mr. Brown explained that Michael had always been an issue between them. She had protected and spoiled him and had never really allowed Mr. Brown to be a "real father" to him. Both Mr. and Mrs. Brown agreed that Michael sensed that he was different from the other children. He did not look like anyone else in the family and had once angrily asked if he was adopted.

With the therapist's help, Mr. and Mrs. Brown were able to discuss how this secret had affected the way in which they had raised Michael and their inability to work together and parent him together. They finally decided to raise the issue with their son and to be clear with him that emotionally they were both his parents. The children were called back into the room and Mr. and Mrs. Brown discussed with Michael this "secret." Mr. Brown was able to share with him the fact that he had accepted him long ago as his son. Michael and the other children looked at each other often during this report. When the therapist inquired as to what was going on between them, Michael reported that a cousin, who had stayed with the family the previous summer had implied that he was an "outsider" but had never told him the details.

In future sessions, the therapist was able to restructure the family by asking the mother to encourage Michael and Mr. Brown to spend time alone together in order to develop the relationship between them. Both parents were able to talk openly about setting clear limits for Michael without this toxic secret between them.

Another type of fatherhood secret may have to do with other children, another family, or another woman in a father's life. Like the secrets discussed above, these issues may be known on some level, but either denied or never discussed by family members. In many cases, these issues surface only when there is a family crisis or major loss such as a death of the father. The following case illustrates this dilemma:

Connie Jones, a 40-year-old Black woman, had come for treatment requesting help for her son Darryl, aged 15. Darryl had two other siblings, Mary, aged 10 and Robert, aged 9. Their father had been killed suddenly in a fatal car accident 6 months earlier. Darryl had been very angry and had been acting out since his death. He stayed out late at night, was truant from school, and was often angry and hostile toward his mother. Darryl had had a very problematic relationship with his father prior to his death and had taken his loss "hard." It was clear that the whole family was struggling with this and had never fully mourned or shared their pain.

In a family session, the father's death was discussed. Darryl reported that his father had really "done wrong by them." At the funeral, another woman had appeared with a child 2 years younger than Darryl and reported that this was his father's child. Darryl's mother reported that she had suspected this and had heard rumors but had never really confronted her husband or let the children know. Michael was furious. He was finally able to tell his mother that he had felt betrayed at having to find this out at a time like that (i.e., during the funeral). He was angry at his father and at her. Once this issue was discussed openly by Mrs. Jones with Michael and the other children, they were able to talk openly about their hurt and anger and their sadness at the death of their father. The family's mourning process could then begin.

Bowen (1976) has discussed the emotional shock wave that a death can precipitate in a family. In many Black families funerals are particularly loaded because they are a time when these secrets often surface. By helping the family to openly discuss their hurt and anger, an issue very central, painful, and harmful to family functioning was defused and they could begin to support each other through the mourning process.

The Discussion of "Secrets" in Family Therapy with Black Families

Family therapists have been known to err in one of two directions in relationship to family secrets with Black families. One type of error involves opening up these secrets prematurely before a bond of trust has been established. The other type of error has often been made by well-meaning therapists who have been exposed to the cultural issues around "dirty laundry." Some of these therapists have therefore been afraid to open up such issues for fear of "losing the family." Clearly, the key issue here is one of timing. It is essential that the therapist join with the family well so that a bond of trust can be formed. This creates an atmosphere in which even the most difficult issue can be raised. The therapist can then make a decision as to which "secrets" need to be opened and explored. This need for a careful joining with Black families is crucial to overcoming resistance and to successful treatment.

This chapter has explored the diverse extended family patterns and the role of informal adoptions that are so central to the lives of many Black families. Within these complex kinship networks, it is extremely important that roles be both flexible and clear. Sometimes, however, these roles can become blurred or confused. The next chapter will explore in detail the issue of role relationships in Black families.

CHAPTER 4

Role Flexibility and Boundary Confusion in Black Families

INTRODUCTION

Role relationships are very complex in many Black families, particularly those with an extended kinship system. This chapter explores different aspects of those roles, including: (1) role flexibility, (2) the response to and role of Black men in American society, (3) roles of Black men as fathers, (4) the mothering role in Black families, and (5) the grandmother role. While this role flexbility is clearly a strength in many families, it can lead to role confusion and boundary problems in some of the Black families who come for treatment. The last part of this chapter explores such problems as the nonevolved grandma, the three-generational family, and the parental child.

ROLE FLEXIBILITY

As the previous chapter on the extended family has indicated, there is a great deal of reciprocity and role flexibility within both nuclear and extended Black families. Hill (1972) refers to this as the "adaptability of family roles." It was his work that described this as a source of "strength and stability." Because of the economic realities faced by many Black families, this role flexibility developed as a survival mechanism. In order for both parents to work, Black women have sometimes had to act as the "father" and Black men as the "mother." The previous chapter has already established that other relatives such as grandmothers, grandfathers, aunts, uncles, cousins, and so on, may assume parental roles. In addition, when all of the adults are working, children are often required to assume "parental child" roles necessary for family survival (Minuchin, 1974).

This role flexibility, while clearly a strength in many Black families, can sometimes result in role confusion or situations in which one individual becomes overburdened. In order to understand the roles Black men have in their relationships, families, and as fathers, one must first explore some of the ways in which Black men are often viewed by American society as a whole.

THE RESPONSE TO AND ROLE OF BLACK MEN IN AMERICAN SOCIETY

The issues of racism discussed in Chapter 2 are particularly relevant when one is exploring the roles of Black men in society and in their families. The legacy of slavery and oppression have definitely had an impact on the way in which Black men are perceived (Franklin, 1988; Gary, 1981; Grier & Cobbs, 1968).

There are many stereotypes that are often applied to Black men, including assumptions that they are "lazy," "peripheral," or "unavailable." This perception totally ignores the discrimination within the job market that often allows little access for Black men. Despite the gains of the 1960s and 1970s, Black men are still unemployed in great numbers. Many individuals in American society adopt a "blaming the victim" view of this phenomenon.

In addition, Black men in therapy often have described to me blatant examples of the discrimination they experience. They are often very aware that their mere presence may invoke fear in some White individuals. Franklin (1988) has described this as the "invisibility syndrome," a paradoxical process in which Black men, because of their high visibility, are perceived with fear and distrust and are often ignored or avoided. This can lead to a feeling of "invisibility." In a recent presentation, Franklin (1988) described a number of examples of this process. He described the experience of a young Black man who was dressed in sneakers, jeans, and a cap and was waiting for an elevator. Two White women came in, eyed him suspiciously, looked very uneasy, and eventually refused to get on the elevator with him.

In another situation, a Black vice-president in a business suit who had just attended a very important meeting at his bank came downstairs onto a busy Manhattan street and signaled for a cab. He waited for a half hour and watched cab drivers consistently pass him by in order to pick up a White person.

Thus, the high visibility and the fears about Black men contribute to either an overt or a subtle form of discrimination, which leads to further fear, distrust, avoidance, adding to the anger many Black men feel about this form of treatment. This negative message can influence a Black man's feeling about himself and his ability to function in his role in the workplace, his role as a lover or a spouse, and his role as a father. Roles of Black men in couple relationships will be discussed in Chapter 13. The first role to be explored here is that of Black men as fathers.

BLACK MEN AS FATHERS

There is, of course, considerable variability in the responses of Black men to fatherhood, as there is in all ethnic groups. Some live in the home and are very active in childrearing; some live in the home but are peripheral to their children's lives; some are involved but living outside the home. Some acknowledge their children, some do not; some provide support, others do not. Despite this obvious variability, there has been an assumption in the social science literature that the Black man is peripheral to the lives of his children (e.g., Moynihan, 1965). This image is somewhat misguided since it was based on a study of families on welfare, an economic situation in which the role of fathers could not be acknowledged lest the family jeopardize their welfare payments.

Black fathers are perhaps the most misunderstood group within Black families. In an earlier study, a colleague and I (Hines & Boyd-Franklin, 1982) pointed out that although there is great variability in the role of the Black man as father and husband, the fact that his identity is tied to his ability to provide in notably adverse economic circumstances could easily give rise to perceptions of Black men as non-family-oriented or uncaring.

> Black males have had the highest job loss rates in the labor force. When employed, the number engaged in managerial and professional jobs is relatively small. The essence of these realities is that Black males may have to expend great time and energy trying to provide the basic survival necessities for their families. This investment of Black fathers in providing for their families has been overlooked by those who stress peripheralness, or the absence of participation and interest on the part of Black fathers in daily family activities (e.g., Moynihan, 1965). (Hines & Boyd-Franklin, 1982, p. 88)

The next section examines more carefully the Black fathers who are peripheral and the ways in which Black families have attempted to compensate for this and provide support for growing children. It is the opinion of many scholars who have studied Black families, however, that the issue of peripheralness has been vastly overstated in the litera-ture (Gary, 1981; Hill, 1972; McAdoo, 1981, 1985; White, 1972, 1984).

In his careful review of the social science literature on this topic, John McAdoo (1981) found that the "exploration of the Black father's role in the socialization of his children is almost non-existent in social science literature" (p. 225). There is clear evidence that many Black men are involved in an egalitarian manner in childrearing, particularly in decision-making patterns (Dietrich, 1975; Gary, 1981; Hill, 1971; Lewis, 1975; Staples, 1971; Willie & Greenblatt, 1978). Childrearing engagement patterns do reveal differences based on class and socioeconomic level, with middle-class fathers in both Black and White homes more involved in childrearing (Cazenave, 1979; McAdoo, 1981). Many of these Black, middle-income fathers were equally involved in raising their children and making decisions about their lives. They were traditional, however, in their childrearing values. Good behavior and respect were demanded of children. Children were expected to respond immediately to their fathers and angry temper trantrums were very rarely allowed. Verbal nurturance was much more likely than hugs or kisses (McAdoo, 1981).

"Peripheral" Black Fathers

One possible family pattern is that of the "peripheral" Black father, who lives in the home but is not really involved in the family's daily life. This, of course, is also quite common in many different ethnic groups where fathers are absorbed in their work or other interests and spend relatively little time with their wives and children. There are some Black fathers who are divorced or separated from their families and are not involved on a regular basis. Clearly, the divorce and separation rates in this country have risen sharply in the last 10 years among all ethnic groups. There are many more single-parent families in the American population as a whole. Although the number of Black single-parent families has risen along with that of the rest of the country's population, as Chapter 11 will indicate, it would be a serious error for a therapist to assume that because a Black father is not living in the home that he is not involved with his children.

The Father's Extended Family

In addition to the individuals who directly "raise" a Black child, there may be a number who interact periodically but in a major way. In addition to the contact with the father or in spite of the lack of direct contact, the father's extended family, particularly his parents and his sisters, may be very involved in the child's kinship network. Because many of these individuals do not live in the home, families often forget to mention this contact. For many Black children, this maintains a tie to their father whom they may in fact never see. As Stack (1974) states:

> A child's father's kin play an active role in the nurturing of children, and as a result they may have the right to observe and judge whether a woman is performing her duties as a mother. If a young woman is unable to care for her child, nothing prevents a father's close female relatives from claiming parental rights. . . . In crisis situations, such as a mother's death or sickness, a child's kin through his mother and father are equally eligible to assume responsibilities of jural parenthood. (pp. 52–53)

Because of the difficulties inherent in the cycle of unemployment in which many Black men are trapped, they are often unable to contribute financially to their children. In these situations, if the father has acknowledged the child,

> the community expects a father's kin to help out. The Black male who does not actively become a "daddy" but acknowledges a child and offers his kin to that child in effect is validating his rights. . . . By validating his claim as a parent, the father offers the child his blood relatives and their husbands and wives as the child's kin—an inheritance so to speak. (Stack, 1974, pp. 51–52)

We, as family therapists, must understand the fundamental nature of these subtle kinship bonds if we are to work effectively with Black families who come to our clinics. Often when we inquire about relatives or draw a genogram (see Chapter 7) with a Black family, they may first tell us more about certain blood/nonblood ties or disclose certain other ties at this juncture. One must be aware of these patterns in order to know the correct questions to ask and thus to locate other resources for the child and the family. This concept is significant particularly for the family therapists who work in clinics, community mental health centers, hospitals, schools, and social service agencies that provide services to poor Black families. Often, if a parent is hospitalized or becomes disabled or is unable to care for her or his children, the children are quickly removed by social service agencies before a careful study is made of the significant others who may be willing to adopt the children informally. Many families of children have been divided in different foster homes because no inquiry was made into supports from the father's extended family as well as from the mother's.

Male Role Models in Black Families

The involvement of many extended family members—both blood and nonblood kin—in the rearing of Black children multiplies the number of potential role models. Unfortunately, many therapists are unaware of this wide range of individuals who are a potential resource for a child or for a family in trouble. As demonstrated above, these resources may come from the father's extended family or the mother's kin network or from close male friends of the mother. Often men who are involved with the mothers of these children become like husband, boyfriend, or friend "play daddies" and are often seen as the person who raised them. Frequently such a man brings his own extended family, who may then become a part of a child's kinship network. The following description of a family highlights both types of kinship support:

> Take my father, he ain't my daddy, he's no father to me. I ain't got but one daddy and that's Jason. The one who raised me. My kid's daddies, that's something else, all their daddies' people really take to them—they always doing things and making a fuss about them. We help each other out and that's what kinfolks are all about. (Stack, 1974, p. 45)

The support of these individuals is often overlooked by our clinics. When I was working on my doctorate at Columbia University, I was assigned a case of a young Black male child (age 12) who was acting out and aggressive. The clinic coordinator first assigned the case to me and then changed her mind. When I questioned her as to why, she answered that "since the child had no male role models," she felt that he and his family should be assigned to a male therapist. I asked her how she knew that he had no male role models, and she replied that he was living in a single-parent family. She had made an assumption based on the family's stated structure during their initial intake presentation about the availability of male role models.

I convinced her to allow me to treat this family. During the course of treatment, a number of male role models emerged who were utilized to help a very overburdened single-parent mother with a number of male children. These Black male role models included in this case the mother's boyfriend, her younger brother (aged 20) who sometimes stayed with them, and the boy's maternal grandfather.

Involvement of Black Men in Family Therapy

Men, in the population in general, are less responsive to treatment than women. Black men bring with them much of the suspicion discussed in the first chapter (see also Grier & Cobbs, 1968), in addition to a feeling of defensiveness about how the therapist may judge them in the fathering role. Given this reality, it is important that the therapist make a special effort to engage Black men directly in the treatment process. Chapters 8 and 13 describe many creative aspects of this engagement process.

My colleague and I (Hines & Boyd-Franklin, 1982) have described this process in detail:

> We may find, for example, that a father who is working two jobs cannot afford to take time off from work to participate in ongoing family therapy sessions. The same father, however, may be willing to come in for a single, problem-focused session. Therapists have to be creative in their use of phone contacts and letters to keep fathers abreast of the developments in their families' treatment. This communicates respect for their position in their families. Even limited involvement in their families' therapy can decrease the potential for sabotage and may well be sufficient for beginning structural changes that can promote the attainment of the goals that the therapist and the family are working toward. (p. 88)

"MOTHERING" ROLES IN BLACK FAMILIES

There are a vast range of role expectations of Black women depending on a number of issues, including age, class, generation, marital status, and the question of whether or not she has children. Many different aspects of such concerns are discussed in other chapters of this book—for example, self-concept and skin-color issues (Chapter 2), and male/female role relationships (Chapter 13). In this chapter, the aspects of female role issues to be addressed primarily surround the "mother" role in Black families. For most Black women, irrespective of the above differences, family is extremely important. Many Black women have numerous models within their extended families of strong, self-reliant women who have helped to keep the family together. The majority of Black women have always worked as well as raised their children. Therefore, many Black women grow up with models of mothers, grandmothers, and aunts who have served both roles in their families. Many Black women place an extremely high value on motherhood. I have repeatedly found in my work with Black women that no matter how problematic their early years may have been or how much they value their careers, they feel strongly about the need to raise children.

Motherhood, then, is a very important part of the role image of many Black women. It is, however, a complex, compounded image. Many Black women grow up with multigenerational models of "mother." Mothering is usually not an isolated activity but is shared with others. "Multiple mothering" is so common that many Black women who raise their children far away from the extended family create substitute "mothers," "grandmothers," and "babysitters."

There are also generational concerns involved in the consideration of the mothering role. Many older Black women (aged 60 and over) have the expectation that they will always mother. They know that even if

they are working, the well-being of their children often requires reciprocal help with babysitting and child care.

Teenage Pregnancy and Young Motherhood

A number of scholars have discussed the role of young motherhood in
Black families (Hill, 1977; McAdoo & McAdoo, 1985; Stack, 1974). This
phenomenon has implications in a number of areas, including feelings
about single parenthood. Attitudes toward the care of out-of-wedlock
children are quite different in Black and White populations. Studies
conducted in the rural South show that the majority of Black children
born out of wedlock are cared for and raised within the extended family
network (Hill, 1977). This pattern was very much the norm in the South
but has undergone some changes in Northern cities where foster care
agencies have placed large numbers of these children. Attempts are now
being made in many states to consider extended family placements first.

The pattern of out-of-wedlock pregnancy among Black teenagers
often creates a family dynamic that can lead to role and boundary
conflicts as the child grows older. Stack (1974) gives an example of this
process:

> A girl who gives birth as a teen-ager frequently does not raise and nurture
> her first born child. While she may share the same room and household
> with her baby, her mother, her mother's sister, or her older sister will care
> for the child and become the child's "mama." This same young woman may
> actively become a "mama" to a second child she gives birth to a year or two
> later. (p. 47)

We will explore in later chapters how the boundaries and roles can
become confused in such families as the teenage mother becomes an
adult and wants to assume parental responsibilities for her first-born
child. This child not only has a particular significant tie to another
"mama," but may also be either designated as "special" or scapegoated
by his or her other siblings because of it.

The Grandmother Role in Black Families

The role of the grandmother is one of the most central ones in Black
families. It can also be one of the most complex and problematic.
Grandmothers are frequently very central to the economic support of
Black families and play a crucial role in child care. Many Black children
raised in informal adoption situations are raised by grandparents (Hill,
1977). They represent a major source of strength and security for many
Black children.

One of the reasons for the complex nature of the role of grandmothers, however, has to do with the fact that in many Black families this role has never fully evolved or takes an extra generation to evolve. For example, if a young teenager becomes pregnant and has a baby, that infant is often raised as a sibling of her mother. The biological grandmother often becomes "Mama" or "Big Mama" and the biological mother is called by her first name as if she were a sibling of the child. The grandmother then assumes the mothering role and does not experience any of the often advantageous situational characteristics of being a grandmother.

The process becomes more complex as the family matures and the children grow older. As the biological mother becomes an adult, she may want to take on the task of mothering. This transition is very complicated because to do this she must (1) displace her own mother; (2) change her family's perception of her as a sibling; (3) change her child's and mother's perception of her mothering role.

To further complicate this process, often there are multigenerational issues involved in the young mother's attempts to validate her role as mother (Bowen, 1976, 1978). In many of these families, the biological mother may not have been raised by her mother but by her grandmother. Therefore her mother has never had a real chance to mother and is delighted to have the chance to "mother" her grandchild. Many grandmothers in Black families are in fact fairly young women (35–48) who had their own children in their teenage years and were also raised as siblings to their children. The role confusion that can result is a common treatment issue for many Black families and extended families.

ROLE CONFUSION IN BLACK FAMILIES AND ITS THERAPEUTIC IMPLICATIONS

While role flexibility is clearly a strength in many Black families, the extended family structure is one that is particularly vulnerable to boundary (Minuchin, 1974) and role confusion. This occurs in many different forms. The next section explores three of the most common forms of this type of confusion—the nonevolved grandmother, the three-generational family, and the parental child—as well as the therapeutic implications and interventions designed to restructure such family systems.

The Nonevolved Grandmother

Colon (1980) has termed the situation described above "the nonevolved grandmother." This is a situation that for a number of reasons is clearly ripe for role confusion. First, it goes counter to the notion in mainstream American society of a mother and father in charge of raising children. Second, the roles are constantly evolving and changing as individuals mature and grow. Third, the grandmother role in many Black families is particularly susceptible to role overload or burnout.

The fact that this role goes counter to many of the expectations of society has an impact on family life, particularly as a child reaches school age. Schools expect a "mother" to appear to register a child and sign important papers. This is also still true of many of our clinics and community mental health centers. Thus, in many situations, the primary caretaker, that is, the grandmother, is forced to take a back seat while the mother presents herself to the outside world. This is often very true for hospital or medical care. Pediatricians and therapists taking developmental histories often report that such "mothers" don't seem to remember their children's developmental milestones or give totally unrealistic ones. This is a very strong signal that the mother probably was not the child's primary caretaker at an early age and that she may not be the primary caretaker at this time.

In many of these extended families the grandmother remains a major power in the family even if the mother presents herself as the primary caretaker of the child. Often it is the grandmother who really makes the important decisions in a child's life, including whether or not he or she should receive therapy.

The second aspect of this has to do with the developmental life cycle of such families. In any family, as people grow and mature, roles change. Families often experience difficulties at particular modal points or life-cycle junctures where roles may be changing (Carter & McGoldrick 1980; Hines, 1988). For example, this model may work very well when a young 14- or 15-year-old teenager has a baby. When that mother is 30 and her child is 15, she may want to take on more responsibility but may find that neither her mother nor her child will accept a redefinition of her role.

This life cycle is further complicated by the role of the "elderly" in Black families. Particularly in poor Black families, older individuals often experience an increase rather than a decrease in responsibility in later life:

> What often evolves is a three or four generational family system that is headed by a grandmother, who is responsibile for caring for both her younger children, some of her grandchildren, and possibly her great grandchildren as well. Given the debilatory effects of poverty over a lifetime, in many cases she reaches later life with severe medical problems that further impair her ability to manage this overwhelming task successfully. For the larger family system, the issues remain similar to earlier stages, as there are

usually adolescent and young adult members in the household, as well as young children to be cared for. Additional adult growth for the grandmother is blocked by these continuing responsibilities and the forward thrust of the family life cycle for all family members may become stalled. (Hines, 1988, p. 529)

This grandmother or greatgrandmother then becomes overly central and is a candidate for system overload and burnout. Often these women present at our clinics as profoundly depressed individuals, or their grandchildren begin to act out or develop symptoms in order to get help for this overburdened family system.

This overburdening of a central family member can have quite an effect on the lives of the entire extended family, from exacerbating the harsh exigencies of poverty to embroiling the family at all levels in a conflict of role-related issues (Hines, 1988). The relevance of this issue to the process of family therapy with Black extended families can hardly be overstated, involving as it does a phenomenon that can reverberate profoundly throughout the family structure:

> The active, daily involvement of multigenerational households magnifies the interplay of their own life phase task with the life stage concerns of other family members who can span three to four generations; thus, intergenerational conflicts have a high probability of arising. Reality demands that the aged assume meaningful roles, the therapeutic task is helping them to be useful without overfunctioning. Family therapy facilitated a shift towards new options that freed the multigenerational family to proceed with their intertwined lives without repetition of serious emotional patterns that led to triangling and dysfunction of younger family members. (Hines, 1988, p. 531)

Life-cycle demands of Black families thus are often complex and overwhelming. To use the metaphor of the "train track" of life, the therapeutic task is to help derailed families get back on track and proceed with life-cycle issues appropriate to each family member. In some extended families where these roles have never evolved, the therapist's task is to help the family construct the track, build the structures, or clarify the roles and boundaries that will allow them to grow and thus to move forward with their lives.

The Three-Generational Family

As we have seen in the three-generational family described above, frequently familial roles become blurred, and the mother of the female adolescent with a baby never fully becomes a grandmother while her daughter is never allowed to fully function as a mother to her own child.

Minuchin (1974) has developed a structural approach to working with these families. The goal of this approach in these situations is to help the grandmother support her daughter in learning to be an effective parent, and to help them negotiate a new "alliance of executives" in which they begin to share parenting responsibilities. Thus, the family is restructured so that the child can be given clear signals and messages by both mother and grandmother.

In Black families, many other family members may also participate in childrearing. One child may respond to an executive system that includes mothers, fathers, stepparents, aunts, uncles, grandmothers, grandfathers, and/or older siblings. The structural approach is extremely useful in these cases because, as with the scenario created by the non-evolved grandmother, intervention can occur along direct, practical lines. Contact is made with the key members of this executive group. They can then be brought together to discuss the problem at hand and to clarify who is in charge of various family functions. In Black families that are functioning well, these boundaries are clear no matter how many adults are involved. In the families that appear at our clinics, however, role boundaries and thus the functional family structure have broken down and need to be redetermined and rebuilt. In many cases, a functional structure has never fully developed and needs to be built for the first time.

The following case example illustrates the latter process.

Clarence (aged 12) was referred for treatment by the principal of the Catholic school he attended because of acting-out behavior. His grandmother, Mrs. Long, a 60-year-old Black woman, brought him for his first clinic appointment. She explained that his mother Margaret Long (age 27) was at work. The grandmother herself worked half-time as a school aide at a local public school.

Margaret Long had given birth to her son Clarence when she was 15 years old. He was raised with her and her siblings. Her mother essentially functioned as his mother. Mrs. Long was a strong, domineering woman who held a great deal of power in her family. It was clear that both her grandson and her daughter were afraid to cross her. The therapist learned this quickly when he asked Mrs. Long to bring in her daughter for a session. Mrs. Long was adamant that this was impossible because of her work schedule. She further stated "It's not necessary because I raised Clarence. I can tell you everything important." Clarence's relationship with his grandmother was a very difficult one. She reported with pride that she had always been strict with him at home but that he "didn't listen to anyone at school." The therapist joined and worked with the grandmother and Clarence for two sessions, coming up with a number of strategies that required Clarence to discuss his response to school officials with his grandmother. When Clarence was placed on probation, the therapist moved quickly. He utilized the "crisis" situation in order push the issue of the mother's participation. He told the grandmother that this was such a serious crisis that he would personally call the mother at work and make arrangements for her to attend the family meeting. When the mother appeared, it was clear that she felt very overwhelmed by her mother and was very resentful of her. In fact, Margaret Long's posture in the session was a mirror of her son's. At a number of points when the grandmother became angry and shouted at Clarence, he and his mother exchanged glances and at one point rolled their eyes. Mrs. Long became furious and yelled at both. It was clear that both Clarence and his mother were responding and being treated as siblings. The therapist pointed this out to both the grandmother and the mother, stressing that this was a serious crisis for Clarence and that unless the grandmother and mother were able to work together, Clarence would continue to act out. The therapist moved Clarence out of the discussion and focused the grandmother and the mother on (1) the consequences for Clarence's behavior; and (2) a strategy whereby the whole family and the therapist could meet together with the school officials. He made it very clear that they needed to work closely in that meeting if they were going to present a united front to Clarence and to the school.

The school interview was very successful and Clarence was reinstated in school with a clear understanding of the consequences if his behavior continued. After this interview, the therapist was able to get a contract with both mother and grandmother for ongoing involvement in the treatment process. He began to restructure the family by exploring ways in which the mother could work more closely with the grandmother in caring for Clarence. The grandmother was gradually able to help the mother assume more disciplinary responsibility for Clarence.

It is interesting that in this family, as in many Black families, the therapist was never able to put the mother in charge. He was, however, able to renegotiate an alliance of executives between the mother and the grandmother that allowed both to work together in parenting Clarence. As the rules and the family roles became more clear, Clarence's behavior improved significantly.

The Parental Child

Minuchin (1967, 1974) is also recognized for his clarification of the role of the parental child, a role that is extremely common in Black families. With the advent of working mothers in the population at large and the increasing number of latchkey children in America today, it has begun to appear more frequently in other cultural groups as well. Because of the economic instability that Black families have experienced in this country, the need for all members of the household to contribute in some way to the family's support is and always has been a very pressing reality. Therefore, with all available adults in a family working, the care of younger children falls to the oldest child, placing that child in a parental role. In Black families, this role can be filled by a male or female child, differing from Hispanic families in that in the latter population the role is usually fulfilled by the oldest female child. In functional Black families where this role works well, the parent or parental figures delegate to this child certain responsibilities for the care of younger children when the parent is not at home. Here the boundaries of the child or adolescent's responsibilities are clear and well defined: Parenting responsibilities are delegated and not abdicated, the parent being careful to remain "in charge" and to have the parental child report to her or him. It is important to stress that parental children are most often not a family structure of choice but an economic necessity.

The parental child family structure becomes dysfunctional when the parent or parents abdicate their responsibilities and place an unreasonable responsibility on the child in this position. This frequently occurs in Black single-parent families in which the mother becomes so overburdened that she begins to over-rely on her "right-hand man." The parental child may then become parent to his or her parent, so that the structure is maintained at the cost of the child's normal, age-appropriate thrust toward interaction with his or her peer group, and the mother is cut off from interaction with her other children.

The therapeutic goal in such situations to "realign the family in such a way that the parental child can still help the mother. . . . The parental child has to be returned to the sibling subgroup, though he maintains his position of leadership and junior executive power" (Minuchin, 1974, p. 98).

In summary, it is the therapeutic task to recognize and support the strength and stability that role flexibility has provided in many Black families without perpetuating the role confusion to which the extended family system is particularly vulnerable. The next chapter explores another strength in Black families: the role of religion and spirituality.

CHAPTER 5

Religion, Spirituality, and the Treatment of Black Families

Family therapists, in assessing the strengths and coping skills of Black families, must be sensitive to the role that religion and spirituality play in the lives of many Black people. These two concepts are listed separately because although many Black people have been raised with and have internalized a sense of spirituality, not all are members of organized religions or churches. Brisbane and Womble (1985–86) state this very clearly:

> Many Blacks who "grew up" in the church—most frequently of Baptist or African Methodist denomination—while continuing to claim a belief in God or to be religious, do not attend church. They vigorously maintain a conviction about spiritual power and unquestionably believe something or somebody greater than themselves is watching over them; and it provides relief and fulfillment. In fact, it may be as fundamental in the lives of Blacks as is religion. Organized religion and the church are viewed as means and places to express one's spiritual beliefs and to have spiritual needs fulfilled. (p. 250)

Training in the mental health fields largely ignores the role of spirituality and religious beliefs in the development of the psyche and in its impact on family life. In the treatment of Black families, this oversight is a serious one.

SPIRITUALITY AND THERAPY WITH BLACK PEOPLE

Knox (1985) states that "spirituality is deeply embedded in the Black psyche" (p. 31). Mbiti (1969) and Nobles (1980) have demonstrated that this sense of spirituality has its roots in the tradition of African religions. As Nobles has stated,

Religion permeated every aspect of the African's life. . . . Religion was such an integral part of man's existence that it and he were inseparable. Religion accompanied the individual from conception to long after death. (p. 25)

Thus, rather than being a systemized set of religious beliefs or practices, the African sense of spirituality was woven into the very fabric of society and was a central characteristic of the African psyche.

Knox (1985) argues for a careful understanding and assessment of the role of spirituality in the lives of Black clients and their families. Her approach utilizes spirituality as a tool in the assessment of Black alcoholics and their families, but her findings are relevant for a much broader Black population. Her work has provided a number of examples of the ways in which spiritual beliefs have become a part of the survival system of Black people and the ways in which they may manifest themselves in the treatment process:

Clues to spirituality, which suggest its use as a coping mechanism, are expressed during initial interviews. These should be explored as any other psychosocial area in the assessment process. The most commonly expressed clues by believers of spirituality are likely to consist of (1) "God will solve my problems"; (2) "God is punishing me for having sinned"; and (3) "The Church is my salvation." (p. 32)

Spiritual reframing is a very useful technique with Black families. Mitchell and Lewter (1986) point out that people who grow up in a "traditional Black community" are spontaneously equipped with a system of core beliefs (p. 2), particularly spiritual ones. One reframing that will often be heard is the notion that "God will know what your needs are and will supply" and "He gives you no more than you can carry" (Knox, 1985, p. 2). This highlights the inner strength of the person and the power of this faith and belief system. These beliefs manifest themselves in many different forms clinically and can be utilized as part of family therapist's reframing who is aware of them.*

Belief statements such as those cited above often function as metaphorical communications of a generalized spiritual orientation. It is of utmost importance to therapeutic effectiveness that the presence of this manner of coping be recognized and incorporated into the therapeutic process. Failure to do so can jeopardize the joining pro-

---

*When I first began my doctoral training at Teachers College of Columbia University in 1972, I had the opportunity to work with Black children and their families at the Harlem Interfaith Counseling Service. Reverend Fred Dennard (the Executive Director) and Mrs. Doris Dennard (the Clinical Director) taught me a great deal about utilizing the spiritual strengths of Black families in therapy. Their therapeutic model, known as the "psychospiritual" approach to therapy, incorporates the basic belief systems of Black people into the treatment process.

cess and impede progress in therapy via client resistance and/or a lowered level of trust.

Black Churches

A more concrete manifestation of the widespread spiritual orientation in Black families is the very central role the community church plays in the lives of many Black people. The intersection between spiritual attitudes and the church can be seen in the extent to which the spirituality expressed within the church setting spills over into the experiences of everyday life (Knox, 1985). "While spirituality exists outside organized religion," Knox explains, "it finds its deepest expression and greatest influence in the Black family, in weekly, if not nightly participation in church activity." She continues,

> The organized church is by far the most profound instrument available to Blacks when it comes to coping with the multiplicity of problems that beset their lives. Church members as well as non-members accept the spirituality embodied in the church and use the church to confront their own helpless and depressive attitudes and oppressive practices toward them by others. Therefore, knowledge of the client's church affiliation and the minister often proves to be a valuable resource to the therapist. (pp. 34–35)

Although, as has been stated, strong religious and spiritual beliefs have always been an integral part of the lives of Black people in Africa (Hines & Boyd-Franklin, 1982), the spiritual heritage of Black Afro-Americans is of combined origins. Frazier (1963) has documented how Baptist and Methodist churches sent missionaries to work with Black slaves in the South. Gradually, an "invisible institution" (Frazier, 1963) developed, made up of Black preachers who interpreted the Bible for Black people. The African tradition of storytelling incorporated Christian teachings and a strong oral tradition, a hybrid specific to the Black Afro-American situation, developed. The custom of preaching in the dramatic narrative style that is such a central part of Black church services today evolved from this tradition. Frazier states that "preaching meant dramatizing the stories of the Bible and the way of God to man. These slave preachers were noted for the imagery of their sermons" (pg. 18). This imagery is still a very important part of Black church services.

The Role of the Church Historically

The overt segregation that existed in most of the South and the covert discrimination in the North had a major hand in the Black church becoming a central force in the lives of many Black people as the sole institution that belonged entirely to the Black community. Black churches thus became multifunctional community institutions. They often established their own schools and Bible societies, serving the varied and widespread needs of a disenfranchised population and becoming what Frazier (1963) describes as "a refuge in a hostile white world" (p. 44). They were, and often still are, one of the few places where Black men and women could feel that they were respected for their own talents and abilities. A Black man or woman who might have a job as a domestic worker during the week could achieve status in the church as a deacon or deaconess. The community church became one of the most important sources of leadership experience and development in the Black community. Many Black people have used this as a major coping mechanism in handling the often overwhelming pain of racism and discrimination. As Frazier (1963) and DuBois (1903) have shown, the churches have provided an escape for Black people from their painful experiences.

It is no accident, therefore, that the churches also became a focus of political activity in Black communities. This was true from the slavery days of activists such as Nat Turner and can still be seen in such religious/political leaders as Martin Luther King, Jr., Malcolm X, and Jesse Jackson (Wilmore, 1973).

Religious Denominations and Groups in the Black Community

There are many different denominations and distinct religious groups represented in Black communities within the United States. These include Baptist, African Methodist Episcopal, Jehovah's Witness, Church of God in Christ, Seventh Day Adventist, Pentecostal churches, Apostolic churches, Presbyterian, Lutheran, Episcopal, Roman Catholic, Nation of Islam, and numerous other Islamic sects.

Of these groups, the Baptist and the African Methodist Episcopal groups account for the largest proportion of Black people. After the Civil War, because of the racist attitudes of most White churches, Black churches separated and formed their own congregations, eventually evolving into the Black Baptist churches and the African Methodist Episcopal churches as we know them today.

Frazier (1963) cites studies of churches in Chicago, arguing that there was stratification in many Black communities, with Black middle- and upper-class families attending more "ritualistic and deliberate" churches such as the Episcopal, Presbyterian, and Congregational churches.

Churches in Black communities are not always large congregations. Many Baptist and African Methodist Episcopal ministers began as pastors of small "storefront churches" (Frazier, 1963). This is also often true of many of a growing number of Pentecostal and Apostolic Churches in Black urban communities. These denominations might include the Church of God in Christ and Seventh Day Adventist. Many of these churches, because of their small size, have an intimate relationship with members of the congregation. For family therapists and other mental health practitioners who are working with these families, some knowledge of the religious beliefs and practices of these groups is important. For example, there are often strict codes of dress, and rules that prohibit drinking, smoking, drugs, dancing, partying, and so on. This often causes generational conflicts for the children and adolescents in these families.

The Church "Family"

It is extremely important for therapists to understand the concept of the church family as it relates to Black people. I will use the example of a Baptist church to illustrate this point, although there are many similarities in different denominations of Black churches on this concept. For many Black families a Black church functions essentially as another extended family. The minister is usually a central figure in the life of the family and may be sought out by family members for pastoral counseling in times of trouble, pain, or loss. After the family and extended family, the church is the most common source of help to Black people. Larger churches have two or more ministers who each may handle different functions within the church. The minister's wife often also serves a very important role; in some congregations, particularly smaller ones, she may also be sought out by church members for help and advice.

Many Black churches have a board of deacons and deaconesses who assist the pastor in carrying out the duties of the Church. This is a position of some status. If a family member tells you that he or she holds such a position in his or her church, this is clearly a strength and a sign of some leadership ability. Often deacons and deaconesses are sought out by other church members for help and counsel. Black churches have complex networks, relationships, and dynamics involving the entire church hierarchy and provide spiritual and social activities for the whole family. There are Sunday School and Bible Study classes that are offered to everyone from very young preschoolers to elderly members. Women in the church volunteer to teach Sunday School and to care for children in the nursery while their parents are attending services.

Members of the Usher Board seat church members on Sunday and collect the donations from the congregation. There are often a number of choirs, including a gospel choir, which draw members into the services.

There are also a number of parallel organizations for young people, including a junior usher board and junior choirs. As has been mentioned, many successful Black professionals today received their initial training in leadership in these organizations.

Preaching is a very important part of the church service and often arouses strong emotions in the congregation. It is an art among Black ministers and this special training accounts for the unique gifts of oratory as evidenced by such powerful speakers as Martin Luther King, Jr. and Jesse Jackson. Because of the degree of emotions aroused by the sermons, most churches also have a Nurses' Aid Association, whose nurses are available if members become overwhelmed with emotion (i.e., "feel the spirit," "get happy," or "shout") during the service. It is preaching that conveys the messages of hope, the route to salvation, and the capacity for survival as a people.

Black churches also serve a social function. Meals are often served on Sunday after services, providing an opportunity for families to mingle socially. Many Black single-parent mothers will tell a therapist, "I raised my children in the church" or "He was brought up in the church." These mothers mean literally what they say: Black churches often function as surrogate families for isolated and overburdened single mothers. Many Black families when moving to a new community will quickly find a Black church as a way to become connected to the community. The ways in which some of these same strategies can be used by family therapists to help build new networks for isolated Black families are discussed later.

One of the most important "family" functions that a Black church serves is that of providing a large number of role models for young people, both male and female. These individuals represent resources who can be utilized when a child or an adolescent is in trouble. Black churches often provide non-church-related activities such as Boy Scouts, basketball teams, youth groups, and so on. Because of the need for services in many Black communities and the deep concerns about the education of Black children, many churches have begun to provide day-care centers and schools on the premises. These are community resources of which therapists should be aware. The following case illustrates this process:

The Porter family was a young Black family consisting of Mr. Porter (aged 28), Mrs. Porter (27), Oscar, 10, and three younger daughters (aged 6, 3, and 1). They came to our clinic seeking help for their son Oscar. Oscar was having a number of serious behavioral problems in the public school that he was attending. He had been truant on a number of days and had not been doing his homework. The school had suspended him a number of times. When the parents entered the first session it was clear that they were both overwhelmed. They reported that they had gotten married when Mrs. Porter became pregnant with Oscar at age 17. They were too young for parenthood and had always found Oscar a "difficult child." The parents felt that things had become much worse as the younger children were born because they could not give Oscar the time and attention that they felt he craved. Both the father and the mother worked and the children were often left with Oscar for a period after school. Mr. and Mrs. Porter reported that they often had to shuttle the children to three different schools and babysitters in the morning. Therefore Oscar was often left to go to school alone and would frequently not go.

This family presented as an overwhelmed sibling group with no functioning executives. The therapist, in an attempt to help support the parents in their parental function, asked them to discuss what they felt would help Oscar most. They replied that they wished that they could find a good school where they could find help with monitoring him. Mrs. Porter also expressed a need for a closer day-care center so that all of the children could be dropped off and picked up more conveniently.

The therapist knew of a small Baptist church in the community that had started a school and a day-care center. The therapist contacted Mrs. Clodhill, the minister's wife, who served as the school principal, and asked if she would help this family. The parents readily agreed to go and meet with her and were able to arrange to enroll all of their children in the school and the day-care center on the church grounds. Mrs. Clodhill and Oscar's teacher then met with the parents and the therapist and worked out clear ways of monitoring his school attendance. There was an after-school program available that took the burden off of Oscar in terms of caring for his younger siblings until his parents returned home.

Mrs. Clodhill, the teacher, and the therapist all worked together to support the parents in their efforts to begin monitoring Oscar's homework more closely and to set clear limits for him.

The Black elderly make up a significant part of the congregation in many Black churches. There is often a respect and caring for these individuals that can continue to provide a sense of family as they grow older, particularly since it is more common today that their adult children are more mobile. The minister will often make visits to the home of an elderly person who is ill. Some churches will provide a car or van to bring in elderly members who could not otherwise attend services. These are resources of which family therapists are often unaware.

Jehovah's Witness Families

One church group that has gained in membership in Black communities has been that of the Jehovah's Witness faith. Largely through the "pioneering" and missionary work of its members, many more Black people have now been exposed to and joined this religious group. The Kingdom Hall is the focus of church activities and it has become an educational center as well as a religious one. Bible study is often an important part of this religion, as is spreading the word of God by passing out pamphlets and discussing the Bible with people in their communities. Jehovah's Witnesses adhere to strict rules about dress and conduct, which can lead to generational conflict of the type described above. Since holidays such as Christmas, Thanksgiving, and Easter are not observed, this may lead to conflicts with other family members. Children often find themselves "in the middle." Jehovah's Witness families often come into conflict with medical establishments because of their refusal to allow blood transfusions in hospitals. Often these families are very hesitant to seek mental health services, tending to rely more on the counsel of the elders at their Kingdom Hall and the other members of their fellowship. When they do approach mental health services, it is often in extreme cases, such as a child who is hallucinating, a suicidal adolescent, or the hospitalization of a family member.

Nation of Islam and other Islamic Sects

There are within the Black community many small Islamic sects which maintain consistent followings, particularly in urban inner-city areas. In the late 1960s and 1970s, the Nation of Islam gained a considerable following. Based on the teachings of the Honorable Elijah Muhammad and preached initially by Malcolm X, this religious group is particularly worth discussing with regard to practicing therapy because of the conflicts that often arise in families due to the strictness of many of its practices.

Edwards (1968) has done one of the few studies that have compared Muslim beliefs with those of Black Christian families from similar lower-class backgrounds.

These differences in belief and practice between the Nation of Islam and Christian denominations often produces major problems for Black people who have converted to the Nation of Islam and their families of origin. The following excerpt summarizes the differences Edwards found, particularly in the beliefs about male and female role issues:

> A number of situations determined the break between the Muslim spouses and their relatives. In those cases where the parents and in-laws of the Muslim spouse lived within the area, "uniting with" the Nation of Islam was contrary to the wishes of these relations. This assumes added significance since the majority of these parents and in-laws belonged to Christian churches. Also of significance in the break between Muslim spouses and their parents was the inflexibility of the Muslim spouses in their adherence to the behavioral codes of the Nation of Islam. It was found that conscientious Muslims did not smoke, drink or curse, nor did they tolerate these prohibited indulgences within their homes. Since many of the Muslims' relatives did in fact indulge in these habits, a situation of mutual

intolerance and estrangement soon followed. Of relevance here also were the reactions of the parents and in-laws to the Muslims, particularly as these reactions focused upon the behavior and activities of the Muslim female spouse. Muslim females never straightened their hair or wore make-up of any kind. The resulting appearance of the female was often a point of criticism and mockery from relatives, particularly it seemed from the female spouse's mother. (pp. 380–381)

Edwards' work is illustrative of the kinds of multigenerational conflict that can result in a Black family when a member or a part of the family converts to the Nation of Islam or another Islamic sect. The following case example demonstrates how a family therapist utilized such knowledge in her work with such a family.

Amena, a 30-year-old divorced Black woman entered our clinic requesting help for her son Abdullah, aged 10. They had been referred by Abdullah's school after he was suspended because of his involvement in a fight with other boys. Amena reported that she had been raised in a Baptist home but that she and her husband had converted to the Nation of islam when Abdullah was 3 years old. Amena had never had a good relationship with her family, particularly her mother, and this already tenuous relationship had been exacerbated by her conversion. Her mother was very active in her Baptist church, and Amena's father, who was deceased, had been a deacon. Her mother accused her of taking her grandson away from the family and the church. She particularly objected to Amena's having changed her own name from Vivian and Abdullah's from Kerry. During her marriage, Amena relied on her husband to keep her family at bay. She saw very little of her relatives for most of the years of her marriage. In the last year, when Abdullah was 9 years old, his parents divorced and Amena found herself with no job or training and was forced to move back into her mother's home. Abdullah's father did not visit him or contribute to his support.

The year prior to seeking treatment had been a very difficult one for the entire family. Amena found a job and enrolled in a training program and was forced to leave her son in her mother's care a good deal of the time. Amena and her mother would battle about everything from her choice of clothes for herself and Abdullah to her choice of names. Abdullah was very torn between his mother and grandmother and would often withdraw and cry. His grandmother persisted in calling him Kerry in spite of Amena's objections. Finally, a number of children at school had begun teasing Abdullah about his name and his clothing. His fights at school were his distress signal for the pain he was experiencing in his family.

The therapist saw Amena and Abdullah together in the first session and quickly realized that the grandmother was a crucial person in this family structure. With Amena's permission, the therapist called the grandmother and asked her to attend the next session. In that session, it was clear that the hostility between Amena and her mother was very intense. They engaged in a number of loud, angry shouting exchanges. As they yelled at each other, Abdullah seemed to shrink in size and began anxiously biting his nails. The therapist stopped the argument between Amena and her mother and focused their attention on what their fighting was doing to Abdullah. He began to cry at this point, followed quickly by Amena and her mother. The therapist then reframed Amena and her mother's tears as signs that they obviously had a lot of love and caring for Abdullah but that their fighting was tearing him apart. They agreed to work together in family therapy to help Abdullah. In future sessions, Amena was able tearfully to tell her mother how hurt and angry she had been when her mother criticized her appearance and her choice of religion and life-style. Her mother was eventually able to share her own hurt and sadness as she perceived Amena as pulling away from her and from the church beliefs of her youth. In a later session, the grandmother was able to acknowledge that her greatest fear had been the loss of her daughter and grandson.

The therapist was able to help the grandmother see that she was losing them both by this attack. The therapist was also able to help Amena and her mother negotiate a truce in their relationship so they could work together in raising Abdullah and stop giving him contradictory messages. The grandmother was able to support Amena in going together with her daughter and Abdullah to discuss his behavior with the school authorities and to help stop the teasing that he was experiencing in school.

Abdullah was helped to express clearly to his mother and grandmother the bind that their fighting had created for him. His behavior improved dramatically at home and in school. His two parental figures were able to put aside their differences and work together on his behalf.

IMPLICATIONS FOR FAMILY THERAPY

Therapists Who Ignore Religious Issues With Black Families

As we have seen, Black families sometimes frame issues in religious terms. If the therapist does not understand this process, a value conflict can sometimes erupt in which the family ends up disengaging from treatment. The following case example illustrates this point:

Kevin, a 14-year-old Black adolescent, was referred to a community mental health center because he was hearing voices and evil spirits. The family consisted of Mrs. Clark, Kevin's mother (40), his father, Mr. Clark, and his sister Janice (17). They were seen by a resident in training who asked the entire family to come in for a number of family sessions. In the second session, the entire family attended and the daughter voiced the family's dilemma. She felt that the therapist was only dealing with Kevin on the "natural side" and not on the "spiritual." She went on to explain that she felt that the therapist was dealing only with Kevin's mind and not with his "soul and his spirit." She stated that she felt that his problems had begun when he had stopped attending church. The therapist, instead of using this as an opportunity to pursue and explore the family's belief system, closed the door immediately. She stated "You're right, we don't deal with the spiritual or religious aspects." When the sister pursued her point of view, the therapist was even more adamant. She stated that "we are a mental health center and our orientation is psychological and psychiatric, not the spiritual, not the religious." She suggested that she could not provide that kind of service and that it "could be provided probably by some kind of minister or religious person but not us." The family left treatment and did not return. (Hines, 1987, personal communication)

The family members undoubtedly left treatment with a sense that the therapist was not sensitive nor inclined to value their way of thinking. With Black families such as this one, it is usually counterproductive to dismiss their definition of the problem as related to religion. Often religious issues are used as a metaphor by Black families and may be their way of testing to see if the therapist respects their beliefs. It is important in these situations to pursue such family signals and to encourage family members to explain their points of view. In this example it would have been important for the therapist to explore whether the mother, the father, and the son agreed with the sister's perspective on the situation. The therapist also missed an opportunity to explore the power issues in the family more closely by exploring the sister's comment that her brother's problems had begun when he had stopped attending church. In fact, this was a very religious Black family in which Kevin's refusal to attend services had created a major conflict. He felt trapped by their strong beliefs and saw no way to differentiate between himself and his family except through his psychosis. This would have been an opportunity for the therapist to explore the strategies that this family had used to try to reinvolve their son in the church network. The family thus would have been given the opportunity to recognize their concern for their son, and the therapist then would have had the opportunity to help them to give him some of the "space" necessary for a growing adolescent. The therapist might have normalized this need for individuation and reframed it for the family by telling them that it was clear that they had instilled strong spiritual and religious values in their son and that many teenagers go through a period of questioning these before accepting certain values as their own.

For some very religious Black families, church attendance and adherence to a religious code is enforced with such rigidity that adolescents choose this most restrictive area in which to rebel. The therapist would have even had the option of involving the minister to help the family cope with this transitional stage in their son's life. Unfortunately, by refusing to discuss this further and ignoring the family's repeated attempts to bring up this issue, a door was closed.

Once the family therapist is aware of the significance of religious values and the resource that churches can provide in the lives of Black people, there are a number of ways in which this knowledge can be utilized in the treatment process. The last section of this chapter is divided into four different types of intervention: (1) involving a minister as a consultant, co-therapist, or integral part of the treatment process; (2) mobilizing the resources of a Black church network to help a family in crisis; (3) utilizing church networks as a support for a family during times of illness, death, or loss; and (4) helping isolated Black families who are cut off from their original networks to create or recreate new ones.

Utilizing Ministers and Other Church Members

The minister or pastor of a church has the potential of being a valuable resource, particularly in situations where he has already served as pastoral counselor for family members and knows them well. At the very least, with the family's permission, a minister who has served in this role should be contacted for information about his involvement. It has always been amazing to me that mental health practitioners will routinely contact other clinics, hospitals, or therapists who have worked with our clients but will not follow up on or often even inquire about help that the family may have sought from a minister, deacon, deaconess, or another church member.

The involvement of the minister in the process of therapy can take many different forms. He might simply be asked for information and asked for his help in encouraging the family to seek and follow through on treatment. He may, in special circumstances, be asked to serve as a consultant or a co-therapist. The following case illustrates this type of involvement:

Anthony Hill, a 27-year-old Black man, was brought to the emergency room by the police and was admitted to the inpatient unit of a large state hospital in the Bronx. He had threatened to attack his wife and was obsessed with thoughts that she was cheating on him. He was very withdrawn in the ward and isolated himself from other patients. Attempts to arrange family sessions with his wife and/or his parents who lived in an apartment in the same building had not been successful. Our staff on the inpatient service had learned to pay close attention to the visitors a patient received during his hospitalization. Anthony's father had visited a number of times accompanied by what the staff described as a "very distinguished older gentleman in a suit." The therapist stayed for visiting hours and met with the father and discovered that the gentleman who accompanied him was their minister in a small Church of God in Christ. Both were very concerned about Anthony. The therapist stressed the importance of getting the family involved in order to help Anthony and hasten his discharge. She asked the minister's help in arranging such a session and asked if he would participate. He explained that the family was very frightened by the hospitalization and that he would be willing to bring them in.

In the session that followed, Anthony, his wife Mary, his father, his mother, and his minister were present. It quickly became clear that this was a very enmeshed extended family in which the parents frequently intruded into the lives of Anthony and his wife. In addition, Anthony's church family consisted of the minister and small tightly knit congregation of a storefront Church of God in Christ. The minister had been used as a confidant by all family members and had been inducted by the family into its system dynamics. When the therapist asked Anthony and his wife to discuss the circumstances which had brought him to the hospital, his mother intruded a number of times. The therapist blocked her intrusion and this time asked the minister if he would help the couple to discuss this issue between themselves. With the minister's help, Anthony and Mary painfully recounted the fact that Mary had been raped and mugged. Anthony had reacted with rage and had blamed Mary for this. He now accused her of having invited the sexual assault. Mary burst into tears. The therapist asked the minister to speak directly to Anthony about this. The minister was able to help Anthony see that sometimes bad things happen to good people, that people do not necessarily provoke the things that happen to them. He also helped Anthony to recognize his wife's pain and led both of them in a prayer for strength to survive this devastating experience. In subsequent sessions, the minister and the therapist worked with the couple alone (without the parents), to further support the development of some measure of autonomy for them.

The minister and his family are often central members of a community and an important aspect of many extended family networks. Just as families can become "enmeshed" (Minuchin, 1974), so too can church families, as can be seen by the entangled relations of the minister and family in the case example above.

Utilizing Church Help in Times of Crisis

Church networks can be a very valuable resource for a family in crisis. Often they can mobilize quickly and offer aid to a family without the bureaucratic process of many social service agencies. The following case illustrates this process:

The Reid family, which consisted of Mrs. Reid and her three teenage daughters, was being seen in family therapy at our community mental health center. An arsonist had set a fire in their building and the family had lost all of their possessions. No one was injured but the entire family was badly shaken by the experience. The family found themselves homeless and after spending one night in a city shelter, the mother became very frightened for her children's safety. She then contacted the minister of her church and the church network was mobil-ized. The minister and his wife arranged for a temporary home for the mother and her daughters in the home of a member of the congregation. Church members donated food, clothing, and necessary household articles and helped her to find a new apartment.

Helping Isolated Families Create Church Networks

Some of the Black families who enter our clinics and community mental health centers are very socially isolated and emotionally cut off from their extended families (Bowen, 1976). These families often present with the most overburdened, multiproblem situations. Some of the most dysfunctional families are those who seem to have no network. In Chapters 3 and 4, I have already discussed ways to help such families resolve the cut off from their own extended families. Sometimes, however, this is not possible, and the family faces the difficult task of building an entirely new social support system. For families who have had a religious orientation or a church connection in the past, helping them locate and identify a new church network can be a very significant intervention. This is particularly true for single parents who may be struggling to raise children alone. Discharged hospital patients who have no connections to family can also benefit from this process.

A word of caution: This intervention is not for everyone. It should be made only if it appears syntonic with the family's belief systems and earlier experiences.

Some of the more cogent historical and psychosocial experiences of Black Afro-Americans and their families are strongly rooted in religious and spiritual background and experience. The vignettes presented in this chapter highlight problems and dilemmas that frequently confront the therapist who works with Black families. The various theoretical approaches that the therapist can employ in addressing this great vari-ety of social, familial, and historical issues relating to treatment are explored in depth in the following section.

II

MAJOR TREATMENT THEORIES, ISSUES, AND INTERVENTIONS

CHAPTER 6

Therapist's Use of Self and Value Conflicts with Black Families*

The previous chapters of this book focused on cultural and racial issues related to the treatment of Black families; subsequent chapters address the theoretical contributions of the major schools of family and systems therapy and present a model for a multisystems approach to the treatment of Black families. There is, however, a missing link between these two areas of discussion. If we are to successfully treat Black families, we must first explore ourselves as people, as men and women, and as therapists. In this context, this chapter provides an opportunity to explore the therapist's use of self and the values, perceptions, and cultural similarities and differences that have an impact on our personal frame of reference and on our work as therapists. Without this essential link I risk the possibility that the later theoretical chapters will be applied in a rote fashion, without careful attention to the human element—that is, the essential relationship between the therapist and the family.

Although this relationship is central to effective therapy with all clients and families, it is particularly crucial with Black families because of the many psychosocial factors specific to this ethnic group that can complicate this process and lead to premature termination [e.g., race (Chapter 2), resistance (Chapter 1), and mistrust of mental health services (Chapter 1)]. Given these factors, the most important process in working with Black families is "joining," that is, initiating therapeutic intervention by building a relationship with the family. The first half of this chapter is intended to help therapists explore the general issues and assumptions they bring to therapy and be sensitive to those of the Black

*The author would like to express her appreciation to Dr. Cheryl Thompson and Dr. Sandra Lewis of the University of Medicine and Dentistry in Newark for their suggestions and contributions to this chapter.

families they treat so that the therapy process can be facilitated. It will also point out some of the obvious pitfalls for both Black and White therapists in working with Black families. The second half of this chapter deals more specifically with common value-related areas of conflict between the clinician's own biases, perceptions, and cultural orientation and those of certain Black families.

GENERAL ISSUES OF THERAPEUTIC INTERACTION WITH BLACK FAMILIES

The Concept of "Vibes"

Scheflen (1973) and Birdwhistell (1970) have sensitized the social science and mental health fields to the ways in which social cues such as body language, tone of voice, and social distance influence social interactions. Scheflen (1973) has had a major impact by raising the awareness of the mental health field of the differences in sensitivity to social variables among different ethnic groups. Black people, because of the often extremely subtle ways in which racism manifests itself socially, are particularly attuned to very fine distinctions among such variables in all interactions—with other Blacks, with White people, and with "White" institutions. Because of this, many Black people have been socialized to pay attention to all of the nuances of behavior and not just to the verbal message. The term most often applied to this multilevel perception in Black culture is "vibes." A clinician (whether Black or White) needs to be acutely aware that every Black client and family member is "checking out" her or him in terms of appearance, race, skin color, clothing, perceived social class, language, and a range of more subtle clues such as warmth, genuineness, sincerity, respect for the client, willingness to hear the client's side, patronizing attitudes, condescension, judgments, and human connectedness. While in many cultural/ethnic groups (e.g., White Anglo-Saxon Protestant and Jewish), the intellectual connection tends to be the more important for many of its members, in Black culture the vibes or the human connections are most often of greatest significance in establishing bonds with another person or group of people. These perceptions are not just based on what is seen or what is said but on a very basic "gut feeling" level.

Subsequent chapters stress the importance of making this gut level joining connection with Black families before extensive historical or family background information is taken. Because of the history of racism and experiences with welfare and other social systems, Black families are particularly sensitive to information gathering that is perceived as prying when conducted before the joining process has gotten underway and a bond of trust has been established. Well-meaning therapists can lose a family by doing this prematurely. Chapter 8 details specific suggestions for facilitating the joining process with Black families.

One very important vibe among Black people is the sense of whether they are being treated with respect. Many Black people are very sensitive to clinicians (Black or White) who convey that they know a great deal about Black families. It is far more productive for the clinician to assume that each Black family is somewhat different and to make no other assumptions, allowing families to teach her or him about themselves and their own cultural backgrounds. Once again, there is no such thing as *the* Black family. Clinicians sometimes make the error of using their cultural knowledge to show families how well they are acquainted with Black culture. It is far more useful to treat cultural material of the type presented in this book as hypotheses to be explored with each family.

Therapists are often surprised to learn that they have to establish credibility with Black families. This is very different from some other cultural groups. Many Hispanic families, for example, will give automatic respect to "the doctor," "the therapist," or any person who is perceived as holding a position of authority. With Black families that credibility has to be earned. Many Black family members will be constantly assessing whether they can trust the therapist.

Thus, the person-to-person connection is the most important in work with Black families; without it, all of the therapist's carefully applied treatment techniques are useless. Black families will leave treatment very quickly in the initial stage if this connection is not made with *each* family member.

Another vibe to which some Black people are particularly sensitive is that of "missionary racism." In this situation, the clinician (often without conscious awareness) conveys to the family that his or her goal is to "save them from their plight" or "take care of these poor people." This is often a very subtle vibe, particularly notable as an attitude characteristic of the well-meaning clinician (Black or White), who can unwittingly convey a patronizing stance to a Black family without intending to.

The Insidious Nature of Racism

In Chapter 2, I attempted to convey the insidious and pervasive nature of the racism that Black people experience in this country. The issue of race is almost never a neutral issue for most Black people; it is always present on both a conscious and an unconscious level. It is important to reiterate at this juncture that because Black people comprise the only ethnic group in this country that was brought here almost exclusively as slaves, the slave–master aspects of racism have persisted in the psyches of Black and White people alike (Grier & Cobbs, 1968). Since this psychological structure has persisted in both subtle and overt negative stereotypes and discrimination, race is a lens through which many Black people view the world and by extension the therapist, be she or he Black or White. Race is equally a lens through which many therapists (often unconsciously) view Black families.

Racial Countertransference and Racial Stereotypes

The term countertransference has not been a popular one in the family therapy literature. It is, however, particularly relevant here when it is applied to the conscious and unconscious racial stereotypes that we all hold and that inevitably influence the treatment process. It is extremely important that *all* therapists (Black or White) explore their own stereotypes (positive and negative) about Black families. Part of the development of any clinician who wishes to work effectively with Black clients and families must include the process of "soul searching." This chapter is intended to help therapists explore and struggle with their own subtly manifested, ingrained beliefs. For example, many clinicians, Black and White, harbor a subtle fear of Black men. Unless they are made consciously aware of this, they will convey this on a number of levels to their clients.

Other clinicians have struggled with a belief that Black people are to blame for their problems. This may be articulated conceptually as, "They are poor because they want to be" or "They should pull themselves up by their bootstraps" or "All other ethnic groups made it; why can't they?"—a process called "blaming the victim." These particular beliefs have been reported by some Black as well as some White clinicians.

In Chapter 1, a very common assumption, the "class not race" view, was explored. In this view, the clinician totally ignores the racial and cultural differences and sees the problems of Black families as arising primarily from a culture of poverty (Boyd, 1977). Still other therapists make the reverse error, seeing only the strengths of Black families and therefore having difficulty identifying the true pathology in the Black families they treat. They deny problems or collude with families to avoid opening up "secrets" because they have been told that Black families are sensitive to prying. This book is intended to assist therapists with the struggle to strike a balance in the handling of such sensitive areas in their treatment of Black families.

With these factors in mind, the next two sections of this chapter explore particular issues for White and Black therapists in developing a cultural sensitivity when working with Black families. It will also explore some of the common errors which are often made. If therapists can be sensitized to their own issues, they can then be consciously aware of them and thus can give their attention to the family whom they are treating. They will also be less likely to reject Black families who are difficult to engage initially. The therapist's use of self is his or her most powerful intervention tool in the treatment of Black families. It can be refined and sharpened by this exploration.

The Importance of Exploring One's Own Culture

One of the important contributions of the Bowenian school of family therapy has been the emphasis on the therapist exploring his or her own family of origin (Bowen, 1978). In addition, it is very important that each therapist explore his or her own cultural identity (or lack of it), family values, beliefs, and prejudices. Chapter 14 will address in detail the ways in which this can be incorporated into training programs. However, for many clinicians in the field, this process may need to be done on a more personal level. It is important for therapists who work with Black families to find an informal support group of other clinicians so that they can share and get feedback on their observations. Many national conferences of mental health associations now have workshops on ethnicity and working with Black families. In working with any ethnic group, the ability of the clinician to effect change is greatly increased by the exploration of what aspects of his or her own culture, ethnic group, and family of origin she or he likes and which ones she or he does not. The clinician should be asking her- or himself, "Which parts of my 'family culture' have I accepted and rejected?"

It is also important for clinicians (Black or White) to explore the question, "Why do I want to work with Black families?" Such a question can be very helpful in forcing all of us as therapists to acknowledge any missionary tendencies before they are transmitted to the families we treat. The next two sections will discuss the issues for White therapists and then for Black therapists in working with Black families.

Issues for White Therapists in Working with Black Families

Although this section addresses many of the common issues that White therapists often experience in the process of learning to work with Black families, it is important to recognize that the discussion is not meant to be exhaustive or representative of all White therapists. It is intended to point to some problem areas and encourage therapists to search within themselves for their own particular areas of concern. Many White therapists come to their work with Black families with little or no first-hand experience of Black people. Some may have known Black individuals in their work or school settings but have never been to a Black person's home. Many are very aware of the differences between their backgrounds and those of the Black families they treat. In their eagerness to practice therapy effectively, they often unwittingly make some serious errors.

For example, some beginning White therapists are so afraid of making a mistake with Black families that they adopt a very tentative, subservient, or humble role. This is neither necessary nor helpful and it conveys to the family a lack of confidence on the part of therapist. A variation on this pattern is a situation in which a White trainee is overly impressed with a very street-wise Black client or family member and his or her ability to "hustle" the system. Some Black clients, particularly adolescents, will resent the fact that their therapist is taken in by this. In many of these situations, family members may interpret the therapist's admiration as phony. This may lead to the family leaving therapy feeling very resentful. It is not unusual in these situations particularly for the beginning therapist to mistakenly believe that he or she has connected with and understood this family. Sometimes therapists in this situation will inappropriately attempt to use slang which they believe is representative of Black dialect in a mistaken attempt to join with the family. This is often viewed by Black families as condescending (Hunt, 1987).

There are a number of useful strategies that White clinicians who become aware of this kind of behavior in their sessions can employ. It is often not helpful to a new therapist to simply point out that these attempts are counterproductive without offering concrete changes that can be made. It is important in these circumstances to help clinicians understand when this behavior is occurring. Videotapes of family sessions that can be stopped and replayed are very useful. Ultimately, the goal is for the clinician to be able to recognize when they are doing this and stop themselves during the session. It is also useful for therapists in this position to carefully examine their own racial issues that may interfere with treatment. Black families are often new to therapy, and they need to be clearly joined with, prepared, and brought into the process. These behaviors may interfere with that joining. There is also often a belief among clinicians that Black families are not appropriate for therapy. This is a variation of the "blaming the victim" response. They often report that "these families can't be helped" or that "you can't do *real* therapy with these families." Therapists must explore their own expectations in this regard or these will be transmitted to their clients as feelings of inferiority (Hunt, 1987). Therapists who find themselves caught in this process may need to enlist the help of their supervisors and/or their peers and colleagues to explore these issues. It is also important to seek out training experiences that will equip them with the skills to be effective in cross-cultural and cross-racial situations.

Another type of problem commonly encountered by White therapists who are new to this work is a tendency to expect to do excellent work immediately with Black families, and to judge themselves harshly when they cannot be "supertherapists" (Hunt, 1987). Often these trainees are very high achievers who have done very well in school and who feel totally inadequate when they find that many of the techniques they have learned are either ineffective or have never been translated for use with this population. They often become very sensitive, self-deprecating, and anxious about these perceived inadequacies. Sometimes these clinicians cope with their anxiety by making desperate attempts to acquire knowledge about Black culture in the hope that this will help them in working with these families. Therapists experiencing this issue can change their behavior with Black families by confronting the ways in which their own self-doubts and feelings of inadequacy interfere with establishing a therapeutic alliance. It is also helpful for them to realize that establishing this alliance with Black families often takes time and persistence. Expectations of immediate joining are often unrealistic (Hunt, 1987). It is my hope that this book will provide an anchor in terms of this knowledge and give them permission to relax and be themselves with Black families and to temper their expectations of perfection. Working with families leads to the development of a certain sense of humility in all of us which can be balanced with a feeling of our own competence as clinicians.

The opposite problem can occur. Sometimes therapists believe that they are effecting change but audio or videotapes of sessions or interviews with a supervisor behind the one-way mirror reveal no progress. For apparent change to become actual change, therapists must work with their supervisor's help to (1) allow Black families to express feelings of anger and/or rejection, (2) appreciate their right to reject therapy, and (3) recognize that issues which have nothing to do with the therapist, such as the "healthy cultural paranoia" (Chapter 1) that many Black families feel, may interfere with the initial joining process. Once again, I must reiterate the central theme of this chapter: In order for clinicians to develop this therapeutic alliance with Black families, they must be willing to extend themselves and establish a human bond or connection. Hunt (1987) reinforces this point. Although her work involves largely individual work with Black clients, it is very relevant to family therapy as well. She states that it is not "what you know but who you are and how you use information about a person's cultural characteristics that eventually allows the client to trust" (p. 116). This ability to convey who one is and to be "real" is essential in establishing a true therapeutic bond with Black families.

Raising the Issue of Race in Cross-Racial Therapy

Another dilemma faced by many White therapists in working with Black families relates to the question of when and if the issue of race or racial difference should be raised. Many therapists received their initial training in the psychoanalytic school of thought and have been taught that "transferential" issues should not be raised until they are broached by the patient. Such therapists are therefore very hesitant to raise the sensitive issue of race in cross-racial therapy. Unfortunately this omission can have serious consequences for the development of an open, trusting relationship with a Black family. As stated earlier in this chapter, it is important for the White therapist to recognize that although they may not feel that race is an issue for them, it often is for Black families. Although this does not always interfere with the treatment process, at least on the overt level, the willingness of a White clinician to raise the issue of race with a Black family often gives the message that "anything can be discussed here," clearing the air and removing a possible obstacle to the development of trust. Although there is considerable debate in the field, in my experience it is far better to raise the issue with Black families than to run the risk of it obstructing the therapeutic process.

As stated above, many Black people tend to be very aware of the race of an individual and can usually tell on the telephone if the therapist is Black or White. They are also taught from an early age to distinguish light-skinned Blacks from Whites. This sensitivity is ever present and often operates on a level at which White therapists have no awareness.

Sometimes inexperienced White therapists collude with Black families to deny the issue of race. It may then not be discussed or become an "unspeakable" topic. If a therapist asks a family directly, "How do you feel about working with a White therapist?," the issue is then available for discussion. White therapists need to be prepared for the possibility that this question may elicit feelings of anger, and some family members may even verbalize their reluctance to work with a White therapist. The more able the therapist is to remain nondefensive and nonapologetic while discussing this issue with the family, the greater the likelihood of a therapeutic connection. A word of caution: It is not necessary to belabor this issue with Black families. A young White therapist whom I supervised was so anxious about the implications of cross-racial therapy that she unwittingly raised it repeatedly in a number of sessions with a Black family and thereby conveyed her anxiety to the family.

It is not helpful for the White therapist to try to convince a Black client or family that he or she "understands" their problems and that his or her experiences are similar to theirs. Many Black people experience this assurance as condescending or patronizing. It is far more useful to avoid thinking of the family members in stereotypical ways but to invite them to share their experiences of being Black. This can often open up areas of discussion that will be beneficial to the family and to the therapist's understanding of them. Often Black families have never really discussed or shared the expectations they have of each other that were formed by their childhood experiences, the area of the country in which they were raised, their family structure (e.g., single-parent, intact, or extended family), their religious views, and what they have learned from peers about male–female relationships. The therapist can learn a great deal about the couple's cultural backgrounds and the family's own culture and use it very effectively to reframe their experiences as different from each other rather than as good or bad.

Issues for Black Therapists Working with Black Families

As Black people learn more about treatment they are becoming more sophisticated assessors of what the field has to offer. They will often come in asking for a Black therapist, whether they seek out a private practice or a community clinic. When a Black therapist is available, the factor of shared race often eases the transition into treatment for a family. Sometimes Black clients are less suspicious and guarded when they are working with a Black therapist. Black families frequently expect something different from a Black therapist on a personal level. They are searching not just for an expert but also for someone whom they feel they can trust.

Often Black families are more relaxed initially with a Black therapist and will make assumptions about a certain level of understanding. The therapist is more closely identified with and is therefore drawn further into the family circle, which often results in a more assertive use of the therapeutic process by the family. An easy familiarity is more likely to develop between the family and the therapist, which can be utilized in treatment when appropriate.

Many Black therapists have found that sharing their own experiences can be extremely useful with Black families, as can identifying common experiences such as normalizing the reluctance of Black people to enter treatment. Use of Black dialect, when appropriate, can be helpful if it is comfortable for the therapist and is syntonic with the family. It is most important, however, that the therapist be him- or herself. Since the

Black therapist runs the risk of overidentification with the family and thereby losing therapeutic objectivity, he or she must be aware of this danger in order to guard against it. Use of self-disclosure is best done in a careful, thoughtful way.

Male–female issues are often important in the treatment of Black families and couples. Any couple therapist is well aware of the seductiveness, alliances, and competitiveness that can develop with one or more members of the couple. (See also Chapter 13 for issues specific to couples.) This can be enacted in a variety of ways in the interaction between the Black therapist and the Black family. Black male therapists who were interviewed for this book stressed that they were very aware of potentially competitive postures between them and male family members. A number of these therapists were conscious of attempting to neutralize this competition.

Because of the socialization around "macho" beliefs, for example, some Black men may find it difficult at first to undergo the process of "opening up" in front of another Black man (i.e., the therapist). The husband/father frequently enters treatment afraid that his problems with his spouse and/or children will be interpreted as weakness by the therapist. The Black male therapist may be perceived as a professional, less streetwise, and so on. There may even be suspicions about the therapist's masculinity because he does not assume a more traditional Black male role. An important aspect of the credibility that the Black male therapist must establish in these situations is that of establishing himself as a peer. Nonverbal cues such as the therapist who seats himself behind a desk and thus distances himself from the couple or family often inhibits the development of trust, increasing the possibility of these types of suspicion arising.

For the Black female therapist working with Black couples and families, the issues can be slightly different. She can be seen by the woman as a competitor by virtue of education, appearance, age, socioeconomic level, and so on. Unless she carefully prepares the family and/or couple for treatment, openly discussing the purposes of her actions, her attempts to join with the Black man can be misinterpreted by the women as seductiveness. Given how loaded the issue of fidelity is with many Black couples, this can interfere prohibitively with the treatment process. Some Black men, on the other hand, feel more comfortable initially seeing a Black female therapist because they feel less threatened. It is sometimes easier to acknowledge weaknesses or problems with a woman than with a Black man, a situation particularly true if sexual problems are involved.

It often comes as a very painful surprise to young Black clinicians when they discover that Black families are also "checking them out." The "healthy cultural paranoia" (Grier & Cobbs, 1968) described in

Chapter 1 extends to most "White" institutions, including mental health centers and hospitals. It can, in some cases, also extend to the Black clinicians who work in them. Gerald Jackson (1980) has discussed the fact that some Black clients and families may initially view the Black therapist as a member of "the White establishment" and even as a threat to their existence. These Black families will often question whether the Black therapist is an "Uncle Tom" (someone who meekly serves the white man), an "oreo" (Black outside, White inside), or a "token" (a Black person who is placed in a position merely to meet affirmative action guidelines). In a smaller number of Black families, the Black therapist may even encounter a projection of the family member's feelings of self-hatred, wherein she or he secretly feels that the Black therapist is second rate and not as good as the White therapist. Occasionally a Black family such as this may even refuse to work with a Black therapist.

These responses from Black people are particularly painful, especially for beginning Black clinicians. It is very important that they be discussed openly in the supervisory relationship so that they can be understood. Black therapists who have struggled with their own self- and racial identity will be in a better position to join with such families and to recognize that these reactions are a product of the racism in society and not a personal affront. It is therefore very important for Black therapists to understand that even though the joining process may be at least superfically more comfortably undertaken, they must never neglect it and must not assume that because they are Black, all Black families will immediately give their trust. This trust must be earned by the therapist, irrespective of race.

Black therapists are often very surprised to discover that they may have their own unique issues to resolve if they are to treat Black families effectively. There is a direct relationship between the degree to which Black therapists are comfortable with themselves, their own families, their own racial identity, and their ability to work with Black families. Since Black people vary considerably on the degree to which they view their racial identity as important to consider, it is not surprising to learn that Black therapists vary considerably also. To the degree that a Black therapist denies or rejects his or her own racial identity, he or she may be cut off from Black families and may have difficulty establishing therapeutic bonds (Hunt, 1987). Conversely, if Black therapists overidentify with Black families, they may miss important issues, losing their objectivity and their ability to act as therapeutic agents of change.

In their work in the mental health fields, Black therapists often experience a double bind. It is not unusual for a Black therapist to be the only Black on staff and thus find her- or himself concerned about the treatment strategies that are applied to Black families. She or he may come to feel like "the voice in the wilderness," the sole person repeatedly stating these concerns. Black therapists and most Black people who work in predominantly White fields must struggle with maintaining their ethnic identity while interacting with Whites (Hunt, 1987). Many Black therapists struggle with considerable guilt over having "made it," thus having left other Black people "behind." The class and socioeconomic differences are difficult issues for all middle-class therapists, but they present even more of a dilemma for the Black middle-class therapist who is working with poor Black families. Many Black therapists can recall experiencing the anger of Black families around this issue, a form of rejection by Black clients that often heightens their feeling of not quite belonging anywhere. These are very important issues that must be addressed by every Black therapist at some point in his or her development. Some Black therapists are fortunate enough to have had therapy of their own with a Black colleague. Many find themselves in a dilemma, however, because some White supervisors are not aware of or equipped to address these issues with the Black therapist. When supervisors approach this in an insensitive or clumsy way, it can often be experienced as judgmental or accusatory by the Black therapist.

Black therapists attempt to deal with these dilemmas in many different ways. Some are very productive. They look for other Black mentors and role models outside of their agencies and programs or join Black professional organizations such as the Association of Black Psychologists, Black Social Workers, and Black Psychiatrists. These individuals and groups can be used as support networks for the Black therapists to explore their beliefs about Black families, therapy, and the development of their own self-identity.

Some of the ways in which some well-meaning Black therapists attempt to cope with this dilemma are counterproductive and in fact undermine effective service delivery to Black families. One posture sometimes assumed by Black therapists in training has been referred to as "the saboteur" (Hunt, 1987). Because many Black therapists experience the rage common to Black people in response to racism, they often respond with what Hunt (1987) characterizes as "indirect hostility and anger in their communications with White and Black professional peers" (p. 116). Because of their concerns that some "White theories" often do not work for Black families, these therapists can sometimes resort to stereotypical comments about Black people: "presenting themselves as experts on the black race allows their assumptions to go unchallenged by many peers" (Hunt, 1987, p. 116).

Many of these Black therapists are expressing their anger at a system that they perceive as not accepting or valuing them or their clients.

However, rather than working toward developing ethnically appropriate treatment strategies, they sometimes overprotect their clients and avoid addressing important therapeutic issues. They often engage Black clients and families in an "us against the system" type of discussion, which may confuse the families they treat. Black families often come into therapy in crisis, needing help on a number of problems and thus are suspicious of Black therapists who have the need to present themselves as "protectors of the race" (Hunt, 1987). To further complicate these issues, supervisors are frequently reluctant to raise these issues with Black therapists, which means that they may never be addressed.

Another pattern that can be counterproductive occurs when the Black therapist becomes the "moralizer" who is going to "raise the consciousness of black people" (Hunt, 1987). Instead of using therapy to empower Black families, these therapists sometimes adopt a "preacher/teacher" model in which they "deliver impromptu lecturettes to their unsuspecting Black clients" (Hunt, 1987, p. 117). The key to recognizing this pattern when reviewing video or audio tapes is noticing whether the therapist "preaches" or talks more than the family. In such situations the therapist, instead of addressing the problems that the family brings to the session discusses political or racial problems in society and ignores or minimizes the family's concerns. It is important for supervisors to help these therapists learn to distinguish between lecturing and therapy with Black families.

Due to the increased empathy that Black therapists often feel for Black families, there may be a tendency to set themselves up as the "rescuers," becoming overinvolved in the family's issues and treating family members with pity for their life experiences. Therapists who make this error often "wallow in their client's emotional content as a release of their own personal guilt for having made it into the mainstream of society" (Hunt, 1987, p. 118). It is important to note that although Hunt describes this as a pattern in some Black therapists, it is also quite common among White therapists as well. Sometimes therapists engaged in this pattern overextend themselves for the Black families they treat, so that they "[are] available at all times, make little or no demands on the clients and inappropriately do favors for them, thus creating new dependency" (p. 118). This pattern is not only counterproductive for Black families but it quickly "burns out" the therapist. A Black therapist whom I supervised some years ago paraphrased a line from the play "River Niger" in describing this feeling: "Everybody wants a piece of my toe." Eager young Black therapists who want to do therapy with Black families need to be helped to guard against this pattern and set limits with the families they treat. They need to address the guilt discussed above and the conflict about having "made it."

In conclusion, although the patterns described above clearly do not apply to all therapists, Black or White, they do illustrate some of the common pitfalls and dilemmas. A number of the examples that are described as more common to Black or White therapists can clearly occur in both groups. It is important, however, for therapists to be aware of their own particular issues and to seek out someone in their own lives whom they can trust and with whom they can address these problems [e.g., a therapist, supervisor, mentor, colleague (White or Black), coworkers, other trainees or therapists, sensitive friends].

VALUE-RELATED ISSUES IN THE TREATMENT OF BLACK FAMILIES

The pervasive impact of values on the therapeutic alliance and process has been discussed throughout this book within a variety of contexts. This chapter will present some of the conflicts in this area that may not have been explored or examined in sufficient detail.

In this section, it is very important to reiterate a theme that has been stated throughout this book: There is no such thing as *the* Black family. By the same token, there is no one set of values that is common to *all* Black families. The most important lesson to be learned by therapists is that all therapy is a process of the negotiation of values and beliefs. It is crucial for therapists to clarify their own values for themselves and explore with the family their particular beliefs. It is the ultimate sign of disrespect to any person or family to assume a knowledge of her, his, or their beliefs or values without asking for clarification. Similarly, it is the greatest acknowledgment of the dignity of a person or family to ask them to tell or teach one about themselves and the things that are important to them.

Values Clarification for Therapists

Values clarification is an ongoing, life-long activity. It is not a task done once in training and then completed, but a process of continuously exploring one's own reactions, countertransferances, and beliefs as one works with families. Because family therapy and other systems approaches are such active forms of therapy, the therapist's own values and perceptions are constantly "on the line."

It is important, therefore, for the family therapist, particularly during the training years, to use supervision and peer support to explore his or her countertransference reactions to the families he or she treats. A family therapist who is afraid to confront issues with an authoritarian parent may have some unresolved issues with his or her own parent. If these patterns recur frequently and interfere with the therapeutic interaction, therapy for the therapist may be indicated.

Values and Therapy

Aponte (1985) gives the following statement about the role of values in the therapeutic process:

> Values frame the entire process of therapy. They are the social standards by which therapists define problems, establish criteria for evaluation, fix parameters for technical intervention and select therapeutic goals. All transactions between therapist and family or individual about these aspects of therapy involve negotiations about the respective value systems that each party brings into the therapeutic relationship.
>
> These values, whether they be moral, cultural or political, are the standards by which a person directs his actions and defines, interprets and judges all social phenomena. A person's values are drawn from family life, social networks, educational experience, and community and sociopolitical organizations. These multiple standards converge into the complex configurations that become the dynamically evolving value systems of the therapist and the families and individuals in treatment. (p. 323)

Given these issues, there are a number of areas in which well-meaning therapists can encounter serious value differences and/or conflicts with Black families. The following are among the most significant: (1) "casual" versus "formal" styles; (2) religious beliefs or values; (3) parenting and discipline; (4) the importance of race and discrimination; (5) teenage pregnancy and abortion; (6) class differences; (7) legal marriage; (8) crisis intervention versus ongoing treatment; (9) the "airing of dirty laundry"; (10) exposure (e.g., one-way mirrors); (11) the importance of feminist or other sociopolitical issues; (12) macho versus alternative male styles.

All of these issues have been or will be discussed in detail in other chapters. This section will therefore focus exclusively on the areas of difference or conflict within therapy.

Casual Versus Formal Styles

Most therapists spend many years in school, where attitudes and interaction tend to follow along more "casual" lines than they do in many families. Students call professors by their first names and refer to each other informally. When they begin to join with families and engage them in family therapy, their natural tendency is to view an informal, "first-name basis" style as putting people at their ease. With Black families, particularly older, more traditional family members, this may be a serious error.

The most important lesson here is for the therapist to take his or her cues from the family. Although many younger Black families allow children to call adults by their first names, many older or more tradition-al Black families are offended by this practice, seeing it as a sign of disrespect. In my own family of origin, for example, all of my parents' adults friends were referred to as Aunt or Uncle in order to indicate closeness to the family. It would have been unthinkable for us to call them by their first names alone.

"Old school" Black families often object to children referring to ther-apists, teachers, or other adults on a first-name basis. Similarly, they may object to a therapist, particularly a young one or one whom they do not know well, referring to them by first names. It is usually helpful to start with a more formal introduction and allow the family to indicate their preference.

During my internship at the Philadelphia Child Guidance Clinic, a family taught me this lesson very graphically:

The Jefferson family appeared for a family session. In the waiting room, there were many members of the extended family. Mrs. Martha Jefferson (aged 36) had originally brought her son Jeffrey (aged 12) for treatment. When it became clear that they were part of a large extended family household, the other members were asked to come in.

I was very young and very new to the process of family therapy at the time. As the family sat down, I asked them to go around and introduce themselves. Martha Jefferson began and gave only her first name. Her brothers and sisters (Jeffrey's aunts and uncles) did the same. When we came to Martha's mother, she looked at me directly and said, *"Mrs. Jefferson."* Her message was clear. She was making an emphatic statement about her role and power in this family and about the respect she demanded as the grandmother and as a member of the older generation.

Naming can also be used to elevate someone's status within the family structure. For example, in a three-generation family in which a grand-mother, a young unwed mother, and a child live in a household, the entire family including the child may refer to the mother by her first name as if she were a sibling. The therapist can begin to help draw the generational boundary by referring to her as Ms. or "your mother" in the presence of her child and other family members.

Working with Black Families With Different Political Views from the Therapist

The issue of political views and values can often be a very difficult and painful issue for Black and White clinicians who hold strong political beliefs that they may find are not shared by the Black families with whom they work. It is easier to see this difference and acknowledge it openly if the therapist is a blatant racist or is largely condemning of poor Black families, Black families on welfare, or single-parent families. It is much more difficult to see and acknowledge in more subtle situations. Political views are important parts of our value system and must be addressed and brought to our conscious awareness so that we do not unwittingly impose them on others or reject those who do not share our views or priorities.

The two examples which can best describe this dilemma are the struggles of a young White woman therapist with a strong feminist orientation, and a young Black male therapist who adopted a "Blacker than thou" posture with the families he treated. The struggle in both of these situations involves a well-meaning therapist who wants to help but who encounters a Black family or a family member with radically different views. It is important to underscore here that both of these therapists hold very deeply felt and sincere political views, which contribute positively to their own lives. The important point here is that even the most positive view can become oppressive if it is imposed on someone else.

Gloria, a 28-year-old White woman, was a social worker with a strong feminist orientation. She was a member of NOW and had a great deal of concern about the ways in which women have been victimized by men. She was working for the first time at an inner-city Community Mental Health Center and had a number of single-parent Black families in which mothers were involved with boyfriends whom she felt "demeaned them as women." She routinely denigrated the treatment these women received by men, encouraged them to leave their relationships, preached to them about the role of women in society, and had never included any of these Black men in the treatment process. Black families typically stayed with her through the first few sessions and then dropped out of treatment.

This scenario illustrates the mismatch that can occur when a therapist is so invested in his or her political views that they dominate his or her view of the world. In this case, her strong feminist values did not allow Gloria to truly join with the Black families with whom she worked. It was clear that no matter which issue they brought to treatment, the mistreatment of these women by men became the primary focus. In many of her cases, Gloria had in fact correctly assessed very problematic couple relationships, but she always moved immediately to "politicize" these women rather than to address the presenting problems that they brought to therapy. In addition, Gloria was so angry at men in general that she was unable to reach out to the Black men in these families and involve them in the treatment process. The sad motif in this situation was that Gloria was never consciously aware of these discrepancies. She thought she was helping and raising the family's "political conscious- ness" without recognizing and accepting the family's presentation of their needs.

In an earlier paper (Boyd-Franklin, 1983), I addressed the fact that many Black women prioritize their feminist values differently from many White women. Thus some Black women will respond first to being Black and then to being a woman. Women of different races who presume a bond based on gender can sometimes find that some Black women experience this as patronizing. This is particularly unfortu- nate when the well-meaning therapist is totally unaware of this per- ception and proceeds as if a bond has been formed. It is helpful to ask people their views in an atmosphere of respect rather than in one of conversion.

An example of a similar dilemma for a Black therapist can be seen in the case of Kwame:

Kwame, a 26-year-old Black man, was a psychologist with a strong sense of his African-American identity. He had adopted an African name, wore an Afro hairstyle and often wore dashikis as well. He strongly and genuinely believes in the necessity for Black people to accept their "blackness," and he has worked hard to nurture a strong Black identity in his own life.

In 1970, Kwame was working in a community mental health center and was assigned a Black family in which a young Black woman was referred because she was on academic probation from her college and was profoundly depressed. In the first session, Kwame met with the young woman and her parents. The young woman had an Afro hairdo and wore a red, black, and green pin in the shape of the continent of Africa. She stated clearly that her parents could not accept her Black identity and were very rejecting of her. Her parents were a middle-aged, middle-class Black couple who were very angry at their daughter for trying to act "too Black" and getting involved in Black student political activities rather than focusing on her studies.

Kwame identified immediately with the young woman (whose situation repli- cated his struggle with his own parents). In his mind he labeled her parents as "bourgie" and proceeded to lecture them on how they were making their daughter depressed by not accepting her need to express her own African- American heritage. While this was one dynamic, it became Kwame's total treatment focus. The parents refused to return for family treatment. Kwame then saw the young woman individually and allied with her against her parents.

He told her that they were Uncle Toms who could not understand her. The young woman stayed for two sessions and did not return to treatment.

Kwame's approach has become known as the "Blacker than thou" syndrome. He was genuinely committed to his own African-American identity but had conflicts about it. This young Black woman and her family replicated his own unresolved issues with his family of origin. Kwame believed strongly in his political convictions about his blackness but he was not able to put his values aside and join with these parents to help them discuss their conflicts with their daughter. His politics caused him to become judgmental of the family and to unwittingly lose his therapeutic neutrality. He formed a generational alliance with the young woman and became so overidentified with her that he was unable to conduct treatment on an individual or a family level.

These two examples admittedly are extreme examples of a problem that may manifest itself in many subtler ways. They are presented here, however, as a word of caution for well-meaning therapists of all races who are not in touch with the powerful influence that their political views may carry and the ways in which they may have difficulty in working with family members who hold different orientations, regardless of the color of either therapist or family.

Religious Beliefs

The training of many therapists has tended to disregard religion or spirituality as an issue in treatment (see Chapter 5). The difficulties that can arise from the presence of different religious or spiritual orientations can immobilize the therapist and bring therapy to a virtual halt. As is discussed in Chapter 5, the therapist may be unable to help the generations in the family resolve religious perspectives on differences and renegotiate their rules because she or he is unable to initiate a similar process for the clarification of her or his own religious values. The following case example illustrates this dilemma:

The Williams family consisted of Mrs. Williams, Mr. Williams, and their two boys, Robert (9) and Ronald (10). Ronald was displaying acting-out and aggressive behavior in school. He "talked back" to his teacher and often fought with other children. At home he was described by his mother as being a "bad child." Mr. and Mrs. Williams were active as Jehovah's Witnesses. They were involved in their Kingdom Hall and spent many evenings in Bible study and weekends "pioneering" or doing door-to-door missionary work. The boys often went with them to the Kingdom Hall, and Robert was described as the good child who never gave trouble. Ronald was clearly scapegoated by the family. In the course of exploration about behavior and rules at home, it became clear to the therapist that there were many restrictions on the boys. Mrs. Williams stated angrily that Ronald was a "terrible sneak" who had brought small toys resembling the television characters "Voltron" and "Transformers" into the house. She was very angry because these were considered "demonic" by her religion. The children were not allowed to play with other children in the neighborhood or at school. The therapist was appalled. She felt strongly that this family was stifling the children's social development. Her first reaction was to side with the children and encourage them to stand up to their parents.

Her supervisor helped her to see that she was becoming caught in the family's structure and was actually forming a cross-generational alliance with the children against the parents.

The therapist was encouraged to join with the parents by asking them to teach her about their religious beliefs and their concerns for the children. In the course of this process, it became clear that these beliefs were primarily Mrs. Williams' and Mr. Williams had been going along with her program. She was clearly the strength and power in the family. It also became very clear that Mr. Williams secretly encouraged Ronald's rebellion against his mother. The therapist was then able to help these parents discuss their differences, particularly in terms of childrearing. They were able to agree on the beliefs that they felt were most important for the children to understand. The therapist then encouraged Mr. Williams to discuss these issues with Ronald, who was able to tell his parents how he was often ridiculed by his classmates because of the things that he was not allowed to do. Mr. Williams empathized with his son and asked his son how his parents might help him with this. He was also able to be clear with Ronald about the rules that he had to follow and the reasons for them. Mrs. Williams was able for the first time to stand back and support this process without intruding.

The therapist in this situation was able to recognize her own value differences with the family, discuss them with her supervisor, and avoid a collision with the family that would have exacerbated rather than resolved the family conflict.

Race and Discrimination Issues

While issues concerning race and discrimination could be included under the discussion of political views, it is important to note that racial considerations are often pervasive enough in character to extend beyond the political outlook. Often, the most difficult Black families for many therapists to treat are those who "deny" their Blackness or minimize its importance. This is also an issue for many politically active White therapists. There are some Black people, particularly those who live and work in all-White settings and who may have gone to schools or professional training in an all-White atmosphere, who see a real value in being "color blind." This is particularly difficult for Black therapists who feel strongly about issues of Black pride and racial identification. The question is often compounded because these families tend to come into treatment when they are confronted by the realities of racism and their world view is threatened. The question that frequently arises in supervision is: How does one join with or convey respect to a person or family whose beliefs are radically different from one's own? This is a very basic struggle, and there are no easy answers. In these situations, the therapist must assess his or her own values and clarify his or her own beliefs. The following case example illustrates these issues:

Alice Downing was a 15-year-old Black adolescent who had grown up in an all-White suburb for most of her life. She and her family were referred for treatment after she made a "suicidal" gesture in which she took ten aspirin tablets. Her family consisted of her parents, Mr. Carl Downing (aged 45) and Mrs. Anne Downing (aged 42) and her sister Mary (aged 11). In the first session with the family, the therapist was struck by the fact that Alice looked quite different from her family. She was in fact the only family member with "Black features." She was light brown in complexion. Her mother, father, and sister were very light skinned and "white" in facial features, and her mother and sister had light hazel eyes. In the course of the first few family sessions, it became clear that Alice was scapegoated by the family and had been for most of her life. Her mother and father both stated that she had "always been in trouble." In an individual session with Alice, the therapist discovered that the precipitant for the suicidal incident had been a rejection by a boyfriend, who was White. His family had objected to his seeing a Black girl. She had never shared this with her family.

In a family session, with the therapist's help, she was able to do so. Both her mother and her father became very angry with her and told her that she had created this problem herself by raising the issue of race at all. Ms. Downing proudly stated that race was never an issue for her and in fact she had many relatives who "passed" for white and were married to white spouses. Mr. Downing described his rise in a white corporation and told his daughter how he had always tried "not to stand out or be different."

The therapist, who was Black, had an extreme reaction of tremendous anger toward these parents. She recognized that this family had very different values from her own. In a discussion with her supervisory consultant, she carefully analyzed her own anger at this family. With the consultant's help, she was able to clarify her reaction and separate out her own countertransference. Once this was accomplished she was able to challenge the family's avoidance of the color issue in their home and help them see that their daughter had always felt "different." She helped the daughter to talk directly to her mother about this pain for the first time in her life, and helped the mother to talk to Alice about this and to try to understand her daughter's need to develop her own cultural identity. Mr. Downing strongly objected and stated that he felt that if she focused on her "difference" she would never "fit in." The therapist asked Mr. and Mrs. Downing to discuss what they had been told about racial identity by their own families and to share the times when it had caused them conflicts in their lives. For the first time, they were able to discuss in front of their children their own struggles with racial identity and the reasons why they had made their choice of a "color blind" life-style.

In a future session, the therapist asked the parents to discuss the possibility that they had made their choice but that their daughter might feel trapped and unable to make a choice for herself. She asked if they loved their daughter enough to allow her the right to make her own choice and struggle with her own decision on racial identity.

Although the parents' views on racial identity changed very little in the course of therapy, they were able finally to support their daughter's need to struggle with her own racial identity and her own appearance as a Black woman. The issue of color difference had long been a taboo issue in this family but it was now opened sufficiently to promote some possible differentiation for the children.

The struggle of this therapist was a very difficult one: Her own values conflicted with the family's; her own cultural identification and sense of Black identity contrasted sharply with those of the family; and she overidentified with the daughter. She used her supervisory consultant to work through her own countertransference and value issues so that she could intervene appropriately in the family. Had she simply expressed her anger at the parents, she would have been drawn into the family dynamics and would have repeated the family's pattern of nonacceptance and blame. There is a very valuable lesson to be learned from this example: It is crucial for family therapists to be willing to seek out a consultation with a trusted supervisor or colleague when these reactions occur. This is an essential part of the process of value clarification and the differentiation of one's own beliefs from those of the family that is in treatment.

Teenage Pregnancy Versus Abortion

One potentially explosive issue for therapists and Black families relates to the question of teenage pregnancy versus abortion. Clearly, this is a value-laden issue that taps a very powerful response in many individuals in this country. There are strong feelings and opinions on the part of both "pro-abortion" groups and "right-to-life" groups. Therapists are clearly not neutral or immune to opinions on this question.

There are many different views within Black communities on this issue also. Some Black people, because of religious, moral, cultural, and/or Afro-centric beliefs feel very strongly that children have a right to be born. This often taps multigenerational beliefs and decisions to choose to carry a pregnancy to term that have been made by other members of the family such as a mother and/or a grandmother. Stack (1974) in her description of a discussion between a 15-year-old girl who is pregnant and her mother captures the cultural beliefs of many Black people on this issue:

> Lottie talked with her mother during her second month of pregnancy. She said, "Herman told my mama I was pregnant. She was in the kitchen cooking. I told him not to tell nobody. I wanted to keep it a secret but he told me time will tell. My mama said to me 'I had you and you should have your child. I didn't get rid of you. I loved you and I took care of you until you got to the age to have this one. Have your baby no matter what, there's nothing wrong with having a baby. Be proud of it like I was proud of you.' My mama didn't tear me down; she was about the best mother a person ever had." (p. 47)

This view is by no means universally held by Black people. There are many Black leaders, such as Jesse Jackson, who have argued that "babies having babies" must stop. There are those who feel very strongly that teenage pregnancy seriously compromises both the teenager's and her child's future. Planned Parenthood has extensive educational programs for teenagers in Black communities.

Within one Black family or extended family, many different views may be represented and this issue may be a very loaded, volatile one within the family. In addition, therapists may find themselves in a serious values conflict with a family regarding these issues. This can sometimes result in a premature termination of treatment by the family:

Janice Valentine (a 14-year-old Black adolescent) was referred for treatment by her physician, who had discovered that she was 4 weeks pregnant. Her mother, Connie Valentine, aged 31, appeared for the intake session with her. Both Janice and her mother expressed concern and ambivalence about her pregnancy. Connie Valentine had been pregnant with Janice at age 15 and was very concerned that this was also happening to Janice. When the therapist asked them to discuss the issue, it became clear that the grandmother, Connie Valentine's mother, had taken a strong stand that "nobody was gonna kill my great-grandchild." The therapist, supported by Janice's physician, pushed strongly for an abortion, arguing that having a baby at 15 would seriously alter Janice's life. They became very concerned with the number of weeks the family had in which to make a decision as to whether or not to have the child.

In one session, the therapist, becoming more concerned as the decision point for a therapeutic abortion was approaching, pushed the mother to help her daughter make a decision. The family dropped out of treatment. Many months later, the therapist learned from the physician that Janice had had her baby.

This case illustrates a number of points. First, it is a classic example of a value conflict between the "helping persons" and the family. The therapist and the physician because of their own beliefs became so invested in the outcome, that is, the "decision," that they lost touch with the structural issues in this family. They in fact recreated the family structure by becoming rigid parental figures who accepted both Janice and her mother's definition of helplessness. The family system had presented as two ambivalent, uncertain adolescents, a structure that was never challenged. The mother was never helped or supported to assume a parental stance with her daughter. Secondly, the therapist disregarded information concerning a very important value conflict between herself and the grandmother in this family. She did not correctly read the grandmother's power in the family structure. Since the grandmother was never engaged, the therapist unwittingly became locked in a value struggle with the grandmother over the outcome of the decision. The family structure was not changed as Janice Valentine was once again "in the middle" and being given conflicting messages.

The decision of the family to have the child might have been the same but the family structure could have been altered significantly if the therapist had engaged the grandmother in the therapeutic process and helped her and her daughter to openly discuss their concerns about Janice's pregnancy. This opportunity was lost because the therapist became equally enmeshed in the family dynamics and tried to convince Janice and her mother of her point of view.

Parenting and Discipline

Another area in which therapists often clash with Black families is that of parenting or disciplinary issues. Many Black families take pride in being of the "old school," firmly upholding such beliefs as those expressed by the maxim "spare the rod, spoil the child." McGoldrick (1982) points out that there are often good reasons for this response by Black parents. She discusses the concept of Black parents providing strict discipline for their children as a way of protecting them from the severe consequences of acting-out behavior, particularly as adolescents.

Peters (1981) in her discussion of approaches to discipline among Black people makes the following observations:

> Discipline techniques of Black parents have often been noted by observers of Black parent–child interaction. Although definitive studies of discipline in Black families have yet to be done, many researchers have described the Black parents' more direct physical form of discipline that differs from the psychologically oriented approach preferred by mainstream families, such as withdrawal of love or making approval or affection contingent on the child's behavior or accomplishment. The strict, no-nonsense discipline of Black parents—often characterized as "harsh" or "rigid" or "egocentrically motivated" by mainstream-oriented observers (Chilman, 1966)—has been shown to be functional, appropriate discipline of caring parents. (p. 216)

There have been a number of studies in the literature of childrearing practices. Lewis and Looney (1983), although their study of working-class Black families did not focus specifically on childrearing practices, note that they "were impressed with the firm but supportive and understanding push of children toward responsible autonomy. The concern about keeping children busy in meaningful activities was particularly apparent in the most competent families" (pp. 134–135).

In their work, they cite a number of authors who have studied childrearing practices in Black families. For example:

> Goodman and Berman (1970) provide a vividly descriptive account of children of the struggling poor in their paper "Tract Town Children." They note that in this very poor neighborhood child play is commonly characterized by fighting, and discipline by frequent "whippings." Mothers are authoritarian in their approach to their children, pushing them toward early autonomy but then punishing them corporally for transgression. The children express strong loyalty and affection for their mothers, suggesting that she is the center of the family. "She assigns chores, sees homework, metes out punishment, and warns against hazards" (p. 205). (Lewis & Looney, 1983, p. 133)

Lewis and Looney (1983) also point out that "the most competent adolescents in our sample saw the fact that their parents were strict as a source of family strength" (p. 134). This is extremely important because in many Black families this "strictness" or strength is seen as a protection against the influences of "the street" (i.e., drugs, delinquency, crime, lack of interest in education, etc.).

Peters (1981) reports on her own work with working-class Black families:

> Mothers became more dynamic in their disciplining as their young children began to understand the appropriate behavior parents expected. Most parents emphasized obedience. However, obedience was not viewed negatively; it was an important issue, often of special significance to a parent. Parents said that they believed obedience "will make life easier for my child," "means respect," "is equated with my love," or "is necessary if my child is to achieve in school." (pp. 216–217).

Negotiation of Values in Therapy with Black Families

Upon recognition of the value issues in family therapy, the therapist is faced with a dilemma. Many Black families enter therapy with very unclear notions as to the process of therapy or very different expectations from those of the therapist as to what the process will provide. It is very useful to ask family members directly what they expect from the process. This, however, can lead to another level of difficulty for the therapist. There are many situations in which the family may want one thing (i.e., "fix the child") and the therapist may view the problem differently (e.g., "this is a family problem"). This impasse is extremely common in therapy in general and is particularly relevant to the struggles between therapists and Black families.

In order for this dilemma to be resolved, a negotiation process must occur between the therapist and the family. Aponte (1985) was one of the first family therapists to discuss the negotiation of values and/or perception of the problem between the family and the therapist. Ultimately the inevitable points of difference, particularly in cross-racial therapy, must be addressed by this negotiation process.

When I present workshops on this topic, I am often asked "Can White therapists treat Black families?" Clearly there is no one answer to this question. Although many Black families express a wish to work with a Black therapist, the reality is that it is more likely that they will be involved in a cross-cultural treatment process. This is due to the shortage of Black therapists in many agencies and in training programs. It is imperative that this issue be addressed and efforts be made to recruit Black therapists for family therapy training programs.

At the same time, given this reality, therapists of all races must learn to work with Black families. In my experience the cross-cultural and cross-racial differences are most successfully negotiated if the therapist (of any race) views family therapy as a negotiation process in which the family is asked for their expectations of treatment, these values are clarified, and the therapist is clear on his or her own goals and values. The process can then be negotiated from a position that conveys respect for the family's belief systems.

CHAPTER 7

Major Family Therapy Approaches and Their Relevance to the Treatment of Black Families*

As with most ethnic groups but particularly in working with Black families, the family therapist must be willing and able to be flexible and to draw from the work of many different schools of family therapy. Given the centrality of the joining process to therapy with Black families, the most effective approach incorporates both the use of self and the theoretical approach best suited to the family at hand. This chapter summarizes some of the major family system approaches and views them in terms of their relevance for the treatment of Black families.

The chapter explores first the structural family therapy model, with particular attention to the work of Minuchin et al. (1967), Aponte (1976a), Aponte and Van Deusen (1981), and Haley (1976). The Bowen model is then examined, as well as the contributions of those influenced by his theory (Bowen, 1976, 1978). The last section considers the applications of the paradoxical strategic or systemic approach.

STRUCTURAL FAMILY THERAPY AND THE TREATMENT OF BLACK FAMILIES

Structural family therapy provides a comprehensive model for the treatment of Black families that can be effectively employed in combination with other approaches. Minuchin (1974), Minuchin et al. (1967), and Minuchin and Fishman (1981) have developed this approach. It provides a method for assessing the structure of a family, identifying the areas of

*This chapter, with some editorial changes, was previously published as "The Contribution of Family Therapy Models to the Treatment of Black Families," by Nancy Boyd-Franklin, in *Psychotherapy*, 1987, Vol. 24, pp. 621–629. Reprinted by permission of the editor.

difficulty, and restructuring the family system in order to produce change. Developed initially for work with minority families, it contains many of the strategies that are most effective at engaging and changing their familial structure.

The structural approach is primarily a problem-solving one (Haley, 1976). This aspect of the structural school makes it particularly useful in working with Black families. It is focused, clear, concrete, directive. For many Black families, the idea of going for treatment is a very new one. As mentioned in Chapter 2, historical approaches that appear to pry before trust can be established are often rejected. The problem-solving focus of the structural approach is, therefore, an important way to engage Black families initially. This is particularly helpful for "multi-problem families" who are overwhelmed with life's demands. This approach can help a family to clarify and prioritize its problems. With its focus on change, it directs the energy of the family toward the future and improvement rather than toward the past and blame. For Black families who may feel powerless to change their lives, this approach provides a sense of empowerment and accomplishment as each problem is resolved and the family is restructured.

The use of family prescriptions and tasks serves an educative function and often provides strategies for change. The emphasis on clear treatment contracts at the end of the initial session (Haley, 1976) is also important when one considers that the treatment process is so new for many Black families. This model quickly engages the family in an interaction process with each other and with the therapist. It is also particularly effective in engaging the peripheral members of extended families in the treatment and it helps to dismantle the "resistance" of many Black families. An additional therapeutic benefit is that it gives family members a hands-on experience with change.

Minuchin (1974) and Minuchin et al. (1967) were among the first family therapists to discuss the utilization of Black and Hispanic extended families in the treatment process. They focused on two aspects of extended family organization that are very common in Black families: the role of the grandmother or the three-generational family, and the role of the parental child. Both of these are discussed in detail in Chapter 4.

Boundaries

Aponte and Van Deusen (1981) state that "the structural dimensions of transactions most often identified in structural family therapy are boundary, alignment and power" (p. 312). These three areas are an important part of the early assessment process.

Minuchin (1974) states, "the boundaries of a subsystem are the rules defining who participates and how" (p. 53). Aponte and Van Deusen (1981) clarify this further:

These rules dictate who is in and who is out of an operation, and define the roles those who are in will have vis-à-vis each other and the world outside in carrying out that activity. The unit directly engaged in the operation may be one member of a family with all the others excluded, or any combination of family members plus persons outside the family. (p. 312)

As the first part of this book has established, these boundary issues may be very complex in Black families. For example, a child, his mother, his grandmother, his babysitter, and his child welfare worker may all be involved in an issue around his behavior. The concepts *enmeshment* and *disengagement* are related to boundary issues (Minuchin, 1974). Aponte and Van Deusen (1981) elaborate on these concepts:

at the enmeshment end of the continuum, the boundaries among some or all of the family members are relatively undifferentiated, permeable and fluid. . . . At the disengaged end, the family members behave as if they have little to do with one another because within their families their boundaries are so firmly delineated, impermeable, and rigid that the family members tend to go their own ways with little overt dependence on one another. (p. 314)

Minuchin (1974) proposes a continuum stretching from extreme enmeshment to extreme disengagement:

enmeshed | normal | disengaged

The vast majority of families generally fall within the normal range, while the cultural norm among Black families tends to fall more within the enmeshed range. Normal, functional Black families often have very close relationships, with a great deal of interaction and reciprocity (Stack, 1974). However, this is a very vulnerable area in Black extended families because this closeness often results in the roles and boundaries becoming very blurred. This can be true cross-generationally as well.

At the other end of the spectrum, there are Black families who are more disengaged. For example, a child may be raised in a large family and extended family but he or she may be essentially ignored. Children in some of these families seem to grow up by themselves. They are often sent to school, therapy, and so on by themselves and no one seems to notice them until there is a crisis.

Alignment

The concept of alignment (Aponte and Van Deusen, 1981) within families encompasses two concepts: alliance and coalition. Alliance refers primarily to the patterns of family members working together on something of shared interest (Aponte and Van Deusen, 1981). Haley (1976) defines coalition as "a process of joint action *against* a third person" (p. 109). In complex Black extended families, the alliances and coalitions are often cross-generational and may include key individuals who are outside of the family but who are very involved and often consulted on key issues, such as close friends, godparents, babysitters, ministers, church members, and so forth.

Power

Aponte (1976a) equates "power" with "force" and defines it as "the relative influence of each family member on the outcome of an activity" (p. 434). This issue is often a very complicated one in Black extended families. As it was shown in Chapter 3, which describes these complex extended patterns, often another relative or nonblood relative has considerable decision-making power in a family. This person might be a grandmother, grandfather, aunt, uncle, father, minister, or boyfriend. From a therapeutic perspective, this creates a complex situation because these individuals often do not appear early in the treatment process and are often not mentioned. Therapists may proceed to have many family therapy sessions with a mother and her children and may even begin to see initial changes. These changes can often be sabotaged later by a very powerful family member who has never been involved in the process. These powerful family members can also have a great deal of influence over the family's continuation in treatment. Therefore, the therapist must begin to explore early in family sessions who the true decision makers are. The following questions are some that may be important:

1. To whom did you speak before you made that decision?
2. Did anyone disagree with you on that?
3. Who has the final word on that issue in your family?
4. To whom do you listen when you need advice?

These issues need to be clarified before the introduction of any interventions. Questions regarding such issues should be asked in terms of extended family and people outside the family who may be involved in the therapy.

THE BOWENIAN MODEL AND THE TREATMENT OF BLACK FAMILIES

The work of Murray Bowen (1976, 1978) and subsequent work of Bowenian therapists is very relevant to the treatment of Black and other minority families. However, it has not been modified for use with different cultures nor have its obvious contributions been explored and clarified. The Bowenian approach has two major strengths that can be particularly useful to therapists working with Black families: (1) it provides strategies for exploring extended family dynamics particularly in the midphase of family therapy, and (2) it provides a theoretical framework that can be useful in generating hypotheses about family dynamics. There are important reasons why the Bowenian approach is more useful in the midphase of family therapy than during the initial stage. Given the resistance and suspicion with which many Black families approach treatment, the fact that the Bowenian approach is more historically focused may raise anxiety and cause the family to flee before trust can be developed. The structural approach quickly establishes a problem to work on and a contract between the therapist and the family to solve that problem together. Once an initial problem has been addressed, the therapist has some credibility with the family and the establishment of trust has begun. In the midphase of treatment with Black families, once trust has been established, the therapist often learns for the first time the "real" family structure of a Black family. It is during this phase that one often becomes aware of the presence of a man in the home or of a sibling who has been raised by family members "down South."

Bowen's theory relies on the use of the family tree (later called "genograms" by Guerin & Pendagast, 1976, and McGoldrick & Gerson, 1985) to help the family map its family organization and membership with the therapist. This process should never be conducted in an initial session with a Black family but should be delayed until trust is clearly established. Any attempts to gain this information prematurely will often prove futile and be incomplete. Guerin and Pendagast (1976), Bowenians by training, describe the wealth of family dynamic information that can be gained from this process. Elsewhere, I have given examples of the use of the genogram in family therapy with Black families (Hines & Boyd-Franklin, 1982). A number of points are highlighted. For example, Black families are often complex in organization and frequently have permeable boundaries. Therefore family members may live together and apart at different points in their lives. Because of the process of "informal adoption" (Hill, 1977), extended family members will often raise children during times of crisis. The family therapist must be careful to include both biological and nonblood relatives, many of whom may be very significant in the family's life. For example, a neighbor, church member, minister, boarder, babysitter, boyfriend, or girlfriend may play a very significant role in the family structure. This is often not apparent until a broader genogram is done and careful questions are asked.

The conceptual framework of Bowenian theory also has a great deal to offer family therapists who are working with Black families. The following concepts will be discussed in detail: differentiation, family projection process, multigenerational transmission process, family emotional cut off, extended family issues.

Differentiation

In the complex extended family in which many Black children are raised, it is not unusual for an enmeshment or blurring of boundaries (Minuchin, 1974) to occur. In the extreme, this can be seen as a fusion or lack of self-differentiation (Bowen, 1976). In the more enmeshed Black family, this lack of differentiation of self can be exaggerated. The therapeutic task is to help family members differentiate and still remain connected to the family and extended family. This differentiation issue is particularly toxic for many Black young adults who are going beyond their families in terms of education, profession, and social class. The level of differentiation necessary for this mobility is often frightening to many young Black adults and their families, which can result in the development of symptoms in family members.

The therapist's task in these situations is to help open the channels of discussion in a family where differentiation may be viewed as desertion. In such cases an "emotional cutoff" (Bowen, 1976) can occur. Many Black families who come to clinics are in fact cut off from their support systems. In these families, when the therapist initially asks about family or extended family he or she will be told that there is "no one." When trust is gained, however, and the genogram is constructed (usually during the mid-phase of therapy), one often discovers a fairly extensive extended family—which may even live close by—that has been cut off. This has often occurred because the family system could not tolerate the differentiation of an individual. Since the extended family has been historically so important for Black families, this is a very significant loss and can lead to the emergence of symptoms in individuals in all of the generations involved. The family therapist who is aware of this process can often help a parent who may be recreating that emotional cutoff with his or her own child to reconnect with his or her own parents while maintaining his or her own differentiation of self. The Bowenian technique of "coaching" can be very useful in helping an individual to resolve issues with the family of origin.

Family Projection Process

Bowen (1976) defines the family projection process as the process by which parental undifferentiation impairs one or more children. There are many ways in which a child becomes the focus of this projection process. Sometimes this is related to what the parent may feel toward the child prenatally and at the time of birth. In many Black families, the birth of a child is met with factors that can significantly increase parental anxiety (e.g., financial burdens, unwanted pregnancy). All of these may contribute to the way in which the arrival of a child is viewed by a particular Black family. Secrets often form around the facts of a birth, and these secrets can create a charge of anxiety around a certain child that is never resolved. That child can then become the focus of parental and extended family anxiety and can develop symptoms

Knowledge of this family projection process can be an aid to therapists when exploring the question of parenthood, paternity, skin color differences, and roots, as well as in the exploration of the genogram. It can also help clarify the reasons why a particular child has been singled out in a Black family to become the object of this projection process.

The Multigenerational Transmission Process

Bowen (1976) has clarified the ways in which the family projection process is transmitted through many generations. In ethnic groups that have strong connections to extended family networks, it is particularly important to be aware of this process. The concept of family repetitions is very useful in understanding certain phenomena in Black families. The case of Anna illustrates a fairly common example:

Anna was a 14-year-old Black girl who was brought to a community mental health center by her mother. She was referred by the school because her academic performance had deteriorated in the last year and her behavior toward teachers was increasingly oppositional. Her mother reported that she also "talked back" to her a great deal at home. In the course of her treatment process with this family, the therapist discovered that Anna had not manifested these symptoms until shortly after her 14th birthday. Further exploration revealed that the mother had become pregnant with Anna shortly after her 14th birthday and had been terrified that Anna would repeat her "mistake." She therefore had "cracked down" on Anna at this point and became extremely restrictive, refusing to allow her to leave the house except to go to school. Once this was clear, it could be pointed out to mother. She was then helped to discuss her own history of rebellion from her mother and her agonizing experience of her pregnancy with Anna. Anna's maternal grandmother was invited to join a session with Anna and her mother in order to discuss this. Anna was able to understand her mother's seemingly disproportionate fears for her, and they were able to re-negotiate the rules for Anna. The therapist was then able to help put mother in charge of enforcing these rules in a more realistic way.

This example demonstrates the ways in which a multigenerational transmission process can operate in an unconscious way in a family. In many Black families these family repetitions are all too common. The involvement of the maternal grandmother paved the way for some resolution of the mother's unresolved issues with her own mother. This example also demonstrates the value of combining the Bowenian and structural approaches. Once the multigenerational issues were clarified, the generational boundaries were restructured, placing the mother in charge.

PARADOXICAL/STRATEGIC/SYSTEMIC APPROACHES WITH BLACK FAMILIES

Papp (1981) states that "paradox is primarily a clinical tool for dealing with resistance and circumventing a power struggle between the family and the therapist" (p. 244). In this respect, it can be particularly useful with Black families who are often very resistant to the treatment process. Papp (1981) stresses, however, that "paradox is neither always neces-sary nor always desirable" (p. 245). Careful consideration of when or how this type of strategy should be introduced into the process is very important in the clinical application of these approaches in general.

There is a need for caution in the use of the paradoxical approaches with Black families. These techniques are particularly problematic in the beginning of the family therapy process because of the suspicion with which many Black families approach therapy. Once the family has been introduced to the treatment process and a degree of trust in the therapist has been established, the paradoxical/strategic/systemic approach can play a very important part in a treatment plan with a Black family. It is easily incorporated into an overall structural approach.

Papp (1981) divides paradoxical approaches into three types: (1) redefining the symptom, (2) prescribing, and (3) restraining. The first of these, the process of redefining the symptom, can be particularly useful in the process of reframing a negative interaction in a positive way. For example, in many Black families living in inner-city environments, there is a constant recognition of the dangers of the street. Parents, particularly single mothers who are raising children alone, are often terrified of the street influences of drugs, crime, and death that threaten their children. A frequent outcome of this process is the tendency of many of these families to restrict children to the house. Many parents will frankly acknowledge that they become more overprotective and restrictive as their children approach adolescence.

Aponte (1980) in a masterful video tape interview with a Black single-parent mother and her three teenage daughters, reframed her over-protectiveness as "loving too much" and was able to help her negotiate with her children a balance between legitimate concern and protection and age-appropriate independence. This type of reframing is extremely useful in Black families, who often feel overwhelmed, beaten down, and unsuccessful in their parenting function. By the process of reframing, one can often tap a well-spring of love and concern.

Selvini-Palazzoli, Boscolo, Cecchin, and Prata (1978) have developed systemic approaches for treating very disturbed families. Their approach includes the use of paradoxical letters that contain a prescription for the family. This approach can prove useful in the treatment of Black families in which key members of the family or the extended family are resistant to coming in for treatment. Often this person or persons may hold the real "power" in the family. In Black families typically men and older family members such as grandmothers are the most difficult to engage. Paradoxical letters can be particularly useful after initial structural change has occurred among the family members present and it is clear that another key person must be involved in order for the change to be a lasting one.

Madanes (1981) has developed techniques of strategic family therapy based on the techniques of Milton Erickson described by Haley (1973). These techniques are also very "goal oriented and directed toward alleviation of specific dysfunctional aspects of the family" (Minuchin & Fishman, 1981). According to this approach, the identified patient is viewed as having the symptom to protect the family.

In many single-parent Black families, it is not uncommon for a mother who is raising children alone to become overwhelmed with the pressures and demands. In these situations, because of the absence of a male partner to share the burdens, the oldest child—particularly the male child—can be very vulnerable to a process involving the reversal of generational boundaries. Often this child assumes spousal or parental responsibilities for the parent. The child may become mother's confidant at a very young age. These responsibilities eventually become too much for the child, and he develops symptoms. In such a situation the strategic use of a "pretend" paradigm can be very helpful (Madanes, 1981). The following case illustrates this point:

A young Black mother, age 27, brought her 10-year-old son to our clinic. She complained that he had once been very helpful to her and had taken care of her three younger children (ages 6, 4, and 2). In the last year he had begun to have angry outbursts at home, where he would throw things and become enraged over seemingly small requests. His mother felt that she had no control over him. The therapist asked the child to demonstrate an angry outburst. He did so and his mother threw up her hands in a gesture of helplessness. In the next session, he was directed to pretend to have an angry outburst. Mother was instructed to pretend to calm him down. She was then instructed to pretend to have an angry outburst herself in which she complained about the burdens of her life. Her son was to pretend to calm her down. They were instructed to perform both of these pretend sequences in the evening each day after the younger children were in bed (thereby giving them a special time for themselves). The angry outbursts stopped within 2 weeks.

This approach is particularly useful in Black single-parent families with young children, where protection of an overwhelmed parent is clearly a dynamic.

   A variation of this protection theme is a "sacrificial paradigm," which can be used very successfully in Black families with adolescents involved in serious and potentially dangerous acting-out behaviors such as drug use. Once again, the child's symptom is seen as protecting the family from dealing with other problems. In this case, the behavior is so potentially dangerous that the danger is exaggerated and reframed as a "sacrifice" on behalf of his family. The symptom is prescribed and the family is told that this sacrifice will have to continue until they are ready to deal with the real issues in the family. The case of Jimmy illustrates this process.

Jimmy was a 17-year-old Black male who was brought by his family for treatment because of his truancy from school, poor school performance, and extensive marijuana use. The family consisted of his mother, father, three older sisters, a brother, and his maternal grandmother. The older siblings had left home, and Jimmy was beginning his senior year of high school. The parents were a very child-focused older Black couple who had no relationships beyond their parental tasks. Jimmy's mother had a very close relationship with her mother, who was dying of cancer.

   It became very clear that Jimmy's acting out was serving a very major function in this family by protecting his parents from dealing with their concerns about their pending empty nest. After numerous attempts to restructure the family and put the parents in charge, the therapist learned that the parents exercised considerable denial regarding the extent of Jimmy's problems. He would often sneak back into their home when he was truant from school and smoke marijuana in the basement. Both parents consistently ignored these "signs."

   Finally, a meeting of the entire family was held in which the therapist told Jimmy and his family that Jimmy was sacrificing himself to protect them from dealing with their concerns about having an empty nest. It was obvious that he loved them so much that he would continue sacrificing himself until he flunked out of school and became hooked on more serious drugs. He would then become so dysfunctional that he would have to stay with them forever. The family was told that Jimmy was to continue to sacrifice himself for them until they were able to demonstrate their love by stopping him.

The parents at first were stunned by this reframing. The prescription was repeated in two subsequent sessions. The parents began to discuss ways in which they could work together to set clear limits for Jimmy. Within 3 weeks, Jimmy had returned to school and the parents had become more adept at confronting his marijuana use. Subsequent sessions were held with the mother and father alone to talk about the issues of loss for them, particularly for the mother as all of her children grew up. She was able to ask her husband's support in helping her through her mother's illness and her need to establish a new role now that her job as "mother" was coming to an end.

CONCLUSION: THE INTEGRATION OF THE THREE APPROACHES

The three approaches presented in this chapter can be combined very effectively in an overall process of family therapy with Black families. In my experience, the multisystems model presented in Chapter 8 provides the best overall framework for the treatment of Black families. The other treatment approaches described in this chapter can be easily incorporated. For example, the structural approach with its emphasis on engagement and problem-solving techniques provides the family initially with concrete solutions to pressing problems and establishes the restructuring of the family system. It takes into account the varying constellations of extended family structure in many Black families and provides a structural "road map" for therapists in treating these families.

Once trust has been established and the therapist has gained credibility through this restructuring, the Bowenian approach can be very useful in the midphase of family therapy. By using genograms, the therapist can further clarify the "real" extended family network. A choice can then be made to include specific extended family members in sessions or to "coach" family members to handle their issues directly with their family of origin. Often lasting structural change cannot occur until these significant sources of "power" in the family can be included. The conceptual framework provided by the Bowenian model can be very useful to the therapist in clarifying the family protection processes and the multigenerational transmission process evident in Black families.

The paradoxical/strategic/systemic approaches should be used with caution in the initial stages of treatment with Black families. Because of the suspicion with which many Black families approach treatment, they are best incorporated into an overall multisystems approach. They can then be utilized when necessary with resistant Black families in which the symptom is a metaphor for a particularly toxic family issue.

Many of the approaches described above were designed to work with nuclear and, in some cases, parts of the extended family. There is another level of family involvement that must be explored if effective work is to be done, particularly with poor Black families: the involvement of outside systems or agencies that have an impact on the life of the family. All of these levels of involvement are considered in relation to each family and to the structure of therapy in the chapter that follows.

CHAPTER 8

The Multisystems Approach to the Treatment of Black Families

INTRODUCTION

Many family systems therapists who have worked with Black families have evolved their own unique and special ways of using themselves to join with and engage these families. They have become able via their experience to draw freely from the many different models of family systems techniques discussed in the previous chapter. The multisystems approach presented herein was developed from my own clinical experiences. This chapter is intended, however, for the person who is beginning to evolve his or her own personal model of treatment and who can benefit from a theoretical framework from which to work. This is not intended to provide rigid constraints for the therapist or *the* model of treatment for Black families, but rather a flexible set of guidelines that can be adapted to the needs and problems of different families and can be adjusted to the therapist's own personality and style. It should also be noted that this model has broad-based applicability in the family therapy and mental health fields and has relevance to the treatment of all ethnic groups.

In my experience as a teacher of family therapy, this multisystems model, in combination with a very thoughtful self-examination and use of self by the therapist (discussed in Chapter 6), can help facilitate the crucial processes of joining and engaging Black families. It can also allow therapists to build credibility more quickly by providing a model that is immediately useful in resolving the problems presented by the family.

As the previous chapter has indicated, effective therapy with Black families requires from the therapist a flexibility that allows her or him to draw from different systems theories and incorporate them into an overall treatment plan. It also requires that we be prepared to intervene at a variety of system levels, such as individual, family, extended family, church, community, and social services. Unfortunately, this complexity both overwhelms many therapists and challenges some traditional dichotomies and professional boundaries in the mental health field. It overwhelms clinicians because most have never been given a model within which they can organize their levels of intervention. The multisystems model discussed in this chapter provides this framework, as well as an alternative to a long-accepted dichotomy between modalities of treatment (e.g., between individual and family therapy).

Finally, many therapists were originally trained with very rigid boundaries in terms of therapeutic function. Work with extended families, churches, outside agencies, and so on, was seen as the job of the "social worker" in an agency. If the therapists were psychologists or psychiatrists, they were often not trained to see these levels of intervention as a major part of their work. In the treatment of Black families, this is indeed unfortunate. It is very difficult to divide functions in this way without further complicating the "system" confusion for many of these families. It also deprives the clinician of an opportunity to join first with a Black family around "real life" problems that may require interventions by the therapist to empower the family to obtain basic "concrete services" such as housing, food, clothing, financial help, and medical care. This is one of the most important ways in which therapists can establish rapport and build credibility with many Black families, particularly those who are burdened by the realities of poverty. (In Chapter 9 these issues will be discussed in more detail.)

In order to treat Black families effectively in therapy, a therapist must be able to both conceptualize and intervene at multiple levels and in multiple systems. These systems might include the individual, a subsystem (Minuchin, 1974) of a few family members, a nuclear family unit, an extended family, significant others and nonblood family members, church and community resources, and, particularly in the case of poor Black families, the social services system. This approach has built upon the structural family systems model (Minuchin et al., 1967; Minuchin, 1974) and a number of theorists who have developed ecostructural (Aponte, 1976a, 1981) or ecological approaches (Auerswald, 1968; Bronfenbrenner, 1977; Falicov, 1988; Hartman, 1978; Hartman & Laird, 1983; Holman, 1985). These models are described in more detail in Chapter 9. Unlike most treatment approaches, which are based on linear models, the multisystems approach is composed of two main axes based on a concept of circularity. The first axis is composed of the basic components of the therapeutic process: joining, engaging, assessing, problem solving, and interventions designed to restructure and change family systems. Each of these components does not occur only once, as it might in a linear model; they can and do reoccur repeatedly throughout the treatment process at all systems levels. In order to work effectively with Black families, the therapist must be flexible and willing to intervene at different levels.

AXIS I: THE TREATMENT PROCESS

Haley (1976) has delineated the following stages of the first interview in a problem-solving structural approach: social stage, problem stage, interaction stage, contracting stage, and closing stage. Again, in the multisystems approach, these stages become a part of a cyclical process that can occur at all systems levels.

Within the multisystems approach, this framework is useful as a model for one session, a series of interviews, and an overall treatment plan at each system level. With this in mind, the flow of treatment should be as follows (see Figure 1):

Step 1. Joining and engaging new subsystems
Step 2. Initial assessment
Step 3. Problem solving (establishing credibility)
Step 4. Use of family enactment prescriptions and tasks
Step 5. Information gathering: the genogram
Step 6. Restructuring the family and the multisystems

Joining and Engaging Black Families

Joining has many different aspects. It is important to convey to each family member who attends a family session that his or her input is valued and important. A feeling of respect is an extremely important ingredient in this process; Black families are very sensitive to a sense of being condescended to. For example, many therapists of today, in response to their need to be casual and informal with families, will often address family members by their first names prematurely, as described in Chapter 6. This is a mistake with many Black families, particularly with older family members who may be offended by this gesture by a younger therapist. It is best to refer to people as Ms., Mrs., or Mr. unless the family member indicates otherwise or permission to use first names is formally requested. It is also helpful to ask family members what they would like to be called.

I have devoted a considerable amount of time in this chapter to a discussion of the joining process. In my experience, because of the reluctance with which many Black families come to treatment, the joining process is the most difficult part. As Hunt (1987) has stated, "the

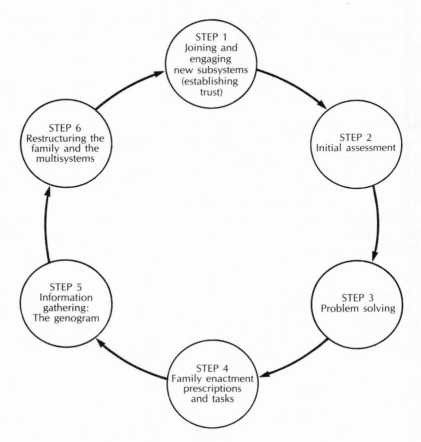

FIGURE 1 Axis I—the therapeutic process.

most difficult aspect of therapy with Black clients is establishing the relationship" (p. 118). Joining frequently involves outreach in working with Black families. Key family or extended family members may be unwilling or unable to come in for treatment sessions. Therefore, it is often important for the therapist to reach out by means of letters, phone calls, and at times home visits in order to engage these crucial family members.

It is important for the therapist to contact family members directly and not to simply send messages through other family members. The engagement of men in all cultures has long been an issue in the family therapy field. This is even more exaggerated in relationships with Black men because of the issues discussed above (see also Chapters 4 and 13).

It is important, therefore, to reach out directly to them. For example, the therapist might tell a mother that it is agency practice to contact all of the key family members and ask her advice as to the best time to call the father (or father figure). She is given some degree of choice but is not asked for "permission" to call him. It is important to underscore here that a man may have a number of relationships to the child and to the child's mother. He may be the child's natural father who may or may not live in the home. He may be the mother's live-in boyfriend or the child's stepfather, and he may be mother's brother or an "uncle" or family friend who exerts a great deal of influence over this child. In joining with this person it is important for the therapist to convey that his help is needed and that he has a very special relationship with this child. Often that statement or reframing will open the door to his involvement.

Many poor Black families have no phone in the home or messages are left and calls are not returned. In these circumstances a letter may "break the ice" between the therapist and this key family member. The following is an example of such a letter:

Dear Mr. _____

Your son Johnny has told me a great deal about you. I am his therapist and I have been working with your family at our clinic now for 3 months. We have been trying to deal with his school problem. I've reached a point where I need your help if we are to go further.

You are one of the most important people in your son's life and there are things he will listen to from you that he won't hear from anyone else.

Please give me a call as soon as possible at [phone number] so that we can figure out some ways to help him together. I know you are working most days but I'd be happy to call you in the evening or to stay later at the clinic to see you.

Many Black fathers will return a call if it is framed in this way. The therapist may also adopt a strategy in which she or he corresponds with a resistant father to keep him informed of his son's progress and to ask his help when necessary.

As stated above, there are often key extended family members who may object to and sabotage certain aspects of the treatment. Contact with these members is essential, as can be seen in the following case example:

James was a 14-year-old Black adolescent who was being treated in a day hospital program. He had come to us following hospitalization. He had been hallucinating, had paranoid ideation, and had threatened to harm his mother during a fight with her. His family consisted of his mother, his stepfather, and his two younger siblings. His father, although he had never lived with him, saw him regularly and was a very important figure in his life.

Family sessions had revealed that there was a great deal of friction between James' mother and his natural father, who was very critical of the way in which she was raising James. An issue arose in our treatment program when James refused to take his medication and began hallucinating once again and had a major aggressive outburst with a staff member. In a subsequent session, James' mother reported that James had been "talking to his father" who was a recovered drug addict and was very opposed to any form of drug. The therapist therefore contacted James' natural father and asked him to come in alone to see her. When his father arrived, he appeared very angry and came right in stating that he didn't want his son on drugs. He reported that he was now a counselor in a drug program and did not believe in them.

Resisting the urge to try to convince him otherwise, the therapist joined with him by asking in what ways he was concerned about James. His father accurately described his observations of James during the period prior to his hospitalization. He was obviously very worried about his son. As he relaxed, he began to share some of his own history of drug abuse. He had begun experimenting with drugs at about James' age and felt very guilty because he had been an addict for many years and had only recently re-entered his son's life.

It became clear that his anti-drug stance was partly a strong belief system but also his way of having some influence in his son's life.

The therapist joined him in his concern for his son and shared her own fears for his safety "on the streets" if he became inappropriately aggressive. The father hung his head and asked her if she had children. She replied that she did. He said, "What would you do if you were in my shoes?" She replied, "I would agonize just like you are but I'd be afraid to leave him with no help. I'd give him the medication but I'd hound the doctors, and get involved so I could monitor what was going on." The father after much thought decided on a trial of medication and agreed to "talk to his son" with the therapist and come in regularly for sessions with his son.

The above example clarifies the importance of joining or connecting with Black men in face-to-face contact. Joining must be accomplished before the therapeutic agenda is pursued. This issue of joining with men or fathers has been carefully discussed by Haley (1976). In his discussion of the initial interview he clarifies some strategies that are useful in this process. He points out that if the mother is designated as the spokesperson for the family, it is very important to also seek out the father's opinion.

This example is particularly important when one considers that men, especially Black men, often do not appear for the first session. It therefore may be important for the therapist, who may have already seen the rest of the family, to "balance the scales" by meeting with the father alone initially or by giving him "his say" in his initial family sessions.

This is also true of other extended family members who may be asked to enter the treatment process at different points. It is crucial that the therapist take the time to join with each of these members before moving on to the agenda or "problem stage" (Haley, 1976) of the session.

The process of joining does not occur at a single point in a linear progression, but is, as stated before, part of a cyclical process. In the course of engaging the many different individuals who are part of an extended family system, the therapist will have to join and engage many different family members at various points in the treatment process.

An important aspect of joining is the willingness to include those who come in. I have repeatedly seen therapists walk out into a clinic waiting room and invite in the "family" for a session and leave the friend or neighbor they brought along outside. With all families but particularly with Black people, it is necessary to find out who these people are and their contribution to the presenting problems.

There is an aspect of joining and engaging that goes counter to the training of some mental health professionals. This involves the concept of outreach to a family or going out of our "ivory tower" to meet with a family in their home or community. Often these home visits are the only way to connect or join with significant family members who are unwilling to enter treatment.

Initial Assessment

The initial assessment phase in a multisystems approach is an observational one. The therapist observes the family and begins forming initial hypotheses about the family structure. Questions that the therapist might consider *internally* and then test out by observing the family are:

1. How do family members seat themselves?
2. Who is the family's spokesperson?
3. Do family members allow each other to speak or are they constantly interrupting?
4. Is this the whole family or are key family members missing from the session?
5. What are the boundaries in this family? Are they clear?
6. Who has the power in this family? Is that person present in the room?

These, once again, are not questions that will be asked of the family but they will help the therapist form his or her own hypotheses about the family structure and the areas that will need to be restructured or changed.

This process of assessment is cyclical and ongoing. It is a process of hypothesis generation and then the gradual testing of those hypotheses in subsequent sessions. The testing of these hypotheses is begun immediately in the initial session.

The other clear advantage of this multisystems model is that intervention begins early and is combined with problem solving and assessment. Once again, the cyclical nature of this treatment approach is important.

The questions listed above are relevant to all families. For therapists working with Black families, a number of other important questions should be considered:

1. How is the family responding to the therapist? Is the joining complete? Are key family members beginning to trust the therapist?
2. Should the issue of race (or class) be raised at this point?
3. Who referred the family? (This is very important since many Black families are not self-referred.) Has the therapist made a clear distinction between herself or himself and the referral agency?
4. How does the family feel about being "in therapy"? How do other key family members (not represented at the meeting) feel? This is important because, as I have stressed throughout the book, many Black people feel that therapy is for "crazy people."
5. Why does the family believe they are coming and what do they want from the process (as distinct from the goals of the referral sources or the therapist)?

Problem Solving

From a systems perspective, problem solving is also a cyclical process. It does not occur one time but throughout treatment. In Chapter 7, the value of the problem-solving focus of the structural family therapy approach (Haley, 1976; Minuchin, 1974) to the treatment of Black families has been discussed. It serves many functions in our work with Black families. First, it serves an educative function in that it quickly initiates families who are new to the treatment process. Secondly, many of our families are "multiproblem families" who feel overwhelmed by a vast number of problems. Clear attention early on to identifying and rating the priorities of the problems that the family feels are most pressing will help to mobilize or empower the family by identifying specific problems that can be solved. Often families who are overwhelmed flit from problem to problem and never really focus on any one issue long enough to reach resolution. Still others feel so powerless to effect change that they feel defeated from the beginning.

The third positive aspect of the problem-solving process at the early stage of treatment is that the therapist begins to gain credibility and a sense of trust with the family as problems are addressed and solved. Depending on the family this initial process may take one session or many; trust too is an evolutionary concept with many Black families.

Use of Family Enactment, Prescriptions, and Tasks

Minuchin (1974) and Haley (1976) have stressed the importance of encouraging families to interact with each other or to enact their family drama in our offices. This is particularly useful with Black families because it quickly involves family members in the process. If individuals feel peripheral to the therapeutic process, they often will not return.

Some Black families who enter treatment think of therapy as a "quick fix." These families often don't see the connections between talking about their problems and actual change. The use of family prescriptions and tasks can be effective in such situations because they continue the therapeutic impact beyond the session. When a family therapist assigns tasks or prescriptions, the family therapy process is brought into the home. This causes other family members who may never come into the office to become curious about and often indirectly engaged in the process of therapy.

For example, in a family where a powerful grandmother has refused to come in, asking a mother to discuss the issues from the session with her mother in private without the children present and to come back and share grandmother's ideas establishes a dialogue between mother and grandmother and between the therapist and this absent family member. The therapist might then follow up with a letter or a phone call.

It is important to remember that tasks and prescriptions are important regardless of whether they are carried out as requested. For example, in the case described above, if the grandmother then resists sharing information with the mother, she and the therapist can explore whether this is appropriate or whether it represents a major structural problem in the family, such that the mother and grandmother do not communicate effectively about important issues.

Another very important task of this stage is the process of enactment. This is a very central process for many Black families. Often, by the time a family comes in for treatment, the lines of communication have completely broken down. A family from an ethnic group with a strong belief in therapy may be more likely to understand that therapy can help to reopen communication channels. For many Black families who are so new to the concept of therapy, enactment or role play that forces two or more family members to communicate with each other in the session gives a very powerful message to the family that the facilitating of communication is a central purpose of family systems therapy. Therapists at this stage should encourage family members to "act out" what they do at home. They might "stage an argument" or have the family enact a family pattern. The therapist can then ask other family members how close this enactment was to the actual interactions at home. This can provide very valuable information for the therapist as well as the family.

Enactment and the assignment of tasks in and out of sessions also comprise a very important component of the empowerment of Black families in the treatment process. This empowerment is particularly essential for Black families who feel powerless to change the "system". Via tasks they begin to feel the power to take control of the reining in of their children and the task of running their families. If the therapist does not actively involve family members—particularly parental figures or adult extended family members—in the process of change, then the therapist will place him- or herself in the parental or executive role in the family. Throughout this book I have stressed the difference between "helping" and "empowering" Black families to change. When a process is initiated whereby the family does the work in the session and members speak directly to each other rather than through the therapist, the likelihood of generalization outside of the actual sessions is far greater.

Information Gathering: The Genogram

It is important to note that information gathering with Black families often occurs at a point later in the treatment process. This is counter to the approach that many mental health professionals have been taught. Because of the issues of building trust with families, clinicians often find that they have to postpone extensive information gathering and the construction of the genogram or family tree until after trust has been established. This often means that extensive joining, initial attention to assessment, and problem solving occur before extensive historical data collection can take place. This is consistent with the structural approach, which stresses the importance of joining and a problem-solving focus in the first session.

The genogram is essentially a family tree. It is a tool, borrowed from the field of anthropology, that can be very useful to clinicians. A number of family therapists trained by Murray Bowen have used the genogram to illustrate his system concepts (Guerin & Pendagast, 1976; McGoldrick & Gerson, 1985). Hines and Boyd-Franklin (1982) have applied this work to Black families. Within this context, the genogram provides a helpful way to organize what is often a very complex extended family in many Black families. A word of caution is important here. Because of the resistance and suspicion that many Black families bring to the treatment process, the therapist must develop an alliance of trust with the family before this process can be completed in a meaningful way. I have often seen therapists who have learned this instrument apply it prematurely with Black families. Inevitably in such circumstances the families have felt as if the therapist was "prying into their business." Often the information given under these circumstances is merely the bare outline of a truly complex family tree. Crucial individuals and circumstances are often left out until the family feels that they can trust.

As this chapter emphasizes, an important step in building this trust is joining with the family around the problems that they feel are most pressing. If this is done in the first session, the therapist can begin exploring the household composition and extended family supports soon after. I emphasize this here because this is the reverse of what constitutes the intake procedure in many clinics, that is, collecting extensive histories in the first interview.

Once trust has been established, the information for the genogram can be collected in a variety of ways. With some families, it may be helpful to sit with the whole family and draw out the family tree. With others, it is useful for the therapist to simply record the information as it emerges and construct the genogram at another time. Often as trust grows, other family relationships are clarified and therapists often discover that their concept of family organization expands over time.

Figure 2 illustrates the family tree of the Bell family. Mary, aged 14, has been referred to a clinic for acting out in school and truancy. Her mother, Sandra Bell, is a 31-year-old woman who had her first child, Annie, when she was 15 years old. That child has been raised since birth by her great aunt, Aunt Mattie, in Georgia. Annie is now 16 and only visits the household for a couple of weeks each summer. The current household composition consists of Sandra Bell, the mother, her daughters, Mary, Martha, aged 6, and Barbara (called "Boo"), aged 3. In addition, Ms. Bell's younger sister, an I.V. drug abuser, died last year of AIDS. Her two children are now part of the household. Ms. Bell's mother, Pearl Bell, lives in an apartment upstairs in the same building. She functions as if she were part of the household and frequently babysits and cooks for the family. The therapist did not learn until some time later that Ms. Bell's boyfriend, Sandford Jones, lives with the family also and that his daughter, Kenya (aged 15), visits occasionally on the weekend. Ms. Bell and Mr. Jones have one child together, Aisha (aged 1), who is also part of their household.

It is important for the reader to explore the questions which were asked in order to obtain this information. The first and often most important question that must be asked is "Who lives with you or who lives in your household?" This is, in fact, much more appropriate than the typical intake forms that ask for mother's name, father's name, and number of siblings. It is important to ask if there are any other children who are not living in the home. In this case example, the mother had her first child when she was 15 and was unable to care for her. Therefore, her Aunt Mattie, who was childless, raised her daughter, Annie. As can be seen from the arrows on the genogram, the informal adoption process often creates a very complicated family tree. Another important question to ask is "Who helps you out?" In this family, the question revealed the presence and role of the grandmother; probing further and asking the mother if she had a special man in her life, revealed the presence and role of Sandford Jones. It is not unusual for the degree of a central male's involvement to be minimized initially. Questioning also brought up the mother's church family, including her minister and his wife, and Mary Word, a godmother to two of the children and the mother's best friend.

Asking about Mary's natural father revealed that he lives in another state and has not had contact with Mary in 5 years. Another important question to ask is whether there is any contact with the father's family. In Black families, two individuals may "break up" or separate or divorce, but often this does not divorce grandparents. In many families, the father's parents or members of his extended family may provide an important connection for the children and a tie to a father whom they may not have seen in a long time. This is worth exploring, even with families where a cutoff has occurred between the mother and children and father's extended family. Children are very important in Black families and "time heals all wounds." A very isolated and overwhelmed mother with little extended family support of her own might be encouraged to reach out now to the extended family of the children's father or fathers. This is an important consideration when placement decisions must be made. The father's extended family, although they may still be angry at the mother, may rally to take a child who is about to be placed in a foster home.

Once a complete picture of the family is obtained, the therapist can explore the involvement of the extended family members, friends, and nonblood kin in the family's life. Questions such as "Who disciplines the children?" or "Whom do you ask for advice when Mary has a problem?" are very helpful. If the therapist stays problem focused he or she can seek the family's advice about who should be involved in a family session regarding a particular problem. "Tribal" or "network" sessions (Kliman & Trimble, 1983), where the entire extended family is asked to be present, are most useful when there is a clear crisis or an emergency problem to be solved. In the following example of the Bell family, the therapist discovered that the mother, her boyfriend, and the grandmother were often in disagreement about how the discipline of the children should be handled.

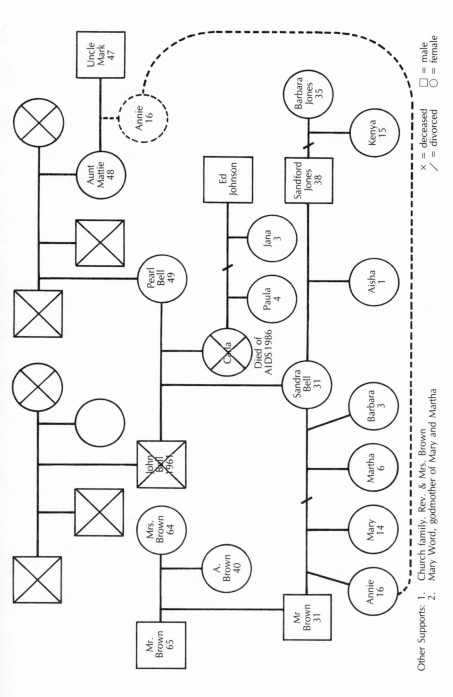

Other Supports: 1. Church family. Rev. & Mrs. Brown
2. Mary Word, godmother of Mary and Martha

x = deceased   □ = male
/ = divorced   ○ = female

FIGURE 2 The Bell family genogram.

145

The next section describes how this was restructured or changed in the family therapy process. The problem-solving focus and the gradual process of structural assessment become the roadmap in restructuring the family system as well as its interactions with outside agencies.

The therapist began with a subsystem of the family (often a mother and her child or children). In interviewing this family she discovered that the child is very oppositional particularly at home toward her mother and at school toward her teacher. The assessment of the family was that the mother has not functioned in an executive, parental role vis-à-vis this child and therefore feels overwhelmed. The following structural diagram represents the first hypothesis about the family structure.

$$\frac{?}{}$$

M	0000
(mother)	(children)

This diagrammatic representation shows that the mother and children appear to be functioning as siblings, with no one effectively assuming the parental functioning. In the early sessions, the therapist began to focus on the problem of the child's acting-out behavior and began restructuring the interaction within this part of the family. She worked gradually to empower mother to feel more in charge in her interaction with her children. The family structure (of this subsystem) would then become:

$$\frac{M}{0000}$$

As the therapist began to develop a relationship of trust and credibility with this mother, she collected a more complete genogram and learned that there are a number of very important individuals involved in the care of these children, many of whom contribute to the feeling of powerlessness that this mother experiences in raising her children.

The genogram segment that clarifies household composition revealed a boyfriend and maternal grandmother. Both the boyfriend and the grandmother were in fact interfering with rather than supporting her efforts.

GM (grandmother)

M   BF (boyfriend)

0   0   0   0
identified
patient

Upon further exploration, the therapist discovered that the grandmother works while the mother is home (receiving welfare payments), and that the grandmother often feels that she therefore has a right to tell her daughter and her grandchildren how to behave. The mother's boyfriend, as the father of the younger child, has been a part of the family system for 4 years. He wants to parent his child but has a very difficult time relating to Mary, the identified patient, because he feels that this girl resents him for assuming the father role.

The therapist then reached out and called the grandmother and the mother's boyfriend to ask them to attend a family session. The conflict between the three adults is very clear:

$$BF \text{ +/+ } M \text{ +/+ } GM$$

In addition, structurally, it appears that in the home the boyfriend and the grandmother assume the parenting or executive role, even though they are frequently in conflict, and the mother is constantly relegated to a child-like role:

$$\frac{BF + GM}{M: 0000}$$

The therapist asked that the children be left with a babysitter for the next family session in order to meet with the mother, her boyfriend, and the grandmother alone. She pointed out to all three that it is their level of disagreement that is contributing to Mary's acting out. She told them that they are all important parental figures to her and that they must work together to decide how they will parent her. The therapist asked the mother and grandmother to talk first:

$$M \leftrightarrow GM$$

They discussed the fact that the grandmother is angry at her daughter for not doing well with her life and feels that Mary is just like her. The therapist acknowledged this problem and asked the mother and grandmother if they could stay focused on the problem of Mary's acting out and how they will handle it. They came to some agreement that the grandmother will no longer deride the mother in front of her children, but will support the mother's rules for Mary.

The mother and her boyfriend were then asked to discuss their differences around the parenting of Mary. The mother's boyfriend pointed out that the mother has never really allowed him to parent Mary. From his viewpoint she is "too easy on the girl." He then feels obligated to be tougher on her. They discussed the need for mother to take the lead in being firm with her daughter as her biological parent.

After these individuals agreed on a strategy of setting limits for Mary and the other children, they could be brought together with the children once again to clarify their decisions.

$$BF===M===GM$$
$$\overline{0 \quad 0 \quad 0 \quad 0}$$
$$\text{(children)}$$

Eventually the mother, with the support of the grandmother and boyfriend, spoke directly to Mary and to her other children about the rules that had been agreed upon to curb their acting out. Thus, the mother is supported and empowered in her parental role by the two other significant adults in the home.

We have looked at the dimensions of the therapeutic process as it impacts on the family. Now it is important to explore the multisystems levels of Axis II.

AXIS II: MULTISYSTEMS LEVELS

One of the complicating factors in the treatment of many Black families is that data collection is often an evolving process. Again, this is contrary to the training of many mental health professionals, who are taught to gain a great deal of background information early in the process. Because of the healthy cultural paranoia described in the introduction to this book, Black families are often resistant to approaches that collect massive amounts of historical and family data in the first session. Working within the multisystems approach, I have found it much more useful to join with a family, focus on the initial problem in the first session, and save extensive data collection until trust has been established. For many therapists, by sessions two to five, it becomes necessary to begin collecting this data. This data may take many forms and encompass many system levels. The multisystems approach provides the therapist with a way of organizing this data so that he or she does not become overwhelmed by it and can use it effectively to produce change.

The multisystems model is a theoretical concept utilized by the therapist to organize complex data and to plan and prioritize intervention. *It does not require that the therapist intervene at all levels.*

Level I: Working with Individuals in the Multisystems Model

The concept of treating an individual using a multisystems model is not a new one in the family therapy field. My students often ask me if I do individual or family therapy. According to the multisystems models,

Multisystems

Level I	Individual
Level II	Subsystems
Level III	Family household
Level IV	Extended family
Level V	Nonblood kin and friends
Level VI	Church and community resources
Level VII	Social service agencies and other outside systems

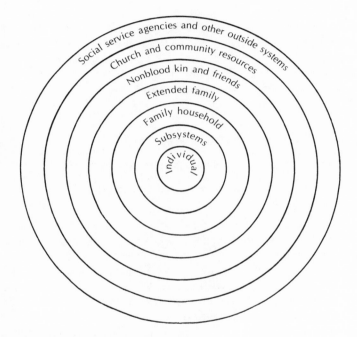

FIGURE 3 Axis II—the multisystems levels.

such a distinction is artificial, unnecessary, and may be counterproductive to effective treatment with many different ethnic groups. The elegance of the multisystems model is that it provides an overall framework that allows a therapist to provide treatment successfully at whatever level or levels (individual, family, extended family, or other systems) that is relevant to the situation at hand. The multisystems model expands the therapeutic frame of reference and thus the ability to provide effective service to Black families. Within the multisystems model, the second axis is comprised of the following multisystems levels (see Figure 3) [this model is consistent with the work of Bronfenbrenner (1977), Falicov (1988), and Aponte (1976a, 1981)]:

Level I   Individual
Level II   Subsystems
Level III   Family household
Level IV   Extended family
Level V   Nonblood kin and friends
Level VI   Church and community resources
Level VII   Social service agencies and other outside systems

Since therapy is so new to Black families, often one individual will be sent for therapy. Seeing that individual first can often expedite the process of building credibility with a Black family. Carter and Orfanidis-McGoldrick (1976) have discussed the concept of family therapy with one person and Bowen (1976) has discussed the concept of "coaching" an individual to produce changes in family relationships without seeing the family. Kliman and Trimble (1983) highlight this process:

> Families frequently are reluctant to bring significant network members into direct contact with their therapists and the participation of nonrelatives in psychotherapy may conflict with agency policy. Even when such obstacles are present, the therapist may conclude that coaching the family is the most efficient means of achieving the desired change. (p. 283)

It is important to note that this approach may be very useful with individual clients as well as families. Once a therapist has a family systems orientation, it will permeate all levels of intervention and even more importantly, it will influence the theoretical construct of change. Family therapists provided with this wealth of cultural information often despair when they cannot engage the significant family members. Coaching provides a model whereby the therapist can help the family members present in therapy to begin to rethink and ultimately to restructure their contact, interaction, and involvement with their extended family.

Kliman and Trimble (1983) have presented a very concise outline of the coaching process:

> The first step in coaching is to introduce the family to the social network concept, through helping family members develop detailed descriptions of their personal networks and teaching some basic principles about the relationships between networks and mental health. The combined family network (i.e., the combined networks of all the family members) is then examined critically concerning both its contributions to the family's difficulties and its strengths and the access it provides to helping resources. Finally, family and therapist develop strategies for changing network patterns, and/or making better use of the network to meet family needs. (p. 283)

The following example describes an intervention involving the coaching of an individual family member whose family, although living in another state, were interacting in a very dysfunctional pattern:

Joan Miller was a 35-year-old Black woman who entered therapy following a major extended family crisis. Her mother, father, brother (19), and two sisters (24, 30) lived in South Carolina. Joan was living in New York City. Her brother, who had been abusing drugs for some time had taken a near-fatal overdose. A quick intervention on the part of the middle sister had gotten him to an emergency room in time to save his life. Joan had been her family's "therapist" for many years and had received a number of calls from frantic family members asking her to come home and "take charge." As was typical of her family pattern, her parents had each "gone helpless" and abdicated their parental role. Joan's first reaction to her brother's crisis was to feel that she should pack her bags and fly to South Carolina immediately. With her therapist's help, she was able to draw out a careful family genogram and a network drawing and to discuss family interactional patterns. She was helped to see that she had taken on "parental child" responsibilities in her family as a young child and that her sister had "filled her shoes" since her move to New York. She explored the issue of her parents' role and their abdication of their responsibility. She decided that instead of rushing home she would call her parents and tell them how upset and angry she was at being called upon to be a parent to her brother. She told them quite directly that he could have died and that it was their choice as to whether they got help for him at this time. She suggested that they call her mother's sister, who was a social worker in South Carolina, in order to find help for him and place him in a drug program. Her parents, frightened by her brother's near death and by Joan's pulling back, mobilized and insisted that her brother enter a drug treatment program. Joan was at first greatly relieved but then gradually began to feel that she was not doing enough. At times she even became jealous of other family members—such as her aunt—who were now more involved. The investment in and pull of old patterns is often very strong. A great deal of Joan's work from thereon centered on her need to take on the role of "helper" and her need to "fix" situations in all areas of her life. As she worked on these issues she was able to stay involved with her family without becoming engulfed by constant demands and crises.

The concept of working with individual family members within a family systems context is relevant here on a number of levels. First, as in the case example described above, many Black adults struggle with Joan Miller's dilemma of how to be differentiated and individuated within a close extended family and yet not become either too enmeshed or totally cut off. Many other ethnic groups that have a collective focus, such as some Hispanic and Italian families, also struggle with this concept of finding a balance between cultural and familial expectations and the ability to meet the needs of the individual. For many Black family members, where the tradition of a collective unity or identity can be traced to their African heritage, this struggle can be very intense. This dilemma can appear in the treatment process and may require individual work with a particular family member.

With some Black families who enter treatment, the therapist may make the decision that one or more family members needs individual work for a variety of reasons. Unfortunately, a rigid dichotomy is often made between individual and family therapy in some mental health agencies. In these clinics, different family members may be assigned to different therapists, which often adds to the sense of feeling overwhelmed and exacerbates the underorganization with which many Black families present. In many of these cases, further systemic confusion can be avoided by a systems therapist who can intervene at many levels, including work with individual family members, the entire household, various combinations of extended family members, and outside agencies.

In my experience, this unnecessary dichotomy between treatment levels and modalities often results in complex treatment case conferences between different therapists, which can ultimately prove more time consuming for the therapist and can actually contribute to the fragmentation of family members. In the worst possible (and often common) scenario, however, overburdened therapists may not have time to communicate with each other and find that they are working at cross purposes. The multisystems model therefore provides a more efficient method of providing mental health services to many Black families. Once again, the flexibility with which the therapist approaches this model is the key to its effectiveness.

Levels II and III: Discovering the Real Family Network or Going Beyond the Subsystem

Many Black families present at clinics as they feel clinicians expect them to appear. This often means that the clinician initially meets only a "family subsystem" (Minuchin, 1974), such as a mother and a child or children. This is where the therapist's work begins. After the first few sessions, as trust begins to build between the therapist and the family, the therapist will inevitably begin to learn more details about the extended family network. The therapist must have some knowledge of Black cultural patterns in order to ask the questions that will help to give a true sense of the real "family." The necessity of this knowledge forces us as family therapists to take a very careful look at the intake forms we use to collect family information, the questions we ask, and the timing of these questions.

After the problem focus of the first few sessions, the therapist will need to begin to explore the network, since in focusing on a particular problem the question of who else is involved in this problem will have been raised and explored. Speck and Attneave (1973) and Kliman and Trimble (1983) have discussed network approaches.

A very basic general question that can be asked in order to explore the support system might be, "Who helps you out with the children?" Families will often open up and give many examples, ranging from grandmothers and aunts to neighbors and boyfriends. Another important question is, "Who lives in the house?" One might learn about many different extended family members. It is also important to explore who visits regularly and whether there are people who sometimes stay over. This will often reveal informal adoption patterns such as those discussed in other chapters. It may also be the first time that a boyfriend or girlfriend may be acknowledged. One might ask a mother directly after trust has been established, "Do you have a special person or a boyfriend in your life?" Many mothers, particularly those receiving AFDC benefits are initially afraid to reveal the presence of a boyfriend for fear of losing their family's income from the welfare department. Rather than the typical intake question of "How may siblings do you have?" one may learn a great deal more about these complex relationships by asking, "How many children live in the home or stay over often?" This may reveal cousins, nieces, nephews, grandchildren, or neighbor's children who interact daily within the household.

Another difficult area to explore in many Black families is the question of the paternity of the children (see Chapter 3). Children may have different fathers, a fact that may not be shared initially. Once a relationship of trust is established, however, one can ask a mother, "Do the children all have the same father?" or "Who are the children's fathers and do they help out?" Often this will reveal other possible aspects of support or involvement by the biological father(s) or his family. As discussed in the previous section, once a father acknowledges the paternity of a child, his extended family may be involved in that child's life even if the father himself is not. Many family therapists make the error of assuming that because a child does not see his or her father he or she has no knowledge of him or of his extended family. As mentioned, one should remember that in Black communities, although individuals or couples may divorce or "split up," one does not divorce grandparents. For many isolated families who are cut off from their network, it is important to explore whether these paternal relatives have ever been involved, since they may once again serve as resources. Also, as children approach late childhood (ages 10–14), they often become very absorbed with the question of "who they are," and will often reestablish contact with their father's extended family as a way of discovering that part of themselves. If this has not occurred, it may be an issue that the therapist can explore with the family.

An extremely important question in Black families is not just "Who is your mother and father?" and "What relationship do you have with them?" but "Who raised you?" Given the prevalence of informal adoption discussed in the previous section, this may be very relevant to the current family dynamics. These patterns of informal adoption are often repeated over generations. One tool that can be very helpful to clinicians in gathering and organizing this information is that of the genogram.

Levels IV and V: Extended Family Organization and Nonblood Kin

Once joining has occurred with the family or family subsystem that originally came for treatment and at least one important problem has been addressed, the therapist is in a position to explore extended family organization and nonblood kin. This can be done in a variety of ways. One very practical way to begin raising the issue of extended family members is to stay focused on the problem or problems that the family has established as being of primary importance and to ask questions such as:

1. How do other family members feel about this problem?
2. To whom do you go for advice?
3. Have a lot of people tried to give you their opinion about this problem?
4. To whom would you listen for advice on this issue?
5. To whom would your child (children) listen?
6. In the past, to whom would you go when you had something serious like this to deal with?
7. Who helps you out when you have troubles?
8. Have you experienced any recent losses (deaths, moves, divorces, fights, cutoffs, etc.) within the extended family, nonblood kin, or friendship network?

As one begins to gather this kind of information, organizing it in the form of a genogram tends to follow naturally.

Once this process is complete and the therapist has a workable understanding of the family's extended support system, specific questions such as the following can be asked:

1. How do family and extended family members interact?
2. How many people have stayed with you (even overnight) in the last year?
3. Do a lot of people turn to you for help? Who are they?

4. Who gets along with whom?
5. Who fights with whom? (Children love these questions.)
6. Who would you say has the last word on things in your family?
7. Have you told any family members and friends about your coming for therapy? How do they feel about it?
8. Do they agree with what you've been doing here?
9. Of these people, who do you feel contributes to the problems we've been working on?
10. Who do you feel might have some ideas that could help us solve this problem?
11. Who's involved in any way with this problem?
12. How long has the problem been occurring?
13. Have there been any major losses, resulting from deaths, moves, separations, fights, and so on in your family during this time?
14. Have any new people come into your life or your family in this time, from changes such as a marriage, a new boyfriend or girlfriend, a new church or religion, an extended family member or other person who has moved in?

Levels VI and VII: Church, Community, and Social Service Networks

Chapter 5 has explored in detail the ways in which religious orientation and spirituality can play a role in the lives of Black people. This section therefore summarizes the levels at which the therapists may need to utilize this resource in treatment. First, the religious or spiritual belief system is so strong in some Black families that the therapist may find it useful to simply explore it as part of general information gathering. For those families for whom religion is of paramount importance, the therapist will quickly receive feedback regarding that importance. It may then be helpful to make reference to spiritual statements made by family members as a help in reframing family impasses.

In times of crisis, the church becomes a very important social service system for many Black families. As Chapter 5 shows, the crisis of fire, homelessness, hospitalization, illness, isolation, and so forth can often be helped by the support of the church "family." For many Black clients and families who are emotionally cut off or geographically isolated from their biological extended family, helping them find a church family and address their fears about doing so can have a long-term therapeutic effect. For many overburdened single-parent mothers who have no particular religious orientation but who are feeling burdened, overwhelmed, and isolated, a Black church can provide a social life for mother and children, free child care and school and after-school programs, and meaningful activities for children to keep them off the streets. For some mothers who have difficulty organizing to seek help, Black churches can provide a structure to help them mobilize. They can also "pass the hat" when a family has lost their possessions in a fire or provide a temporary sanctuary if a family is homeless. Chapter 5 also gives examples of special circumstances in which a minister, pastor, elder, deacon, or deaconess might be included in the treatment process. The key here is that therapists be aware of this level of intervention and utilize it when appropriate in order to mobilize help for some Black families.

Community supports are available on a number of levels, and can range from after-school tutoring services, free lunch programs, day-care centers, or free hospital and clinic care. It is important for therapists within agencies to keep a file on these different services so that they can mobilize them when necessary. For example, some therapists make excellent use of a number of transportation services that are available through state, city, and Medicaid and Medicare agencies for transporting children and families to and from therapy sessions. This kind of tapping of available resources is sometimes the single most important interaction in facilitating the possibility of treatment.

The seventh level, social services and public institutions, encompasses an area that, as has been stated, many therapists are not trained to address as part of the therapeutic process. The realm of public agencies and services is central to the treatment of poor Black families, who are often very dependent on these institutions for survival. Such families are also particularly vulnerable to institution and agency intrusion into the functioning of their families. For these reasons, Chapter 9 is devoted exclusively to the application of the multisystems approach to the treatment of poor Black families and the seventh multisystems level, the agencies that have an impact upon their lives.

CONCLUSION

The multisystems approach expands the "road map" of the therapist in working with Black families, helping to highlight the levels to be explored and allowing the therapist to maintain a problem-solving focus and to explore the ways in which each system level contributes to the problem that a particular family is struggling to resolve. Therapists often have to help Black families in therapy establish clear boundaries between the different system levels, and construct ways in which each level involved can be a support rather than a hindrance. The multisystems approach also enables the therapist to explore systematically each of the levels in looking for resources of people and services that might aid in finding the solution of a particular problem. The next chapter explores the ways in which social service networks can be utilized to function in a more supportive and empowering fashion for poor Black families.

CHAPTER 9

The Multisystems Approach to the Treatment of Poor Black Families

The multisystems approach provides the family therapist with a model for moving beyond the structure of the individual, the family, and the kinship system. It allows the therapist to assess, clarify, and ultimately restructure and change the interaction between poor Black families and the outside systems and agencies that intrude in their lives. These systems include schools, courts, child welfare agencies, housing offices, welfare departments, police, hospitals, and health care and mental health providers. It will often be important for the family therapist to help the family "navigate the system" by meeting with representatives from these various agencies and the family and to assess the boundary, alignment, and power issues involved. Often the family therapist may find it necessary to restructure or help the family to renegotiate and clarify its relationship with a particular agency.

Because of the number of social systems that are involved, often intrusively, in the lives of poor Black families, many of whom feel completely overwhelmed by life's demands and socioeconomic realities, these families often find that they cannot interact effectively with agencies. It is not unusual for a therapist to discover that a number of these agencies are working in opposition, and that the family has been triangulated by them (Minuchin, 1974). Many Black inner-city parents report that they feel manipulated and condescended to by these agencies. This sense of powerlessness when faced with "the system" is often a metaphor for a more general sense of defeat that many of these parents feel in relation to societal institutions. When assessing family dynamics, family therapists must be willing to assess the impact of these external structures on the family and help to support the family in their interactions with these other institutions and agencies.

THEORETICAL CONTRIBUTIONS TO
THE MULTISYSTEMS APPROACH

Aponte (1976a, 1981) has made the most significant contribution to the theoretical and clinical development of this model. Building on his foundations as a structural family therapist, he developed the "ecostructural" model, which examines the role of the family therapist vis-à-vis outside agencies working with poor families. Aponte (1976a) and Aponte and Van Deusen (1981) built upon the work of Auerswald (1968) whose ecological approach addressed a similar need. Bronfenbrenner (1977) utilized an ecology of human development to illustrate these different levels and their impact on the family. Aponte (1974) gives a very clear statement of his ecostructural view:

> In the eco-structural view we recognize the internal structural organization and ecological balance of the many psychological and biological systems within the individual, but we also look beyond the interaction and structural relationship of these systems in the individual's life context. (p. 4)

The ecostructural model offers important contributions to the treatment of poor Black families: (1) it provides the therapist with a conceptual framework within which to organize the large number of agencies and institutions that are involved in the lives of their patients; and (2) it affords a clear path that the therapist can use to assess the structural issues not just within the family but between the family and these organizations. The therapist can then expand the structural concepts of boundary, alignment, and power to assess accurately these broader system interactions (Aponte & Van Deusen, 1981). Third, as Aponte (1974) stated, the ecostructural model allows the family therapist to organize and integrate other treatment modalities and methodologies:

> While the eco-structural viewpoint helps to integrate other methodologies, it also brings with it its own methods and skills. The therapist must be able to conceptualize what he or she sees in terms of systems and their structural bases. The therapist must also be able to talk and behave in such a way that the members of the family system and other systems will themselves be able to experience the relevant issues as phenomena founded on the interactions between people and organizations. The therapist must be able to use himself or herself to promote change in authoritative hierarchies, communication lines, interpersonal alliances and other organizational structures which will change the functioning of systems. The therapist needs to know how to communicably pair himself or herself, and in other ways interact with others so that they will change the ways their particular systems are operating. (pp. 4–5)

Hartman (1978), Hartman and Laird (1983), and Holman (1985) have described an "ecological approach to family assessment . . . [that] acknowledges that families do not exist in a vacuum" (Holman, 1985, p. 18). They recognize the interplay and interaction between families and their environment, presenting a model that describes the complex interplay of organizations and individuals that may have an impact on a family system.

Before we proceed further in exploring specific treatment aspects of this approach, it is important to examine the issues of concern to families that are Black and poor. This will offer the therapist an understanding of the needs of this population and the advisability of adopting a multi-systems approach.

THE REALITIES OF BEING BLACK AND POOR

We have already established that the impact of racism creates a burden that is unique for Black families in this country. This burden is particularly heavy for low-income Black families who also struggle with the oppression of poverty. These are the families whom Wilson (1980, 1987) describes as the Black "underclass" or the "truly disadvantaged." Parents live not only with the financial burdens of doing without and with the inability to provide for the basic wants and needs of their families but also with the seemingly endless cycles of unemployment, poor housing, and inadequate community services. When one adds this information to the national statistics that indicate unemployment among Black people to be the highest in the country, one can understand more fully the feeling of hopelessness in many Black communities.

To be Black and poor is to live in fear. Families are constantly afraid for their children and are well aware of the location of the local "crack house" or the neighborhood pusher. Children at a very young age become enlisted by the "drug culture," first as "runners" and later as pushers or users. When disillusionment grows strong, drugs and alcohol can often lure youth. The process of educating their children is another "mine field" for Black parents. Inner-city schools are often not responsive to parents or to children's needs, and can be viewed by many Black parents as another hostile, overwhelming system and an impossible wall to scale. It is not difficult to understand, therefore, why Black youth have one of the highest dropout rates in the nation.

There are fears on many other levels for Black families living in poverty. Street crime is extremely high and the further discrepancies between Black inner-city communities and the rest of the nation increase the desperation. The rage that this process causes often erupts in domestic violence, child abuse, and "Black on Black" crime. In many Black inner-city neighborhoods, there are many Black families who are struggling to survive and who feel that they have no protection. Experience has taught them not to trust the police or the courts to deliver justice. Thus they avoid these systems at all costs.

EXPERIENCE WITH WELFARE AND OTHER SYSTEMS

One of the issues that has led Black families to resist mental health services has come from confusion about the relationship between clinics and other agencies (e.g., welfare, courts, schools) (Hines & Boyd-Franklin, 1982). Many Black families have a history of involvement with the welfare system, for example, and have reported experiences of intrusiveness and prying by these agencies. As has been stated, the welfare system has the power to discontinue the family's financial security if the father of the children (or another man) is proved to be living in or contributing to the household.

Often if the father of a child contributes a small amount, even if the parents are not living together, he could compromise the family's financial allotment through welfare. This, coupled with the tragic unemployment rates for Black men and the "last hired, first fired" policies in this country, has contributed to the breakup of many Black families and the fragile nature of some family units.

Many of our inner-city families are referred for therapy by the courts. This is a frequent recommendation in child incorrigibility cases for example. In family dispute assault cases, both police departments and courts often refer a family for therapy. This creates a difficult dilemma for the therapist and the family on at least two levels. First, Black families in these situations are often not self-referred. They feel forced to come and in fact they are often forced to do so by probation officers and courts. Second, Black families in these situations are extremely suspicious of the therapist and are dubious about the confidentiality of their treatment. They are well aware, often before the therapist is aware, that the courts or referring agencies will require a report or evaluation of their progress in treatment. Therapists in these situations frequently find themselves asked to make difficult decisions or recommendations in the lives of their clients. These realities must be discussed frankly, honestly, and realistically with Black families if trust is to develop.

Schools are one of the most frequent referral sources for Black children and families to clinics and community mental health centers. In keeping with the system's view of the child or identified patient as the person whose symptoms reflect the distress in the family system and the need to get help for the whole family, it is not surprising that these symptoms or problems often manifest themselves at school. Poor Black families place a very high value on the education of their children; educational orientation is therefore a focus of strength for these families (Hill, 1972; McAdoo & McAdoo, 1985). Such families, however, are often so overwhelmed by survival demands that they have not been able to monitor or intervene effectively in their children's education process.

FOSTER CARE AND PLACEMENT SYSTEMS

Social service agencies have also had a great deal of power in poor Black communities: "Black children are disproportionately overrepresented in foster care homes and facilities" (Hill, 1977). Child welfare agencies have the power to remove children on the basis of abuse or neglect. They have the right to divide the children in a family into numerous foster homes and to petition the courts for "termination of parental rights." Once a child has been removed from a family, the regaining of custody is often a long and difficult process. Poor Black families are often very frightened and resentful of this power. Given this context, it is not surprising that a Black family who is referred for therapy by one of these agencies would tend to be suspicious of the therapist's role. Many fear that they will be "reported" to these agencies if they share personal information. As was mentioned in Chapter 6, Black therapists are often surprised to discover that they are also perceived as part of "the system" and are not trusted initially.

Prior to 1977, it was less common for children to be placed with relatives. In response to lobbying efforts and research documentation by the National Urban League (Hill, 1977), that process has begun to change (see Chapter 3). Today, a greater effort is made by some social service agencies to locate extended family and place children with their relatives. Often these efforts have not been sufficient and many children "fall between the cracks."

The complex interaction of social agencies and poor Black families makes it important to return to a discussion of the multisystems approach and to describe its basic principles, strategies, and interventions. The next section explores four basic principles of this approach: (1) the therapist's own values and assumptions; (2) the family therapist as system guide or facilitator; (3) concrete problems as a legitimate part of the family therapy process; and (4) the concept of empowerment in the treatment of poor Black families.

EXPLORING THE THERAPIST'S OWN VALUES AND ASSUMPTIONS

One of the hallmarks of the multisystems approach is that it forces the therapist to examine and clarify his or her own values and explore his or her own belief systems (see Chapter 6). Therapists must examine their own families and their own cultural identification, as well as their own beliefs about poor Black families. In the process of the clarification of values with the trainees, the author has often heard class biases such as "the poor are lazy," "they want to live that way," and "they like getting welfare." Some clinicians deal with such issues by ignoring the racial component, preferring to state that the issue is one of "class not race."

Once the therapist has explored his or her own beliefs, biases, values, and so on about what it means to be Black and poor, he or she is in a very different position to work with these families. One of the most important issues therapists must handle within themselves is the tendency to "blame the victim," or to see poverty as the "fault" of the person. The approach to treatment presented in this book is based on the concept of empowerment. Parnell and Vanderkloot (1989) have emphasized this point. They state: "Blame is counter to empowerment. It paralyzes everyone, families and therapists alike" (personal communication). Thus, the model of looking for and building upon strengths is essential to our work with poor Black families.

In March 1987, I had the privilege of working with Myrtle Parnell in a workshop on these issues at the American Ortho Psychiatric Association. Her approach allows her to join very effectively with poor Black families around the issue of "wanting something better for themselves and even more importantly for their children" (Parnell & Vanderkloot, 1989). This allows the therapist to reframe the familial position for him- or herself and for the family: "You desperately want things to be better for you and your child and you are struggling against great odds to get there," or, "As I listen to your statements I sense that you desperately want things to be better for your children than they were for you." Parnell and Vanderkloot (1989) have elaborated further on this issue:

We have presented a clinical model which is basically non-blaming and non-pathological for working with poor people. We have shown that in helping the parents of poor children to do well what they most want to do has a powerful effect on the children and the family. *We have searched for that part of the parent that fiercely wants life to be better for his children than it was for them.* We have validated the totality of the person's experience and thereby formed a powerful bond with the parent and children. We are seen as "we" rather than "they" when we work in this way. As one of our patients stated (a convicted rapist) when he asked himself what was different in our treatment of him, "All the other people were nice and helpful, but it is as if I were out in a canoe in rough water. Everyone else is standing on the shore calling out directions. You dove into the water, swam out, got into the canoe and showed me a new way to shore." (p. 461)

THE FAMILY THERAPIST AS SYSTEM GUIDE OR FACILITATOR

Throughout this chapter it has been established that poor Black families often depend on outside agencies for very basic needs and services. With these government services, families must contend with an enormous bureaucracy. Often each agency is perceived as a baffling maze of individuals who do not give clear answers or show respect. Therefore, in addition to helping families to learn to structure their involvement with these agencies, the family therapist is frequently faced with the task of helping families learn how to navigate effectively the social service system. In this role, the therapist often has the task of becoming a system guide or facilitator for the family. In the traditional medical model, this was the role of the social worker. However, family therapists of all disciplines who work with poor Black families have commonly found that the therapist's willingness to assume this role (irrespective of discipline) is an essential part of joining with such a family and building trust.

The concept of a facilitator is important here. It is crucial that the therapist not take over the central role for family members but rather support the parents or parental figures in assuming their respective executive roles.

As an important component of their role as facilitators, therapists should have at their disposal files of information on social service agencies that can provide vital social services. It can be very useful for clinics or community mental health centers to provide files making available this information and to request that each staff member contribute new ideas. It is also very helpful if such clinics establish contact people in key agencies who can serve as resources or expedite the process of obtaining services for a family.

Poor Black families expect involvement from us as clinicians, often waiting for us to take the first step and being afraid to trust us as agents of change. It is thus extremely important for therapists to convey a willingness to get involved and to "roll up their sleeves" and get to work. Parnell and Vanderkloot (1989) have framed this issue as follows:

If we as clinicians are not prepared to "dive in," difficult as that may be, it will be hard, if not impossible to capture the attention of poor children and their families. They are so busy struggling just to stay afloat that there is little energy left to focus on anything that is not immediately useful in the resolution of those struggles. (p. 461)

In conveying this involvement to the family, it is important for the therapist to "take the family where it is," starting with the problems that seem most overwhelming to them.

CONCRETE PROBLEMS AS A LEGITIMATE PART OF THE FAMILY THERAPY PROCESS

A major fact of life for some poor Black families is that they tend to enter treatment with an overwhelming array of life problems. Survival issues such as money, housing, food, and safety are ever-present realities. What role if any do these issues have in the process of family therapy? In truth, most major schools of family therapy have not even addressed these concerns. This is a serious error in working with poor Black families. In my experience as a supervisor of beginning family therapists working with this population, it is not unusual for a family to present their housing problems, for example, as their first priority in family therapy. Many beginning family therapists will quickly ignore this issue and search for problems related to family structure or dynamics. I have supervised therapists who in learning an informed approach to poor Black families feel frustrated by the presentation of these issues and ask, "When do we get to the *real* family problems?"

This a very serious error in working with these families for four reasons. First, families who are homeless or hungry are often so overwhelmed by these realities that they have no energy left to focus on other issues. Second, therapists who ignore these issues miss a primary opportunity to join with and engage these families. Working with them on these survival issues establishes the therapist as a "helper" and a person who can be trusted.

Third, family therapists often miss the opportunity to observe the structure of the family first hand by asking them to discuss this issue with each other or to discuss ways of resolving the problem together. Such observation can provide an opportunity for a clear enactment of the interactions that occur routinely at home. The therapist can then observe these interactions and note where the process breaks down. The ways in which a family discusses and handles these concrete problems also function as indications of their more general communication and problem-solving strategies. By asking a family to interact and discuss one of these concrete issues among themselves, a therapist can gain important data about such issues as family boundaries, seeking to determine, for example, whether the children or the adults lead this discussion. The assessment of concrete problem considerations also provides the therapist with an opportunity to evaluate the family's support system. Questions such as "Whom do you have that you can talk to about this problem?" are often very revealing.

Fourth, the feeling of powerlessness or hopelessness in the face of a racist society is often overwhelming for many poor Black families. It has an impact on many structural levels. Often a mother who feels powerless to solve her housing problem also feels powerless to discipline her children. Empowerment of the family and the parental system is a major task of family therapy in general, and particularly with poor Black families. Empowering a single-parent mother to contact the housing department and begin to get help in finding an apartment for her family can become an empowerment to be utilized in other areas: Her willingness to take charge can then be stated clearly for the family and redirected to the setting of disciplinary rules and structure for her children. The next section discusses the role of empowerment in this treatment process.

EMPOWERMENT AS AN ISSUE IN THE TREATMENT OF POOR BLACK FAMILIES

Throughout this book, the concept of empowering Black families has been emphasized within a number of frameworks. It is important to give this concept careful consideration because it is particularly central to the process of providing therapy to poor Black families. Many of these families have a multigenerational history of victimization by poverty and racism. Unlike other cultural or ethnic groups who can "blend in" or become part of the "melting pot," Black people by virtue of skin color are visible reminders of the inequities of society. With this experience of victimization comes a sense of powerlessness and, for many Black families, a sense of entrapment. This sense of being unable to make and implement basic life decisions in their own lives and the lives of their children often leads to a sense of futility. Empowerment most often involves helping parents to regain control of their families and feel that they can effect important changes for themselves. This is very threatening to many family therapists because it often requires that they take a stand on a decision made by another agency, forcing them to abandon their fantasies of "neutrality" in therapy. As many of the chapters of this book indicate (see especially Chapters 6 and 14), family therapy in general and with Black families in particular is an active therapy that insists upon the examination of the therapist's political, cultural, and religious beliefs and biases and on active intervention.

Empowerment can revolve around the seemingly innocuous issue of encouraging a mother to call her child's teacher rather than having the therapist make the call. If further support is needed, the call might be role played with the therapist first and even made from the therapist's office so that it can be discussed after. This may also apply to avoiding quieting down the children at the beginning of each session and instead allowing the mother to begin doing this herself with the therapist's support.

When many outside agencies are involved, it is also necessary to hold meetings with representatives from the different agencies or schools and the family. When these occur, it can be very useful for the therapist to role play in advance with the executive or parental figures in the family the process of raising issues that they want to clarify at such a meeting. The goal of the therapeutic process is to provide them with a sense of personal control, and to encourage the executive figures to take this kind of active role when confronted by these life events.

It is often a very dramatic and powerful moment in family treatment when a mother who has presented as feeling overwhelmed by her children and perceives herself at the mercy of child welfare agencies and schools can come into a session with her therapist and the representatives of these agencies with *her* list of issues, needs, and questions that she wants to address. This scenario represents a very effective restructuring, and communicates the structural message to the children that their mother is "taking charge." This is true empowerment.

It is through this kind of examination and the therapist's ability to convey respect for the families she or he treats that she or he creates an atmosphere in which empowerment can occur. This holds true whether we reestablish generational boundaries and put the parent or parents in charge, or help a poor Black family to reestablish the external boundary around itself and set limits on the intrusion by outside agencies.

STEPS IN THE MULTISYSTEMS APPROACH WITH OUTSIDE AGENCIES

As indicated in the previous chapter, the building of trust between therapist and family is often a prerequisite to exploring the involvement of other system levels. The following may serve as a guide in working with such families. The processes of joining and engaging, assessing, and problem solving are ongoing and should be addressed early on. The following are a number of crucial issues and steps that should be addressed in the multisystems approach.

1. As has been stated, many low-income Black families are not self-referred. They are sent or forced to come by outside agencies such as the police, courts, schools, hospitals, child welfare agencies, probation officers, and so on. These families are well aware that agencies will expect verbal and sometimes written reports from clinicians regarding the family's progress in therapy. This issue should therefore be addressed openly with the family and done so early on in treatment, with the therapist clarifying the issues of confidentiality.

2. It is important for the therapist to distinguish him/herself from these outside agencies as much as possible and clarify these distinctions for the family. Therapists should pay attention to referral sources and get permission from the family to contact them early in the treatment process. Families often expect that a therapist will speak to referral sources. This can often help clarify the agenda of the referring agency, which might be quite different from the needs or wants of the family. The clarification of the referral source's expectations of the treatment process can help prevent the frequent dilemma of many well-meaning therapists who become triangulated in a battle between the referral source and the family.

3. Once trust has been established with a family, it is often helpful to do a more complete "eco map" (Holman, 1985) with a family in order to assess more carefully the role of outside agencies. The eco map is a drawing of the different outside systems and agencies that have an impact on the family. Hartman (1978), Hartman and Laird (1983), and Holman (1985) discuss this technique for diagramming the interconnections between a family and its ecological system.

Holman (1985) gives the following summary of the data collection process.

> As an eco map is developed with the involvement of family members, it provides the workers and the family with an understanding of the stresses on the family system as well as the available supports, and family members are likely to feel more comfortable and less defensive about providing information (Hartman, 1978). Using a structured map simplifies the procedure for the worker and clarifies for the participating family members how various systems in their ecological field relate to their family. (p. 63)

Holman uses arrows to signify a flow of energy or resources and different kinds of lines to illustrate the nature of connections: a solid line for strong, a broken line for tenuous, and a broken line with slashes through it for stressful (see eco map, Figure 4, for Kelly family).

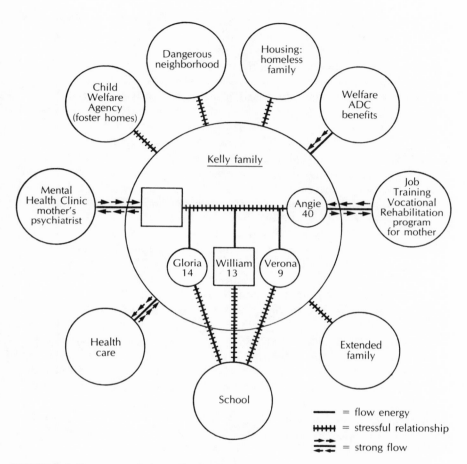

FIGURE 4 Eco map of the Kelly family.

This might indicate that there is considerable friction between this particular family and the school, the social welfare system, and the extended family. The therapist can then choose to explore these issues further and to intervene if necessary in these systems.

The eco map can help not only to clarify the structural involvement of outside agencies but also to determine which agencies are helping the family to resolve problems and which are creating or contributing to the family's difficulties. Sometimes eco maps also provide a quick, efficient method for finding out crucial social services that the family is not receiving.

4. As stated above, many Black families present with multiple problems. A therapist should spend early sessions helping the family to identify the most urgent problems and then to remain focused on these problems first. Many families become so flooded by needs and problems that they quickly become immobilized. Therapists will quickly begin to feel helpless also if they attempt to address too many problems at once. It is important to start with a problem that can be addressed and solved quickly at first in order to establish the process as helpful.

5. As much as possible, family therapists should become facilitators of the process rather than taking over the family's executive role. Enactment and role playing should be used with family members to help clarify their roles with outside agencies. Family sessions should be used to empower family members to delegate tasks and design strategies for dealing with specific agencies.

6. The therapist should function as a source of information for the families he or she treats. It is very important for therapists and agencies working with this population to set up a resource file or person that can be consulted in order to locate the particular services.

7. The therapist should be prepared to call for and to attend meetings with the family with outside agencies or schools. Often the therapist then becomes the system's therapist and must assess the boundary, alignment, and power issues between the therapist, the family and outside agencies. Sometimes this process involves calling for meetings of numerous social service agencies involved with a family. A joint plan can then be designed so that the family does not become overwhelmed by multiple forms of output.

8. Once again, it is important to stress the necessity of going outside of the clinic to meet with other agencies, make school visits, and meet with significant family members at home when necessary.

The following case illustrates this process:

The Kelly family consisted of Angie, a 40-year-old Black schizophrenic woman, Gloria, aged 14, William aged 13, and Verona, aged 9. The family was supported by welfare (AFDC) benefits. The family was referred by a local child welfare agency because all three children were truant from school, experiencing academic difficulties, and had been repeatedly placed in foster homes over the years. In the first session, Angie Kelly and her three children were transported by their caseworker. Angie looked particularly helpless in the session. Her oldest daughter Gloria took charge and described the family's concerns. She stated quite bluntly that they lived in a "hell zone" in which they could not sleep at night. Their apartment had been broken into a number of times but was "better than nothing." The family had in fact been living in shelters for the homeless prior to finding this apartment 6 months earlier. The child welfare worker reported that the family had been homeless a number of times because the children often vandalized the buildings in which they lived. She also reported that the youngest sister had been placed in a foster home the previous week because her mother had burnt her head with a curling iron when fixing her hair. All of the children had been removed a number of times and placed in foster care. Gloria, the oldest girl, had been placed in a foster home but had recently run away and returned home. Angie Kelly expressed a helpless feeling of not being able to "get these children to act right." She was herself seen for medication by a psychiatrist in the adult clinic at the community mental health center and had been maintained on 300 milligrams of thorazine daily for 2 years. She had not had a hospitalization in that time.

The therapist listened to everyone's input and thanked the child welfare worker for her support in bringing the family and then asked if she might meet with them alone briefly. She felt strongly that the family was very guarded and careful in their statements and she wondered if the presence of the child welfare worker might be adding to their reluctance to discuss their family.

The worker understood and waited in the waiting room for the family. The therapist had created a boundary between herself and the child welfare agency. The atmosphere in the session changed considerably after she had left. William immediately jumped in and stated that he wanted his family "back together." Gloria made clear that she felt that their housing situation was urgent. The therapist noted that the children had assumed a "parental role" and began mobilizing the mother by asking her what she wanted. She very passively agreed with her children. The therapist became very concerned about her passivity and was afraid that the generational role reversal in this family would be a permanent one because of the mother's diagnosis and the limitations on her functioning.

The therapist used future sessions to explore the limits of the mother's capabilities and to empower her to take responsibility for her own family. To accomplish this, the therapist worked with the mother individually as well as in family sessions with her children. In an individual session shortly after her daughter Gloria was again placed in a foster home, Angie admitted that she really did not feel that it was in the best interests of her children to live with her at that time. She felt that she needed to find a new apartment in a safer neighborhood and explore OVR (Office of Vocational Rehabilitation) job training opportunities for herself. In a subsequent family session, Angie Kelly was able with the therapist's help to explain this to her children. She told them that she wanted them to behave in their foster placements and that she would begin the process of meeting with the child welfare agency to make plans for bringing them together in the future. Family therapy sessions became a regular meeting place for the family. The therapist arranged for the caseworker to transport the two girls who were in foster homes.

After a number of attempts, Angie reported that she had been unable to find a new apartment. The therapist suggested a meeting of Angie, her children, the therapist, the child welfare worker, and a parent advocate who had been assigned the task of helping her to find a new home. The therapist and Angie had role played her involvement prior to the meeting. Her children were obviously impressed and surprised to see their mother take charge in the meeting and to clearly state her needs and the difficulties involved. The two outside agencies agreed to offer her concrete help with finding an apartment and the parent advocate offered to accompany her on a number of the visits to view possible apartments.

During this period, Gloria again ran away from her foster home. Her mother, with the therapist's help, was able to explain to her in front of the other children that they must work together as a family and stick to the original plan if they were to bring about change. There was a marked sense of empowerment in Angie and the helpless individual of earlier sessions was less in evidence.

William, who was still living with his mother, had been truant from school for an extended period of time. The therapist met with William and his mother to discuss this and learned that he was often afraid to leave his mother alone when he went to school. The therapist helped Angie to discuss this with her son and to tell him about her own plans to enter a vocational rehabilitation program. He agreed with his mother to explore a number of special programs for children who had experienced difficulty in attending classes regularly.

This was an extremely difficult family to treat. Nevertheless, despite constant crises, the therapist managed to help the family identify their most pressing needs and empowered the mother to assume a parental role, involving the social service agencies but drawing a boundary between her work and theirs.

The process of working with outside agencies can be very complex. Often it takes time for the therapist to see the entire terrain and to understand the network of interrelationships. The following case is an example of a situation in which both the therapist and her supervisor missed an essential component of the dynamics between the family and an outside agency. Although serious "mistakes" were made, in this case a mistake is defined in this approach as an opportunity to learn and to grow. This case illustrates this process:

Mrs. Brent, a 40-year-old Black woman, brought her "son" Carl (aged 7) for treatment. They were accompanied by Carl's child welfare worker, Mrs. Black, who had made the initial referral for treatment. Mrs. Brent explained that she was planning to adopt Carl officially as soon as possible. Her child welfare worker had recommended treatment because he seemed withdrawn, depressed, immature, very dependent, and was experiencing academic problems in school. She also produced a number of reports by psychologists that questioned the degree of psychological bonding that had occurred between Mrs. Brent and Carl.

The therapist then learned that Mrs. Brent's family consisted of her children Carol (21), Evelyn (18), Ella (15), and Rashan (5). The family was supported by public assistance. There was a great deal of competition and tension between Carl and Rashan, which often resulted in Carl bursting into tears and withdrawing.

Mrs. Brent had been a babysitter for Carl for brief periods of time during the first 6 months of his life. When he was approximately 1 year old, his natural mother, who was reputed to be an alcoholic and a prostitute in the area, left Carl with Mrs. Brent and asked her to care for him. She had never returned. This "informal adoption" arrangement continued for many years until an eviction created a housing crisis for the Brent family, and the child welfare department became involved. They designated Mrs. Brent an official foster mother for Carl at age 4.

Two years later, when Carl was 6, Mrs. Brent was informed that under the law of the state a permanent adoptive home had to be found for Carl. She was told that if she did not agree to adopt him a new home would be found. Because Carl's natural mother had not contacted him in many years, the child welfare agency was pushing for a procedure known as "termination of parental rights."

The therapist, a psychology intern, worked very hard to engage this family in treatment. She had a number of sessions with Carl and Mrs. Brent in which she attempted to clarify the boundaries between them and to reinforce Mrs. Brent's parental role. She also attempted to schedule sessions with the entire family, which were always cancelled. Finally, Mrs. Brent, who suffered from asthma and a cardiac condition, was hospitalized after a severe asthma attack. During that period, Carl's child welfare worker continued to bring him for treatment. The therapist began to lose contact with Mrs. Brent and to become increasingly angry at her for her resistance to treatment. She was preparing to terminate their case.

Learning from Our Mistakes

The family had pulled back from treatment. Mrs. Brent felt increasingly threatened by what she perceived as observations of and judgments about her mothering. The therapist and her supervisor realized rather late in the treatment process that Mrs. Brent was resistant because she saw the therapist as an extension of the child welfare agency, which she perceived as having the power to remove "her child." A session was arranged in which the therapist and her supervisor met with Mrs. Brent and explored this issue. The therapist asked Mrs. Brent how she saw her role. She also shared with Mrs. Brent that many families in her situation had told her that they weren't sure they could trust the therapist. Mrs. Brent burst into tears. She shared for the first time that she had been terrified for more than a year that Carl, whom she thought of as her child, would be taken away.

Mrs. Brent was also very conflicted about the adoption process in other ways. She and her family were attached to Carl and wanted to keep him. They would have gladly continued in their "informal" arrangement throughout his life. She was very anxious, however, about the process to "terminate" his mother's rights. In her view and in Black culture one never terminates a mother's rights to her child even if someone else raises him and becomes his de facto mother. In a variety of ways she communicated this conflict and ambivalence to Carl, which he interpreted as her hesitancy about keeping him. She was so conflicted that she had difficulty setting limits for him. He was treated very differently by the entire family and was infantilized by them.

In addition, the formal adoptive process brought with it a number of evaluations, which are routine and are designed to evaluate the quality of the psychological and emotional bonding of the parent, child, and family. These procedures were never explained to Mrs. Brent, and she therefore felt that everyone was judging her mothering of Carl and finding problems.

She explained to the therapist that she had read a report that said that Carl was more bonded to her daughter Evelyn than to her and she was therefore afraid to let the therapist meet the rest of her family.

The therapist was then able to help Mrs. Brent to separate her role from that of the child welfare agency. Poor Black families feel very much at the mercy of these agencies and truly do feel that they could "lose their children." The therapist encouraged Mrs. Brent to ask for a meeting with the therapist and the child welfare worker to discuss her concerns about the adoption process and her fears of losing Carl. The worker explained that the evaluations were a "routine" part of the assessment process. At this meeting a child welfare worker was able to help her to see that in her particular case, there was no danger of losing her child but that there were some problems that could be helped by family therapy which needed to be addressed. She was then able to "begin again" in treatment. Unfortunately, as so often occurs in our training programs, the psychology intern was completing her internship and leaving at this point. She was, however, able to help Mrs. Brent "clear the air" and recontract for treatment for Carl and her family.

The Brent family "started over" with a new therapist with whom Mrs. Brent was now able to develop a bond of trust. She met regularly and involved her other family members. By the time treatment was completed, Mrs. Brent and her other children had learned how to work together to provide clear, consistent limits for Carl, instead of setting up a good mother/bad mother dynamic between Mrs. Brent and Evelyn. All family members were helped to verbalize their fears and anger about the protracted nature of the adoptive process, and Carl was able to talk about how jealous he was of Rashan because Rashan was a "real family member." Once these issues were out in the open they could be addressed, and Mrs. Brent could be helped to take charge of handling them with Carl instead of ignoring them or delegating them to one of her daughters.

The therapist also supported Mrs. Brent in calling regular meetings with the child welfare agency in order to get clarification about the lengthy and complex adoptive process.

Although the complexity of the formal adoptive process gives an added dimension to this case, Mrs. Brent's reactions are not atypical of many poor Black families who feel judged and intruded upon by outside agencies. The therapists and supervisor who worked with this family learned a number of important lessons from the early mistakes. They learned to pay close attention to how families perceive therapists. Particularly in cases where a family is brought in or referred by another agency, it is important for the therapist to create some distance between her- or himself and the outside agency and to clarify the differences in roles. This is a difficult process at times because the therapist does need to have contact and work closely with the agencies involved. As in this case, however, it is important for the therapist to help empower the parental figures to call meetings with agencies when necessary and to voice their own concerns. If this is not done therapists become parental surrogates or create a false dependency on both themselves and the therapeutic process.

In this case the therapists also learned not to minimize or fail to address the very real fear of many poor Black mothers that their children will be removed. Most have either had this experience or know of other families in their communities who have had similar experiences.

CHAPTER 10

Demonstrating the Multisystems Approach: A Case Example

The following case example illustrates a number of different aspects of the multisystems approach with Black families. The Jefferson family presented initially as a large, underorganized single-parent family. They were originally referred by the the local child welfare agency because Kinshasha, aged 12, had made a suicidal gesture (i.e., taking pills after having a miscarriage a year prior to this referral) and had adamantly refused to attend school. She was not sleeping and would often "go out" for long periods at night.

The family consisted of Ms. Delores Jefferson (aged 40), a single parent supported by welfare payments, Kinshasha, Carla (aged 19), Gloria (aged 16), and Terence (aged 13). This family lived in the home of Ms. Jefferson's mother, Cora Jefferson (aged 60) and numerous extended family members who were not identified initially. The grandmother's (Cora Jefferson's) apartment consisted of three bedrooms, which were occupied by thirteen people. Ms. Jefferson and her four children had all shared one bedroom in the grandmother's home for the past 2 years.

INITIAL FAMILY SESSIONS

Kinshasha and Ms. Jefferson were seen initially by a therapist who discussed the current crisis with them. Kinshasha was able to share some of her feelings about the miscarriage with her mother but refused to discuss the identity of the boy who had impregnated her. Ms. Jefferson looked helplessly at the therapist and reported that she in fact felt helpless and unable to understand her daughter. She explained that she felt overwhelmed by problems with all family members. She prioritized her problems in the following way: (1) concerns about

Kinshasha and her current crisis; (2) the unsafe living conditions of the family and the need to find a home; (3) problems with her other children. In the next session, Ms. Jefferson was asked to bring in her family. The family session was attended by Ms. Jefferson, Kinshasha, and her sisters Carla and Gloria. The therapist, having greeted the new family members and engaged them in the treatment process, asked the family members to discuss the problem as they saw it. They began to discuss "Kinshasha's problems" but the discussion quickly moved to the entire family's feelings of helplessness and hopelessness, which they had experienced in living in their grandmother's home for the last 2 years. It became clear that the family related many of their problems to their living situation, including Kinshasha's pregnancy. She had been staying out nights in order to avoid having to live in the tension-filled household, which at any one time might include 10 to 14 extended family members. Both Ms. Jefferson and the children were vague initially and reluctant to identify the other persons who lived with them.

The therapist's initial hypothesis was of an underorganized single-parent family in which the mother was so overwhelmed by many tasks and problems that she became helpless and hopeless. The initial impression in the session discussed above was that of Ms. Jefferson being more of a sibling than a mother to her children. The following diagram illustrates this structure.

$$\frac{\text{Parental or executive system}}{\text{Sibling system}} = \frac{?}{\text{Ms. Jefferson} \quad \text{Carla} \quad \text{Gloria} \quad \text{Kinshasha} \quad \text{Terence}}$$

The therapist's initial treatment goal became to help restructure the family by reinforcing the mother taking charge. This was true in the session and in other aspects of her life. The rest of this and future sessions focused on achieving the following goal:

$$\frac{\text{Parental or executive system}}{\text{Sibling system}} = \frac{\text{Ms. Jefferson}}{\text{Carla, Gloria, Kinshasha, Terence}}$$

This was very difficult for a number of reasons. Whenever the therapist attempted to encourage Ms. Jefferson to speak to one of her children about an issue she would say "I don't know what to say" or "I don't know what to do." He therefore asked her to pick the problem which she felt was most pressing for her family. Meekly, she replied in a small voice, "finding an apartment," and "getting out of my mother's house." He then asked her to go around the room, and discuss this with each of her children and get their input and suggestions. The mother appeared helpless and passive at first but gradually began to respond as her children responded to her. At the end of the session, as a task to reinforce this issue and strengthen the family's ability to problem solve, the mother was asked to call a brief meeting each night in the family's room so that she and her children might discuss these issues.

The therapist in this situation was torn between wanting to help the family with their housing problem and feeling as if doing so would divert the focus from Kinshasha's crisis, which he felt was the more important issue. He also felt overwhelmed by the problems in this family. However, it was clear that this family felt overwhelmed by their home situation and needed to discuss this first. As mentioned in the previous chapter, this type of concrete problem is often initially presented by Black families as pressing. If it is not addressed or is dismissed by the therapist as not relevant to therapy, the family will often leave treatment. The therapist therefore decided to use the discussion of this problem as a way (1) to observe the family interactional patterns; (2) to help the family focus on the problem within a problem-solving framework; and (3) to empower the mother to assume her rightful position as the executive in the family, reinforcing her as being "in charge" of the discussion and thereby helping to restructure family interaction.

In future sessions a number of problems were discussed. The therapist was able to use the structural problem-solving model described in Chapter 7 to help the family focus and to help them set clear goals. This family, like so many underorganized families (Aponte, 1976), felt so overwhelmed by problems that they could never focus long enough to resolve any.

SUBSYSTEMS APPROACHES WITH THE FAMILY

Therapists in the mental health fields often become locked into the perception that they are either "individual" or "family" therapists, viewing the two modalities as mutually exclusive. The same assumption is often made in terms of professional boundaries and roles, with the "therapist" providing therapy and the "social worker" or "case worker" providing "concrete services." These are very unproductive and limiting assumptions when working with Black families, particularly poor multiproblem ones. Accordingly, this section discusses subsystems work and the interface of different modalities and the next session explores intervention in the external agency systems.

There were many levels of problems or issues in the Jefferson family. The therapist learned in the second session that Gloria had also made a suicidal gesture (swallowing pills) the year before and that Kinshasha's gesture had in fact followed hers. Both girls reported feeling very depressed at that time and stated that they had been threatened with removal from their mother because of the family's problems. The therapist was concerned about the following issues: (1) the depression in both girls; (2) the issue of suicide; (3) Kinshasha's "secret pregnancy" and her subsequent miscarriage, and (4) Delores Jefferson's seeming inability to "be there" emotionally for her children.

Therefore, in addition to the ongoing family sessions, Kinshasha and Gloria were both seen individually for a number of sessions by the therapist, and in sessions with their mother, in which they tearfully told her of their anger at her for being ineffectual and unable to provide for them. This issue was later brought into a family session with other siblings present and the family was finally able to discuss how the emotional needs of members were often ignored. The denial expressed by all family members of Kinshasha's pregnancy was explored, with the therapist confronting the family on the fact that she was 7 months pregnant and this had been allowed to remain a "secret" by other family members.

Ms. Jefferson was also seen individually by the therapist at a number of points in the course of the treatment process in order to help her work through her own depression and her feelings of hopelessness and powerlessness.

EMPOWERMENT OF THE FAMILY IN COPING WITH EXTERNAL SYSTEMS

There were a number of systems issues in this case that related to the family's involvement with outside agencies. Chapter 9 describes the use of the multisystems approach in helping families to navigate that system. There were a number of issues that the family members felt were important to address with the child welfare agency: (1) the family was missing appointments because they "did not have the bus fare and lived far away"; (2) the housing situation; and (3) the fact that both Kinshasha and Gloria were not attending school.

In their fifth session, Ms. Jefferson, Gloria, Carla, Kinshasha, and Terence met with the therapist prior to the meeting with their child welfare worker. The therapist encouraged Ms. Jefferson to ask the help of her children in making a list of their concerns.

When the meeting was held with the child welfare worker, Ms. Jefferson, in what was perhaps her strongest show of authority, detailed her family's needs and requested help with resolving the above issues. Once again, Ms. Jefferson's executive role was encouraged and stressed.

The following plans evolved: (1) the child welfare agency offered to transport the family to their sessions; (2) the child welfare worker agreed to meet with Ms. Jefferson and work out a strategy for finding an apartment; and (3) the possibility of both Kinshasha and Gloria entering day treatment programs in which they would receive both their schooling and therapeutic help was discussed.

The potential of getting both girls placed in a structured school environment helped to energize the family and mobilize Ms. Jefferson to begin seeking an apartment. The therapist agreed to explore day treatment programs and facilitate that referral process.

In a future session with Ms. Jefferson and her children, the therapist reported that two day treatment programs had agreed to consider the girls. Ms. Jefferson agreed to take responsibility for arranging the interviews and getting the girls to attend. At the last moment on a scheduled interview day, Kinshasha became scared of the new program and threatened not to go. Ms. Jefferson was able to assert her parental authority and insist that she go. The therapist strongly reinforced Ms. Jefferson's new assertiveness and helped her to remain firm and consistent with her daughters during the period of adjustment to the new programs. She was also able to set limits on Kinshasha's curfew hours.

As this process continued, the therapist received a frantic phone call from Gloria one morning, stating that she had been up all night because gun shots had been fired into their apartment. She expressed urgently her need to move out. The therapist asked for a family meeting to discuss this. In this family session, a major secret was revealed: Ms. Jefferson's brother and other members of the house were involved in drug dealing. The Jefferson family often lived in fear of being caught in the middle of the neighborhood "drug war."

Because of the urgency of this session, a special family session was scheduled in which the family's support systems could be discussed and explored for possible help with a move. Although the family had been resistant to discussing the other members of their household or extended family and had refused to allow contact with anyone therein, this "crisis" had given them a great enough sense of urgency for them to see the importance of opening up to the therapist. They also felt that they no longer needed to protect the "family secret" of the drug dealing from the therapist.

EXPLORATION OF THE EXTENDED FAMILY SYSTEMS: THE GENOGRAM

Throughout this book, the point has been made that Black families often resist revealing their "family business" to strangers until trust has been established. By this point in treatment a number of changes had occurred in this family and their therapist had established credibility and trust with them. Both girls were attending their programs and doing well, and Ms. Jefferson was increasingly more assertive.

The family was therefore ready to look at the ways in which the extended family network contributed to their problems, and to look more carefully at extended family networks for sources of support.

In that session, the family painted the following picture. Ms. Jefferson was the oldest of eight children. She and her brother Willy had been sent to live with an extended family member at an early age. There had been family secrets about this that had never been discussed. She was and always had been the "family scapegoat" who never quite made it on her own. She had moved eight times in the last 3 years, for example. This scapegoat role had been passed on to her nuclear family (her children) as well and they were always "in trouble" with other extended family members. (The genogram illustrated in Figure 5 was constructed with the family's help.)

Next the therapist attempted to clarify who was living in the household. In addition to the grandmother, Mrs. Cora Jefferson, it included Delores Jefferson, her four youngest children, her daughter Vanessa and her child, her mother's brothers Willy, age 39, Clarence, age 33, Robert, age 30, and mother's sister Bernice and her son Tarik on weekends.

The issues of the permeable, very loose boundaries within the extended family household became clear. There was no order or structure. It was "every one for himself," with family members often "staying over" or "dropping off" kids on the weekends. Drug dealers and users were in and out constantly and drug paraphernalia was easily accessible. It was interesting that neither Ms. Jefferson nor any of her children were involved with drug use.

The extended family was also explored for possible sources of support or help, particularly with the issue of helping the family to move. Initially Ms. Jefferson responded that she "had no one she could count on." This is not an uncommon initial response from Black families who are feeling isolated or cut off from positive support in their extended families. Each of the members described in the genogram were reviewed in detail.

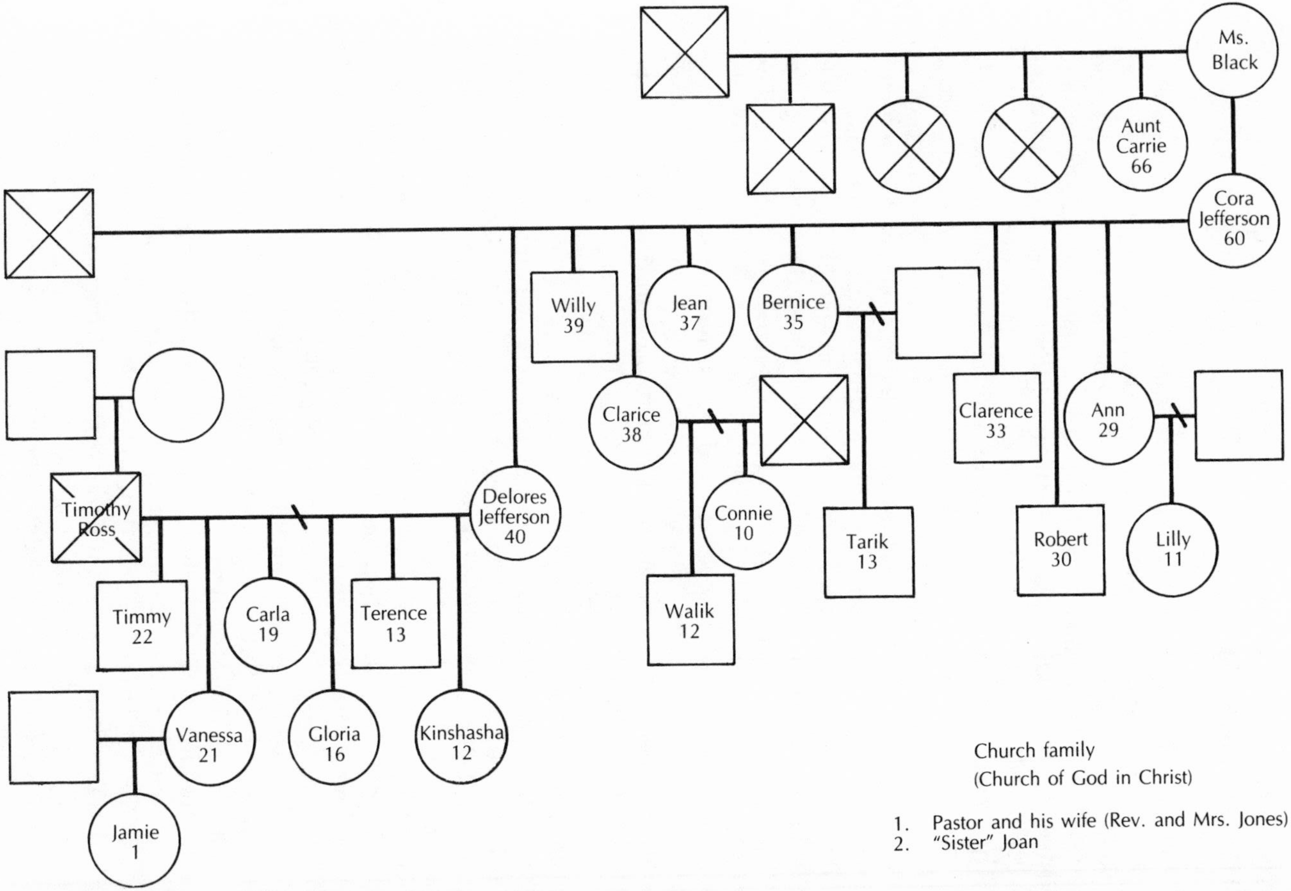

FIGURE 5 Genogram: Jefferson family.

Church family
(Church of God in Christ)

1. Pastor and his wife (Rev. and Mrs. Jones)
2. "Sister" Joan

182

The following possible supports emerged: (1) the mother had a sister, Ann, who lived in a nearby town and who might provide the family with a place where they could "get away" for short periods of time; (2) the mother had two untapped resources in her older children, Timmy (age 22) and Vanessa (age 21), and both she and the children felt that Vanessa might be willing to plan to rent an apartment with them and move into a bigger place together; (3) the family was connected to a church network that had intervened in the past.

Exploring the Church Network

The therapist had been told by the family early in the treatment process that the family's church had helped the mother find a school for Kinshasha some time earlier. However, when earlier on in therapy the therapist had attempted to explore this in more detail, the mother and her children had become resistant and said that they were no longer involved. In the family session, the therapist pursued the ways in which the church family had been a support in the past and the reasons for the cutoff.

The children and their mother reported that up until the previous year, they had been active members of a small storefront Church of God in Christ in which a Reverend Jones was the pastor. He and his wife had "adopted" the family and become very involved in their lives. Another important person in their church family was "Sister Joan," a kind member of the church community who had befriended the family. Reverend and Mrs. Jones had provided the Jeffersons with an extended family and a social service network. The family had had to move a number of times and the minister and members of their church family had helped them find housing. When the therapist inquired as to whether she had asked for their help this time, Ms. Jefferson stated that she was "too embarrassed to bother them again."

Both Kinshasha and Gloria echoed their mother's reluctance in strong terms although for different reasons. The girls reported that the church community had been very important to them also, with Mrs. Jones and Sister Joan serving as mother surrogates. They reported that the members of their church family had been very concerned about the drugs and general chaos in their home and had helped Ms. Jefferson find a residential Christian school for Kinshasha. When Kinshasha became homesick and ran away from the school, it was a great embarrassment to their pastor.

Gloria also reported that she felt embarrassed to go back because Reverend Jones had "shamed" her before the entire Church community. When she had made her suicidal gesture the year before, all of their church family had been very upset and the Rev. Jones had made her stand up and asked everyone to pray for her. Gloria was very ashamed and afraid that they all thought she was "crazy." Kinshasha expressed similar fears.

As the session proceeded, it became clear that all of the family members greatly missed their church family. They were really very isolated and the church had provided them all with a social as well as a spiritual outlet. The therapist asked Ms. Jefferson if she had ever thought about returning. She replied "every day." The therapist asked her if she could go talk with the minister, his wife, or Sister Joan and ask for their help. He asked if there was someone who could go with her. Surprisingly, she stated that her mother Cora would probably accompany her. With the therapist's urging, she went the following week and appeared for her next session looking greatly relieved. Her personal care and grooming were far better and she had begun to pay some attention to her appearance. She also reported that she had convinced her children to go with her the next Sunday.

There was a marked improvement in all family members after this point. Both girls continued to do well in their programs.

FAMILY CRISES

Because the girls were no longer home during the day, Ms. Jefferson was home alone for longer hours. She voiced interest in moving and did go out with the child welfare worker to look at some apartments but was discouraged by the results. She stated that she wanted to find a job but had been disappointed in these efforts. She reported feeling "depressed," sleeping all day, overeating, and so on. The therapist had a number of individual sessions with her in order to help her explore these issues.

Within a week, the therapist received two phone calls from the mother. One stated that Carla, aged 19, was pregnant. The second stated that Terence was now truant from school and staying home.

The therapist asked all the family members to attend a family session. In it, he observed two "strange phenomena" in their family. First, they appeared to have a rule that someone must be at home to protect and take care of Mom. First Kinshasha and Gloria had sacrificed themselves, and now Carla and Terence were sacrificing themselves. The second rule seemed to be that everyone in the family could not be functioning well at the same time. Someone had to carry on their tradition as the scapegoat of the family. The therapist, using a paradoxical approach, stated that the family was changing too fast and suggested that they might all have to sacrifice themselves and fail school in order to keep their reputation as the family scapegoats and stay home and protect their mother. He prescribed the symptoms and suggested that they keep doing this, as the family was not ready to change so quickly.

Within the week, Terence was back in school. Carla had gone to see their minister's wife and decided to keep her baby. Ms. Jefferson had gone to her daughter, Vanessa, and made a clear plan for their move with a list of things that they needed to do. One of the most important tasks was that of Ms. Jefferson finding a job for herself. Her job hunting took 3 weeks and then she proudly reported that she had found a job caring for an elderly woman.

The "protective," "sacrificial," and "scapegoat" themes were repeated a number of times in the next two family sessions. First, the family discussed the ways in which Ms. Jefferson had been seen as "weak" by her family of origin and how her children had begun protecting her. She was able, with the therapist's help, to let them know that she wanted this to change.

Second, Ms. Jefferson reported to her children that she had talked to her brother at some length about their having been sent out to live with another family as young children. He reported that he had tried to speak to their mother about it but she had "burst into tears" and he had stopped. Ms. Jefferson told her children that she needed to talk with her mother about this but wanted the therapist's help. The therapist was amazed at her assertiveness and clarity. They agreed that both Ms. Jefferson and the therapist would speak to Cora Jefferson and invite her to come in for a session.

The therapist then worked with Ms. Jefferson in front of her children, coaching her on her interactions with her mother. Her children were able to support her willingness to speak to her mother and begin her differentiation.

DISCUSSION

There has been a tendency in many disciplines within the mental health field to present primarily the cases that represent the "ideal" or the "success" scenario, a tendency also true of much of the family therapy literature. Therapists, particularly those who are new to clinical work, thus frequently miss a prime opportunity to learn from their mistakes and to utilize clinical crises as opportunities for growth and change.

In this case example there were a number of critical periods in which serious errors were made by the therapist and/or the supervisor. These were utilized and provided important opportunities for therapeutic movement.

One particularly serious mistake occurred at the point at which the family was ready to explore their support system with the therapist and to do their genogram. As stated above, the therapist in this case was a psychology intern, who was a part of a family therapy training program. As a part of the program, supervisors regularly do live consultation interviews for trainees and demonstration interviews, which are done before a one-way mirror with a full group (10–20 of staff and trainees) observing behind the mirror.

In accordance with this practice, the therapist and supervisor asked this family's permission for the observation, obtained a signed release, and showed them the empty one-way mirror room prior to the session. The entire family agreed to have their interview in that room. During the session, however, Gloria became increasingly uncomfortable as she began revealing sensitive areas in her family and her feeling that her family network and later her church network had viewed her as "crazy" because of her suicidal gesture. She began to voice her discomfort with being observed and her fear that people would judge her. She also discussed her fears about confidentiality. She demanded to see the observers behind the mirror. The supervisor and the therapist felt caught, fearful that allowing her to meet the observers would upset her further.

At the end of the session, the therapist and the supervisor made a decision to allow the family to meet the observers. When Gloria saw the number of observers and the fact that many were white, she reacted, became angry, and left the session.

This was a very critical period for the therapist and the family and for the supervisor as well. The therapist pursued the family member and met with her alone and discussed her concerns. He also explored the feelings of other family members. Gloria had in fact been the spokesperson for the entire group. The therapist was able to stay with the process and allow Gloria and the Jefferson family a cooling-off period, and was eventually able to re-engage them in the treatment process.

Black families for a variety of reasons are often extremely sensitive about the use of one-way mirrors, video tapes, and audiotape recorders. They are concerned about rooms in which microphones are strategically placed in the ceiling. (See Chapter 1 for a more complete discussion of these issues.) Any personal resistance, hypersensitivity, fear of judgment, or paranoia is intensified by a generalized cultural paranoia that many Black families bring to this process.

In retrospect one could argue that in this case it was a mistake on the part of the therapist and the supervisor to choose this particular family for a teaching demonstration interview. Often our teaching and training needs must be weighed against the needs of the family, with the understanding that the needs of the family should have priority. On the other hand, this mistake, like so many clinical "errors," creates a crisis in the therapeutic relationship between the clinician and the family that brings the trust–mistrust issue into the session in a very real, vivid, and concrete way. The therapist in this case had a history of trust with this family and an established sincerity that allowed him to acknowledge the mistake and to renegotiate his relationship with the family.

III

DIVERSITY OF FAMILIAL STRUCTURES AND INTERVENTIONS

CHAPTER 11

Single-Parent Black Families

The startling increase in Black female-headed families within the last decade parallels a similar trend in all American families. Since 1970, the number of single-parent households in the United States has more than doubled. These single-parent households include a diversity of family structures (e.g., single never-married, single divorced or separated, and single widowed).

FUNCTIONAL SINGLE-PARENT FAMILIES

The experiences of clinicians often focuses on families who are in trouble or in crisis. It is important therefore to keep a clear perspective on what constitutes a "well-functioning" family. This is particularly important when one is dealing with Black single-parent families because so much of the literature has been derogatory (e.g., Moynihan, 1965). One must be very cautious about the tendency to see families whose structure may be very different from that of the clinician as "deviant." With this in mind, it would be helpful to begin our discussion of treatment with a view toward what might constitute a well-functioning Black single-parent family.

Single parenthood does *not* necessarily make a family dysfunctional. Many Black single parents who have never been married function well as parents and their children grow up to be capable adults. Many divorced or separated Black single parents—a population that is increasing in numbers similar to the White population—are functional as well.

The first characteristic of functional Black single-parent families is a clear understanding of who is in charge of the family. As Minuchin (1974) has illustrated, all family members know precisely their roles and responsibilities in the family. It is a family that has well-delineated, flexible boundaries and in which all of the children have easy access to the parent. The parent may be working or on public assistance; the children are well cared for and their basic needs are met. Emotionally, both parent and children feel free to give and receive nurturance and communicate their own needs.

In some functional single-parent families, there may be a parental child who helps the mother care for younger children. This may be an economic necessity: An older child may care for his or her siblings when a parent works to support the family. Once again, it is not the presence of this structure that is dysfunctional in itself. A single-parent family with a parental child can function quite well as long as the parent does not abdicate parental responsibilities or overburden this child in an inappropriate way. A parent who delegates certain responsibilities to her oldest son or daughter while she is at work but who assumes leadership when she is at home can often support the development of a sense of responsibility in her child. The child must also have access to other age-appropriate peer activities and not feel that the total responsibility for the care of the family is on his or her shoulders. In these functional Black families, single parents keep an open dialogue with each of their children and are sensitive to issues such as the ones described here. Parental children in these situations receive praise and nurturance along with responsibility.

Another feature of well-functioning Black single-parent families is the fact that they have and utilize a support system. This might include blood and nonblood extended family, church members, friends, and community supports. They are not cut off and they are not afraid to ask for help when it is needed. If a father (or fathers) is not involved, other men in the extended family or the broader network are utilized as male role models. Children have a sense of "belonging" to a family. The other extended family members are involved with the children in a constructive way and do not undermine the mother's role or authority with them.

The final aspect of these well-functioning families is that the parents (usually mothers) have a life of their own apart from their children. Among Black single-parent mothers, this can take many different forms. It might involve having a job or a career or having a boyfriend. For many Black women, the church serves a very important social function and often constitutes their only time for themselves apart from their children.

TYPES OF DYSFUNCTIONAL SINGLE-PARENT FAMILIES

Because of the significant numbers of single-parent families mentioned above, it is very important for family therapists who are working with single-parent Black families to be aware of the common issues in these families and the different ways in which they may be present. The following section discusses the clinical implications of a number of different presentations of single parent families: (1) the underorganized family; (2) the overcentralized, overwhelmed mother; (3) the dysfunctional parent; (4) the boyfriend, the hidden member; and (5) the three-generational single-parent family.

The Underorganized Family

One clinical presentation of Black single-parent families is that of the underorganized family in which children seem out of control and mother appears totally overwhelmed. Aponte (1976b) describes this type of family as one in which

> power is loosely distributed . . . the power of any one individual is not effectively woven through the various operations in which he or she is involved, nor is it balanced flexibly. . . . In the underorganized family, a parent may not be able to take for granted his/her power and may be able to exercise it only when he/she asserts it with exceptional force. In such a household, one is likely to see a mother repeatedly yelling or striking her children to obtain some order. (p. 438)

Boundaries in this type of family are usually very vague. There is no clarity as to the rules and responsibilities of the members. Alignment patterns in this type of family tend to be extremely inconsistent and chaotic, with different family members siding with each other randomly and inconsistently. Power is weak and force is inconsistent—excessive at times and nonexistent at others. If one visits the home of such a family, one is met with a sense of underorganization at the front door. Family members often function in a manner reminiscent of "bumper cars," colliding with one another and interacting briefly but never really relating. Mothers in these families tend to be totally overwhelmed, often having "stairstep" children very close in age and being unable to manage the pressures and burdens.

In some underorganized Black families, there is inconsistent extended family involvement; when it occurs, it is usually erratic, unpredictable, and destabilizing rather than supportive. In other families of this type the family is very emotionally cut off (Bowen, 1976) from extended family supports and there is no one to support the parent in assuming executive parental responsibilities. The degree of dysfunction in these families is often directly related to their degree of isolation or lack of utilization of their supports.

On the continuum of family involvement described by Minuchin (1974), these families are often characterized as "disengaged." The feelings of being overwhelmed cause underorganized families to be "in crisis" often and to present with one or more children in serious trouble at home, in school, and/or in the community.

Overcentralized Mothers

The second type of a single-parent Black family that often presents at clinics is characterized by Aponte (1976b) as "overcentralized" or having power overconcentrated in one person, usually a very overwhelmed and overburdened mother. She is in fact the "switchboard" for family communication. He states that

> a single or a few family members may possess an inordinate amount of control over all operations, regardless of function. Since any single person, or even an exclusive few can never, by the force of their talents, make every family undertaking work, this kind of overconcentrated power is inefficient. If a mother holds on to all the family controls, her young children may be very well-behaved in her presence, but very disorderly and negligent about carrying out household duties whenever she is out of the home. (p. 437)

On the structural axis of family boundaries, these families are often closer to the "enmeshed" end of the scale (Minuchin, 1974). While this structure may function adequately with young children, it is one that often leads to difficulty in adolescence, when this rigid, mother-dominated structure is challenged. Behavior problems in adolescent children usually present at this time, including stealing, lying, running away, and oppositional behavior at home and in school. Often other children or family members collude to undermine the power of the overly central mother. Aponte (1980) in a masterful videotape illustrates the strategy of working with such a family:

The R. family was a Black family composed of a mother, aged 38, and four children, teenage girls aged 17, 16, and 12½ and a son, aged 18. The mother and the three daughters attended the session. Mother began by characterizing herself as "overprotective" of all of her children. She was the central force at home and usually "preached to" her kids rather than talked with them. She expressed particular concerns about the lying and behavior problems of her 12½-year-old daughter and the school problems of her 16-year-old. With careful questioning, the therapist learned that the mother had kept a very high degree of control over her children when they were young but as they reached adolescence, each became more oppositional in school and at home. In focusing on the acting out and the lying of the youngest child, he learned that the two older girls often protected their younger sister from their mother's censure and "took her off punishment." The therapist relabeled the entire family's involvement as "loving her too much" and helped the mother to ask for the help of her older children in working together to provide limits for her younger child. He helped her to learn how to delegate responsibility when she was at work and to involve her adolescents appropriately in the decision-making process.

The therapist then encouraged the mother to talk about the reasons for her "overprotectiveness" and her own experiences of growing up. He helped her to see that a part of what she must teach her children is how to be strong and stand on their own two feet as she does. By helping her to involve the older children in this process, he facilitated her move to decentralize herself and delegate responsibility appropriately.

The Dysfunctional Parent

Another type of presentation in single-parent Black families is that of an obviously dysfunctional parent whose children are actually "running the family." Often this is characterized by an overburdened parental child. This can occur for a number of reasons. The mother may have (1) a medical illness, (2) an emotional or psychiatric disorder, (3) a drug or alcohol addiction, or (4) a low intellectual level or mental retardation. In some of these families, a highly functional parental child essentially runs the household and the family often does not present until this role conflicts with the developmental thrust toward age-appropriate independence in the adolescent.

Frequently, however, these families resemble the first category of underorganized families, in which the mother presents as a member of the sibling group rather than as the head of the family. The strategy outlined in the first example applies here also. The therapist's task is to help build a family structure that can function predictably and help meet the needs of all members. In this case, however, the family therapist is faced with the dilemma that the executive member may in fact be dysfunctional and unable to assume those responsibilities. The therapist must first assess the mother's capabilities and support her in exercising what power she has. In some cases the therapist's task will be to seek support for her outside of the family in order to help her function in her role and relieve the burden on her children.

A more extreme example of this type of parental-child-controlled/ dysfunctional parent system is that of the alcoholic single-parent family. Often as the mother becomes increasingly incapacitated by the alcoholism, an older child will assume the parental child role for the mother as well as for the other children. In Black alcoholic families this child is often female and becomes what Brisbane and Womble (1985) call the "Black female family hero." These "family heroes" assume total responsibility but receive little or no nurturance. Brisbane and Womble state that in alcoholic families there is "a greater possibility that [the family hero] will not receive nurturing which is necessary if she is to pass through the various stages of her own development with a sense of fulfillment and mastery" (p. 254).

Because of her central role, the involvement of this "family hero" is crucial in the treatment of such families. It is also important to note that these families come to our attention via two main routes: (1) by extreme acting out in the younger children and/or (2) a threat by an outside child welfare agency to remove the children. Often the latter is necessary to produce a sufficient crisis for the family to mobilize and for the alcoholic member to even consider a treatment program. The following case example illustrates this process:

The Glenn family was a Black family referred for treatment after Ms. Glenn, the mother, was reported to the local child welfare agency by neighbors for neglecting her children. The family consisted of Mary (aged 15), the "family hero" who cared for the younger children, Brian (aged 6), Nikki (aged 4), and Kenya (aged 2). As her mother's alcoholism worsened, Mary took on more and more family responsibilities and ultimately became frustrated and unable to cope. She gave up and began neglecting the younger children. The child welfare agency removed the three younger children and placed them in separate foster homes pending an investigation. Mary was sent to a group home for adolescents. As often occurs in these cases, the referral to our clinic was made for Brian, the 6-year-old, who became aggressive in the foster home and at school. When he was first seen, he was extremely angry and frightened at being separated from his family. The family therapist mobilized the child welfare agency to transport all family members including the mother to a session at the clinic. The mother had been given an ultimatum by the agency to enter an alcoholism treatment program or her children would not be returned. She was very frightened of losing them and expressed that fear in the session. Mary, true to her role, quickly moved in to comfort her mother.

The therapist emphasized the love and caring in this family and the desire of the mother to be with her children. The mother discussed her fears about the alcoholism treatment program. With the support of her children and that of the therapist, she agreed to enter an inpatient alcoholism treatment program at an affiliated hospital. The therapist was able to arrange for her to participate in family sessions during this time. In the initial detoxification period, Ms. Glenn was extremely irritable and "snappish" with her children. Mary again tuned in to her mother's distress and tried to quiet the other children. The therapist talked with Mary and her mother about this impossible job that she had taken on of trying to be "super mom." This theme was stressed for a number of sessions. As Ms. Glenn became more functional, the therapist encouraged her to take more responsibility for talking directly to the children and planning for their return. As she soothed and talked with the children, Brian's aggressive behavior decreased in the foster home and at school. Mary was initially blocked from intervening by the therapist. The mother was helped to talk openly with her daughter about the burden that had been placed upon her. In these discussions in subsequent sessions, the mother was surprised to learn how serious Mary's neglect of her own needs had been. She had been truant half of the school days in the last year. Because of her alcoholic haze, the mother had been oblivious to her daughter's distress. In one very tearful session, she expressed her sadness and sorrow about this to her daughter.

After discharge, the alcoholism treatment program required a long-term follow up and intensive outpatient and AA (Alcoholics Anonymous) involvement. During that time, the therapist worked with Ms. Glenn and her children to discuss carefully how things would be different when the children returned home. Although Mary and the other children were still in foster homes, Ms. Glenn (at the therapist's urging) arranged to go with Mary to school and to discuss her needs. At the mother's request, the therapist accompanied her on this first visit. The mother also made a visit to Brian's school and was pleased to learn that his aggressive behavior had decreased. For the first time in many years, she was assuming appropriate parental responsibilities.

As the time for the children's return home approached, the therapist helped to arrange for a homemaker from a social service agency to care for the younger children and help with some household chores while Ms. Glenn attended her AA meetings and treatment sessions. Family therapy continued throughout the first year of the return home. The focus was on emphasizing and reinforcing mother's competence and helping Mary to give up the "family hero" role and become involved with her school and her peers. Ms. Glenn became directly responsible for the care of Brian and the two younger children and Brian's aggressive acting out stopped completely within the first month of his return home. At the time of completion of treatment, Ms. Glenn had been abstinent from alcohol for over a year and was an active member of AA.

The Boyfriend: The Hidden Family Member

In many Black single-parent families there is often a "hidden" family member: the mother's boyfriend. The mental health field has been in a dilemma as to how to label this role in Black families. He has been referred to as the "paramour," in more long-term unions as the "common law husband," or in other cases where a marriage eventually occurs and he has been absorbed into the children's lives as the "stepfather." The role of the boyfriend is a complex one in Black single-parent families, because it is often "hidden" initially when the family presents for treatment for a number of reasons discussed in previous chapters.

This section focuses on the three major ways in which the boyfriend can become an important focus in family therapy: (1) the secrecy about his presence; (2) the issue of his involvement in the treatment process; and (3) the definition of his role in the family.

The issue of the secrecy about the presence of a boyfriend is an issue that many family therapists must address in the treatment of these families. Often, the mother presents initially with her children as a family unit and no mention is made of the boyfriend, or his presence is so minimized and denied that his involvement is at first very unclear. Because Black families often do not trust clinics and therapists initially and are dubious about confidentiality, the issue of the boyfriend is usually not available for discussion until trust is developed. Once the family, particularly the mother, trusts the therapist, the boyfriend will often be mentioned much more openly. Sometimes the children in the family will begin discussing this person. Many Black mothers initially deny the relationship even to their children and these boyfriends might be called "uncles" by the children. The entire family often colludes to deny the true relationship. Once a family raises the issue of the boyfriend, the therapist should definitely pursue discussions of his role and function in the family and consider including him in a session.

One of the most helpful ways in which to raise the issue of the boyfriend with a single-parent mother is to ask her frankly, "Who helps you out?" This can be pursued by a question such as "With all of these responsibilities for taking care of everyone else, who takes care of you?" Asking a mother if she dates or goes out herself can help focus attention on her role as a woman apart from her role as a mother. This is a very important intervention with Black single-parent mothers. If the therapist has communicated support and not censure, these issues can then be discussed more openly.

Once the boyfriend's presence can be discussed, the family therapist can begin to explore his role and the amount of time that he has been involved with the mother and with her children. The answers to both of these questions tend to vary because many Black women choose not to involve their boyfriends in their children's lives unless a clear commitment has evolved between the partners.

At this point, it is often helpful to include the boyfriend in the treatment process. The first task is the issue of engagement. It is often helpful for the therapist to contact the man directly by phone or letter and to try to talk or meet with him alone before bringing him into the family sessions. If a man is living as part of a household or even "visiting" or "staying over" on a regular basis, he has an impact on the family alignments, boundaries, and roles within the home. It is often necessary to state how important he is to the family and to let him know that his input will be valued and respected.

The role relationships that boyfriends develop within such situations vary considerably. Some are essentially peripheral to the running of the household and the care of the children, visiting primarily for sexual encounters with mother. Still others may "stay over" regularly, eating meals at the home and keeping clothes there. In other cases, there is a long-term "live-in" relationship from which there may be children. In many states, if this persists for 7 years or more, it is considered a "common-law marriage." There are also situations that begin as one of the above and eventually evolve into a marriage. Although this situation would officially qualify as a "stepfather" relationship, some of the issues are similar to those discussed above. Despite the label or the surface description of the relationship or the period of time involved, one must carefully clarify the degree of involvement that the man has with the children and the amount of his responsibility for parenting, child care, and discipline.

One of the most common issues in the involvement of boyfriends in Black single-parent families is the protectiveness that many Black mothers exercise in the involvement of their men with their children. Often, even if a man has been living in a home for many years and expresses a desire to be involved in parenting, the mother in this situation will create a "buffer" between her children and the man. This may continue to be true even after the relationship evolves into marriage. The Jacobs family illustrates this point:

Ms. Jacobs, a Black woman in her 30s, initially presented at the clinic with her three children, aged 16, 15, and 2. She was very careful to avoid mention of her boyfriend of 6 years. The identified patient was her son Anthony, age 16, who was having academic difficulties in school and who would often have loud arguments with his mother. He refused to follow her rules and often came in beyond his curfew in the evening. He had been suspended from school after having been picked up by a truant officer outside of school during class hours. The therapist worked initially to help the mother to set clear limits for her son and to be consistent in her discipline with all of the children. She had great difficulty in doing this, and eventually shared with the therapist that John, her live-in boyfriend, was always "after her" to discipline Anthony. She stated that her boyfriend felt she was "too soft on the boy." They often got into arguments in which the mother would tell her son to do one thing and her boyfriend would criticize her openly in front of the boy. The therapist, recognizing the triangulation that was occurring in this process, called the boyfriend and asked him to join a family session.

In the session, it was clear that the boyfriend sat on the periphery of the family. Ironically, the family member seated closest to him was Anthony. During the course of the session, it became clear that Anthony had had a rather good relationship with his mother's boyfriend until 2 years ago when his little sister had been born. At that point, the boyfriend had begun to live with the family. He had attempted to take over some of the disciplinary responsibility but was always blocked by the mother, who would yell, "Don't you touch my son!"

The therapist asked the mother and her boyfriend to sit together and asked them to discuss the question of the parenting of Anthony and who should do it. The mother stated that she didn't feel her boyfriend should take over and was very fearful of this. Her boyfriend stated that he just wanted to help and became angry when she allowed her son to "talk back" to her. The therapist helped these two individuals to discuss a consistent policy for handling Anthony, including the establishment of clear rules and consequences. They agreed that Ms. Jacobs would present these to Anthony with her boyfriend there to support her statements. They agreed, for example, that if Anthony was truant from school or was late coming in in the evening, he would not be allowed out with his friends for a week. They were able to reinforce it together.

The therapist also helped Ms. Jacobs to create a regular time when she could talk with her son alone about his needs, and she was able to encourage him to spend some "man time" working on the car with her boyfriend.

Often the therapist's role is one of helping a family in transition to negotiate the inclusion of a new member. This transition is often made more difficult by the mother's own ambivalence and possibly by her earlier experiences with men. For example, a woman who has had a number of painful relationships may find it very difficult to trust a new man and allow him to become involved with her children.

In other situations, the family therapist's task is to help a young single mother to place a protective boundary around her children and separate them from her transient relationships with men. Laura Tate and her children illustrate this situation:

Laura Tate was a 25-year-old Black single parent who came into treatment after a referral by a sexual abuse unit at a local hospital. Her 5-year-old daughter, Imani, had been raped by the mother's boyfriend. This boyfriend, although he did not live in the home, had entered frequently. The therapist learned that the mother had in fact been raped as a young child by her "uncle," but had never discussed the experience with anyone. Imani was having night terrors since the experience and would frequently have angry outbursts at her mother. She had also been involved in some sexual play at school.

A strategic "pretend" strategy (Madanes, 1981) was utilized in which Imani was asked to pretend to be frightened of an assailant and her mother would pretend to protect her. The mother would then pretend to be frightened of an assailant and Imani would pretend to protect her. This scenario was prescribed every night before bedtime. Imani's symptoms disappeared within a few weeks. Her mother was able to talk about her own unresolved experience of sexual assault as a child and to discuss ways in which she would protect her daughter in the future. Ms. Tate was able to create a protective boundary around her child and to discuss openly the need to be careful about exposing her daughter to her male relationships. Most importantly, however, she began to establish a relationship with her daughter such that the daughter could feel safe in speaking to her mother. A channel of communication that had been closed was opened between them. This was the beginning of trust.

Lindblad-Goldberg and Dukes (1985) have compared "functional vs. dysfunctional Black single-parent families" and have made the following observation regarding boyfriends:

Mothers of less adaptive families more frequently relied on boyfriends to help with their family's functioning. These network males may be a less stable type of support for the single-parent mother in that their role definitions and functions within the family might not have been clearly defined.

This observation is certainly a challenging one. It is particularly relevant in families in which the mother continually changes boyfriends or has very short-term relationships and has either very negative interactions with her extended family or is cut off from them. In these situations, she and her children may rely too heavily on her current boyfriend for emotional and financial support, which may result in his overload or a burnout of that relationship because of the premature burden of caring for a family. In these circumstances, it may be the task of the therapist to help the mother resolve her issues with her own extended family and/or to create other supports for her family that are not dependent on the survival of her relationship with a current boyfriend.

EXTENDED FAMILY AND NETWORK INVOLVEMENT FOR BLACK SINGLE-PARENT FAMILIES: POSITIVE AND NEGATIVE CONSEQUENCES

In Chapter 3, the importance of the extended family as a strength for Black families has been clearly documented. However, many Black single-parent families that present at clinics may have experienced a breakdown in the support function of the extended family. In some cases, the presentation of a child as the identified patient may in fact be a symptom of a dysfunctional structure or pattern of relationships within the extended family. This is a complicated issue for many clinicians and family therapists. As therapists, we have often been trained to take the "single-parent family" at face value when they appear at our clinics. Too often, however, this is a serious error because the family that presents may well be a subsystem of a much more complex extended family. The presenting problem brought by a member of a Black single-parent family may well be a symptom of a dysfunctional pattern in the extended family.

Lindblad-Goldberg and Dukes (1985) make the following observation in their study of functional and dysfunctional Black single-parent families:

One primary implication to be drawn for ecostructural therapy with low income female-headed families is not to assume that an extended kinship network necessarily operates as a support system. In working with these families it is important to assess how the presenting problem relates not merely to dysfunctional structure within the nuclear family but rather to the dysfunctional structure(s) in the extended kinship system of both blood and non-related persons. Thus, the definition of the "family" becomes the definition of the extended kinship system.

Findings such as those of Lindblad-Goldberg and Dukes are very relevant to our clinical assessment of these families. The primary concern of these researchers was "to discover if there were differences in the social networks of functional and dysfunctional Black low-income female-headed families." In looking at a clinic and a nonclinic population of Black single-parent families in Philadelphia, they found the following results: (1) there were no significant differences in the numbers of family members involved; (2) more female than male network members were reported for both groups; (3) the importance of support categories were reported in the following order: "family," "friends," and "relatives." The three categories were described to the interviewers as: (1) family—mother's children, mother's siblings, mother's parent(s); (2) friends, both female and male; and (3) relatives—grandparents, aunts, uncles, cousins (female and male), nieces, nephews, and inlaws (p. 9).

Lindblad-Goldberg and Dukes (1985) and Lindblad-Goldberg et al. (1988) identified other variables including those described by Pattison (1977) in the "neurotic type" of network. "Less adaptive" mothers more frequently listed people who were deceased as important to them. They also tended to list more people who were important because they were disliked or because they caused these mothers difficulty. This type of network can be impoverished and isolating (Pattison, 1977). The unresolved mourning and subsequent longing for a lost object may prevent these mothers from interacting meaningfully with those available to her. In addition, real life interaction may be limited by avoidance of contact, especially when there are negative emotional influences in some of these relationships.

This distinction is important because sometimes these families present with severe problems, especially after the loss of a very significant family member such as the mother's mother or grandmother who may have "held the family together" or been "Big Mama" to everyone. This often leaves a very real emotional and executive vacuum in the family, which the single-parent mother who has suffered such a loss may feel that she is unable to fill. The Wilson family illustrates the emotional impasses that can arise in such a situation:

The Wilson family entered treatment when Vernette, aged 12, began fighting with her peers and acting out in school. The teacher reported that when she was not fighting she appeared isolated from other children and somewhat withdrawn. The teacher encouraged Vernette's mother, Ms. Wilson, to take her to the community mental health center for treatment. The Wilson family consisted of Ms. Wilson, aged 26, Vernette, 12, Willy, 9, and Paula, 7. When asked by the therapist when Vernette's problems had begun, all of the family members became very quiet. Finally Ms. Wilson stated that they had started a year earlier. When the therapist explored what had been happening in the family at that time, at first all of the family members looked puzzled. The therapist then asked if there had been any changes in the family at that time, whether anyone had died, left, and/or entered the family. Ms. Wilson then reported in a very tearful voice that her mother had died about a year ago. Vernette had been very close to her grandmother and took her death "hard." All of the family members looked very sad and found it difficult to talk about her death. The therapist very gently helped them to talk about that period. She learned that the grandmother had been the real "mother" in this family. She had been the family switchboard and most of the family's communications had passed through her. She had "held the family together." When she died suddenly of a heart attack, Ms. Wilson found herself alone raising her children, and she felt completely overwhelmed. At the time of her mother's death, Ms. Wilson's sister Martha and her two children, who had also been living in the grandmother's apartment, moved in with Martha's boyfriend. Ms. Wilson felt betrayed and abandoned and had not spoken to her sister since then. Ms. Wilson had become more depressed in the last year and had withdrawn from her children. She had begun to stay in her bed, frequently for much of the day, leaving the care of the younger children to Vernette. No one in the family had mourned the grandmother's death, and both Vernette and her mother were feeling sad, overwhelmed, and abandoned.

The therapist's first task was to help this family mourn. In a number of very emotional sessions, Ms. Wilson talked with her children about their sadness. Vernette and Ms. Wilson were able to talk about their feelings of being alone and having to take on all the family responsibilities. The therapist had a number of sessions with Ms. Wilson during this period and placed her on antidepressant medication. As Ms. Wilson felt given to or "fed" by the therapist, she was able to give to her daughter.

It became clear that Ms. Wilson's mother had held all of the decision-making power in the family and that Ms. Wilson needed help to evolve into her role as "mother." A number of sessions were held with Ms. Wilson and her children in which the therapist supported her in assuming a parental role with her children. This included concrete issues such as (1) a planned visit to Vernette's school, (2) homework, and (3) discipline at home.

As the family's depression began to lift, the degree of isolation in which they functioned became increasingly clear. A number of sessions were spent in helping the family construct its genogram and look at its former support systems. The emotional cutoff of Ms. Wilson from her sister was very loaded for her because they had been very close. The children were very close to her also. In an atmosphere of increasing trust, the therapist was able to challenge Ms. Wilson's assumption that her sister had left because she "didn't want to live with her anymore." In the discussion of her possible reasons for leaving, Ms. Wilson was able to acknowledge the possibility that her sister may have felt freer to live with her boyfriend after their mother's death and that her move had not been related to her sister at all. The therapist, with the children's support, encouraged Ms. Wilson to go talk to her sister about this. After many weeks of discussion and coaching (following Bowen, 1978), she was able to call her sister. Their reconciliation was a major step in reconnecting with the rest of the extended family.

Both Vernette and Ms. Wilson were not depressed at the completion of treatment and Vernette had shown significant improvement in school.

There were a number of other areas of difference between functional and dysfunctional single-parent families that Lindblad-Goldberg and Dukes (1985) have identified in their study. One key area was an imbalance of reciprocity in the extended families:

> Being able to count on someone for concrete assistance such as helping with domestic tasks, finances, child care, is a critical factor for all low-income families. A significant difference found between these successful and non-successful families was that perceived help from family network members was less for families in trouble than for those doing well. The groups did not differ in the amount of help they felt they gave to network persons.

This is an important piece of information for the family therapist who is working with such families. An imbalance in the reciprocity loop or "kin insurance" (McAdoo, 1981) can give rise to a situation in which the usual, culturally prescribed patterns are not occurring in a particular family. The task of the therapist with a broader systems perspective is to help the family or the individual single-parent mother find a way to balance the scales. This might involve renegotiating relationships in her extended family and/or helping her to find other sources of support. In some families this support may exist, but the single mother and her children may not be benefiting because of an emotional cutoff that has occurred. In other situations the single mother may have become over-central and overburdend, but because she has been playing that role for so long she has never learned how to scream for help or how to accept it when it is given.

CHAPTER 12

Black Middle-Class Families
in Therapy

The majority of the literature on Black families has focused primarily on low-income families. In recent years, however, a number of researchers have begun to explore patterns of upward mobility and middle-class status among Black families (Billingsley, 1968; McQueen, 1971; Stack, 1974; Bagarozzi, 1980; McAdoo, 1981). McAdoo (1978) discusses two different views of the role that the extended family or the kin network may play in the upward mobility of Black families. The first view describes a positive impact of the Black extended family on upward mobility and states that Blacks have moved up the economic scale because of the help of their kin network (Billingsley, 1968; Hill, 1971). The second viewpoint, represented by McQueen (1971) and Stack (1974), states that although Black families have developed patterns of mutual help and kin support that help in the struggle to cope with poverty, the extended family becomes a liability once a Black individual or family become middle class (McQueen, 1971). McAdoo (1978) summarized this viewpoint as follows:

> McQueen and Stack seem to indicate that only by cutting him/herself off from the family can the black of poorer circumstances move up to a more stable level of living. This isolation does not exclude casual visiting and joint holiday and ritual celebrations. It also does not exclude support of aging parents or occasional help. It does mean that to some degree, upwardly mobile blacks separate themselves from the draining process of dealing with the everyday needs of their families of orientation. (p. 764)

In contrast, McAdoo's (1978) results indicate that Black families in the middle-income group in general maintained their close ties to their extended families and did not have to avoid these ties in order to become upwardly mobile. The data from such findings challenge the notion that economic well-being removes the need for bonds of culture, race, and family.

DIFFERENT TYPES OF BLACK MIDDLE-CLASS FAMILIES

McAdoo (1981) has identified four different mobility patterns in Black middle-class families.

1. In the first group are individuals who were born working class and are newly mobile. Generally, they became "middle class" by acquiring professional degrees and moving into higher status jobs.
2. The second group is composed of those who have been upwardly mobile over three generations from lower class, to working class, to middle class.
3. The third group was born into middle-class status and had less educational achievement than their parents.
4. In the fourth group of families the grandparents, parents, and the current generation had all maintained their middle-class status (McAdoo, 1981).

One disturbing aspect of Black family mobility, which does not tend to have the same effect when it occurs in White families, is the difficulty Black families have in maintaining their middle-class status in the subsequent generations. McAdoo's (1978) research supports this reality and indicates that in some families there may even be a decline in future generations, educational achievement—and the ability to achieve a particular socioeconomic status—having peaked in the generation that was upwardly mobile. McAdoo hypothesizes that being born into middle-class surroundings may reduce the success drive that is often a very central concern in lower socioeconomic brackets. Middle-class status can provide instead the freedom (due to a great extent to financial security) to follow a career or educational bent because of individual interest rather than economic need (McAdoo, 1978, pp. 767–768).

Although this "downward mobility" does in fact occur in other ethnic group mobility patterns, the impact that such a change in status has on Black as opposed to White families differs significantly. The most obvious disadvantage of Black families in this situation is the concrete result of being a less established population—that is, the rarity of a level of financial security that could provide a cushion for a subsequent generation that does not achieve a high educational or career level. The maintenance of a middle-class life-style is such situations is thus dependent upon an inherited wealth that must be sufficiently large to afford the nonachieving generation the same opportunities of education and social standing that would otherwise require that generation's own concerted efforts. Since this kind of accumulated wealth is unusual in Black families, a failure to achieve most often means a failure to maintain middle-class status (McAdoo, 1978, p. 768). Therefore, for many Black families the failure to maintain economic stability jeopardizes not only their middle-class status but ultimately their sense of personal and family security.

BICULTURALISM AND BLACK MIDDLE-CLASS FAMILIES

Although the problem of living in two worlds is clearly an issue for all Black families, it becomes more of an issue as a family moves into the middle class and further up the socioeconomic ladder because contact with people of different cultures is increased.

Elaine Pinderhughes (1982) maintains that "values from all three value systems—African, American, and victim—are found in Afro-American families" (p. 110). The attempt to incorporate a solid Black identity within the multicultural scenario that characterizes American society requires an ability to adapt: The flexibility necessitated by this biculturality serves in some families to strengthen their sense of cultural identity and to increase their tolerance for cultural difference and ambiguity. In other families, the sheer difficulty of both adapting to different systems and forging an identity leads to a confusion of values and roles and a sense of powerlessness in the face of this cultural complexity (Pinderhughes, 1982). This has often given rise to a self-defeating cycle: Identity confusion, role and power conflicts, and rigidity in relationships reinforce one another in the process in which powerlessness begets more powerlessness (p. 114). This struggle to maintain one's own cultural identity while living in a bicultural world has its unique impact on Black middle-class families.

Irrespective of the socioeconomic level of the family, however, the therapist must be keenly aware of the impact of racism and oppression on the lives of Black people. I am in total agreement with Pinderhughes (1982), who states that "as long as racism and oppression maintain the victim system, the goal of family treatment must be to enable the family to cope constructively with those stresses and to counteract their pervasive influence" (pp. 114–115). Ultimately our goal is to empower families to reverse the effects of this racism and produce changes in their lives.

DIFFERENCES BETWEEN BLACK AND WHITE
MIDDLE-CLASS FAMILIES

Black middle-class families differ from their White counterparts in a number of areas that are important to consider if one is to attempt to understand the intricacies of Black family functioning (Bagarozzi, 1980). First, although many White middle-class families do not themselves fit with the family life-cycle model that some sociologists have proposed (e.g., Rodgers, 1972), the life cycles of Black middle-class families often diverge sharply from the proposed model. An example given by Bagarozzi of this divergence is the fact that the "launching phase" (Dietrich, 1976) of a family life cycle is often marked in Black families by the entrance into the household of children of the extended family. Such children may be those of relatives who are teenage mothers, who are divorced working parents, or who are otherwise unable to provide care. Thus, at a stage in which a couple is, under "normal" circumstances, engaged in adjusting to an empty house and to refocusing on each other, the house of a Black family may be quickly filled with children, extending the time period in which the spouses fill parental roles.

Another area of difference is the character of male–female power structures in each racial group. Prior to the 1970s, many White middle-class families tended to exhibit a male-dominant power dynamic, while Black families showed a greater incidence of a structure in which power is shared more or less equally by the spouses. Some sociologists (e.g., Scanzoni, 1971) have hypothesized that this greater egalitarianism may often be the result of the fact that Black wives were more likely than White wives to be employed—and often to contribute substantially to the family income. This difference in power dynamics has decreased in recent years as both Black and White women have entered the labor force in increasing numbers, a fact that supports the connection between working wives and the balance of power in the family structure. Black families, however, have a longer history of finding this type of balance.

Family boundaries constitute another area in which race functions as a difference in family dynamics. Black family boundaries have been considered by many sociologists (e.g., McAdoo, 1978, 1981) to be more permeable, more open to outside influence—be it from the extended family or from the Black community. White Anglo-Saxon Protestant families, in contrast, are relatively closed to such influence, tending to maintain more of an isolated family nucleus. It should be noted, however, that Black family boundaries may be unusually impermeable where input from the White community is concerned (Grier & Cobbs, 1968).

THE VULNERABILITY OF BLACK MIDDLE-CLASS FAMILIES AND ITS IMPACT ON TREATMENT

Racism, Discrimination, and Black Middle-Class Families

Bagarozzi (1980) has examined the issues related to therapy with Black middle-class families. Black middle-class parents have been found to share similar goals and expectations for their children with white middle-class parents. Bagarozzi states, however, that "[w]hile their basic goals do not differ significantly from their white counterparts, Black middle-class families find their attainment more difficult because of discrimination and prejudice which is inherent in many social, cultural and economic institutions in the United States" (p. 161).

After the Civil Rights movement in the late 1960s and early 1970s, there were many strides in attempts to give equal opportunity to Blacks in various fields. However, many Black middle-class families are becoming disillusioned as they increasingly find that the roads of access stop short of widespread, high-level equality, obstructed by more subtle forms of the racial injustice they faced two decades ago. McAdoo (1981) summarizes this reality:

> there are now fewer Black middle-class families than there were in the mid-1970s. There has been a steady erosion of the proportion of Blacks who are preparing for and being employed by the traditional professional careers. (p. 158)

This disparity was also evident for what McAdoo calls the "golden cohort" of young Black male and female professionals, aged 25 to 35. Initially, many of these bright young Blacks complete their educations at White institutions and enter the job field at much higher levels than their parents. However, as they climb the occupational ladder, many find that they are viewed as "second-class citizens," or as having been hired to fill affirmative action guidelines. For many of these young Black people, there is considerable disillusionment as they attempt to enter higher management and executive levels. With the loss of many affirmative action programs in the 1980s, many Blacks become victims of the Black "job ceiling" and are unable to realize their true potential. Davis and Watson (1983) have explored the issues faced by Blacks who are working in corporate America.

The inequities of the social system are felt by Blacks across the socioeconomic spectrum. It has clear consequences for family life. Most Black middle-class parents struggle with the knowledge that although more doors have been opened for them these same doors may be closed again for their children and grandchildren.

Some of the Black middle-class families whom I have seen in treatment have talked openly about the insecurity that they feel. Although
they may have good, well-paying jobs, there is the fear that their
"advantages" will all disappear. Some of these individuals work in large
White corporations or institutions in which they perceive their positions
as at best tenuous.

These fears are not without a basis in reality. *The New York Times*, for
example, in a number of articles in 1987 highlighted the "last hired, first
fired" experience for Black managers and executives. One particularly
depressing article featured a Black network executive who found herself
on the unemployment line. Many Black professionals were in fact hired
by White companies to fill jobs in human resource areas or affirmative
action and equal opportunity programs. In times of cutbacks, these jobs
are the first to go.

In a more recent *New York Times* article (July 14, 1987), Williams states:
"More than two decades after civil rights victories have made equal
opportunity in the workplace a matter of law, many black professionals
say they still face formidable obstacles to success." Based on interviews
conducted around the country, Williams describes a work scenario in
which Black employees in both public and private industry are still
inhibited in their professional advancement due to the color of their
skin. This situation creates a very real internal pressure for Black employees, a pressure to constantly prove themselves in a system that may
never recognize their efforts. Many aspects of the sense of alienation
that Williams describes are in fact subtle indications of racial barriers that
clearly add to the emotional burden of Black employees and interfere
with the development of good mental health and self-esteem. The speci-
fics of this subtle racial bias are described by Black professionals in
various ways. Some tell of the "glass ceiling" sensation, that "invisible
but very real" barrier that prevents the Black professional from reaching
the top of his or her field (Williams, 1987, p. A16). Others describe
instances of obvious prejudice, such as indications that their White
co-workers believe Blacks to be lacking in intelligence, while others
speak of having the sense of being always monitored and judged.
Williams's interviewees also mention as a factor the sense of "social and
professional estrangement . . . among White colleagues" (p. A16).

In relation to this first factor, Williams notes that the level of "integration" in the workplace is also deceptive. In a section entitled "Integrated
Offices, Segregated Lives," this issue is explored:

Specialists in black advancement say that more than 50 percent of black
executives are graduates of predominantly black universities, and black
executives are frequently the first from their families and neighborhoods to

move into the upper echelon of American society. While they may work in integrated offices, the lives they lead outside the office are in many ways segregated. (p. A16)

The Emotional Price Paid for "Advancement"

The subtle and overt forms of discrimination described above have their impact on the Black middle-class individual and can cause persistent feelings of low self-esteem and constant anxiety about one's position. This constant pressure has its impact not just on the individuals but on their couple and family interactions as well. Since it is typical for both spouses to work in many Black families, both individuals may be bringing these issues home.

The stress is often displaced onto spouses, children, and other family members: It is not uncommon for an individual who feels powerless in his or her work situation to abuse power in their home environment, since this feeling of powerlessness can result in intense anger that gets acted out in a sphere where the individual can exercise some amount of power. The following sections address the issue of handling this anger in treatment with Black families.

The Theme of Power

The influences of racism and discrimination greatly affect the issue of power in Black couple relationships, particularly in terms of the misuses and abuses of power in these relationships. This is very true at all class and educational levels.

The following example clarifies the existence of this struggle beyond the class barrier of an upper-middle-class Black family:

Mr. and Mrs. Smith, a Black couple in their 50s, entered treatment following an incident in which Mr. Smith had come home from work as an upper-level manager in a major White corporation and had yelled at his wife and knocked the food she had prepared off the table. Mrs. Smith became frightened and took their three children (aged 14, 10, and 6) to her mother's house. It was during this brief separation that she called to make an appointment for marital therapy.

When they appeared for the first session, both Mr. and Mrs. Smith looked very uncomfortable and somewhat rigid. Mrs. Smith reported that for the first time in her 18-year marriage, she had been very frightened of her husband. Mr. Smith, threatened by this crisis in his marriage, had agreed reluctantly to come in for treatment.

As the work with the couple progressed and both members became more comfortable with the therapist, Mr. Smith shared the root of his concerns. He had been in line at his job for a promotion to vice-president. He was clearly one of the most qualified people within his organization and had been expecting the promotion. His corporation had never had a Black vice-president. At the last moment, another White colleague was promoted to the position. Mr. Smith was devastated and felt strongly that he was passed over because of racial discrimination. He was in a rage but felt impotent and powerless to change the system.

He was intensely embarrassed by this and had not been able to discuss it with Mrs. Smith until this particular couple session. She was very surprised at the intensity of his anger and shame, and for the first time, she began to understand the reasons for his angry outbursts. The therapist was able to help both members of the couple see that as a Black man, Mr. Smith felt angry and somewhat powerless in his work situation and he passed on this anger to his wife and family. He had more of a need to exert his power at home as he felt more powerless and out of control on the job. The process between them was reframed as the need to support each other in spite of the racism from the outside world.

As this example demonstrates, this experience of racism cuts across class levels for Black people. Because of this issue, the impact of the pressures of racial discrimination plays a very significant role in the treatment of Black people. Often Black individuals, couples, and families feel themselves to be without recourse in the face of this racism. Therefore, the issue of empowerment is a very prominent one in the treatment process.

Anger in Black Middle-Class Families

The sense of vulnerability, of powerlessness in the face of entrenched racism, thus gives rise in many Black people to an anger that must be confronted in therapy if one is to treat Black families effectively. The contradictions that arise from the position of the Black middle-class family in a social structure dominated by White culture often serve to obscure the sources of such anger. Also, the increased social and economic similarities between Black and White middle-class families run counter to the often unexpected experiences of prejudice (Bagarozzi, 1980). Thompson (1987) stresses the need to help Black clients distinguish between racism and neuroticism. Family therapists who treat Black middle-class families need, therefore, to aid these families in the process of recognizing the extent to which their problems are influenced by their involvement in the external racist social structure and when they result from their own personal issues:

> The family therapist . . . must help family members become aware of how anger at societal injustices may be displaced and acted out within the family context. He/she also should help families determine how much of their difficulties stem from the effects of discrimination and how much they result from personal dysfunctional behavior styles, faulty communication

patterns, unverbalized expectations or coercive interpersonal behavior change attempts. (Bagarozzi, 1980, pp. 163–164)

The following case vignette illustrates one example of the types of anger that therapists often sense in Black families. It often surprises therapists that Black middle-class families who appear to have "made it" still have a tremendous amount of rage in reaction to the subtle injustices and racism that they encounter.

Earl Owens was a Black 40-year-old executive at a major White corporation. His position was that of Director of Human Resources. There had been a series of cutbacks and "job abolishments" at his organization for the last 3 years, and he had lived in constant fear of losing his position. His family consisted of his wife, Martha Owens, who had been a homemaker for many years and was when the family entered therapy in her first year of a masters program in social work. They had 3 children, Leticia (aged 16), Amena (aged 10), and Earl Jr. (aged 6).

The family came into treatment originally around the issue of Leticia, who was acting out in school. The school had also reported the family to the Bureau of Child Welfare because there had been large welts on Leticia's legs, arms, and face. The bureau had investigated and discovered that Mr. Owens frequently flew into a rage and abused Leticia.

When the family entered treatment, it was clear that they were embarrassed by the referral and very angry that they had to come. The father felt that he had been forced to come. Mrs. Owens described herself as feeling both hopeless and helpless to intervene in the struggle between her husband and her daughter.

Leticia was an attractive adolescent who spoke extremely well and was assertive in communicating her ideas.

The entire family reported that up until, 3 years ago. Leticia and her father had had a very special relationship. She was a "daddy's girl" who followed him around. Approximately 3½ years earlier, however, a number of events occurred simultaneously. Mrs. Owens went back to school to complete work on her B.A. Mr. Owens' job became more unstable and Leticia began reaching out to her peer group more, asserting her independence and becoming more involved in age-appropriate activities.

It became clear in subsequent sessions that Mr. Owens had begun to feel very threatened at work and very abandoned by his wife and favorite daughter at home. He had always been verbally volatile, but as pressures increased he became more physically abusive of his daughter, hitting her with a belt. Initially, Mr. Owens tried to dismiss these as related to the cultural norm of spanking children in many Black families. The therapist was able to challenge this, eventually helping Mr. Owen reach a point where he was able to acknowledge that he was so angry and out of control at these times that he had far exceeded the accepted level of "spanking." He began to talk about how everything in his life felt out of control, his work, his home life, his children. He couldn't make anything go "his way."

It became clear that Leticia had become a scapegoat and a focus of all of this anger. The therapist acknowledged Mr. Owens's pain and anger. She helped him to talk to his daughter about why he "flew off the handle" with her. The therapist had a number of sessions with the couple alone in which Mr. Owens's pain and pressures were normalized and the couple was encouraged to address the distance between them and their increasing inability to support each other. The therapist pointed out that Leticia, who was asserting herself as a normal adolescent, had become the target of that anger.

Mr. Owens was able to tell his wife how he had felt abandoned by her at a time when he was feeling very vulnerable at work. This was very hard for him because he repeatedly stated that he did not want to "appear weak" in his wife's eyes. Mrs. Owens was able to tell her husband that she had felt his withdrawal from her, was very angry, and as a result had immersed herself increasingly in school.

As the couple worked out some of their own issues they were able to honestly discuss the feelings of vulnerability, castration, loss of control, and rage which Mr. Owens experienced at work. He was able to get his wife's support and the therapist's for looking at other options that would allow him to take back his sense of control.

The couple was then able to have a number of sessions with their children and the therapist in which they were able to set clear limits regarding curfew, study time, chores, and so forth with clear consequences. Mr. Owens was able to begin to tell his daughter how angry her acting out made him, rather than displacing his rage from the work situation on to her.

THE EMPHASIS ON KEEPING UP APPEARANCES

For many Black middle-class families there is a tremendous pressure to "keep up appearances." Often there is a desire not to let the outside world know the difficulties they face. "Respectability" becomes an important theme for many of these families and "shaming the family" is viewed as one of the most negative acts. Clearly, this is not totally unique to Black families, but it often takes on a more intense form. Black middle-class and upper-middle-class families frequently find themselves held up as examples by other members of their communities. Many children of Black professionals report a "fish bowl" type of childhood in which they were constantly expected to behave and bring honor to the family. In Black communities children of doctors or ministers in particular tell of growing up with the sense of having to live up to being the "preacher's kid" or the "doctor's kid." When a family such as this seeks mental health services, there is often a tremendous sense of shame and guilt. For families who are viewed as the pillars of their communities or the backbone of their churches to seek help is to admit failure—failure here especially to live up to community perceptions.

As has been noted, many middle-class Black families live essentially in a bicultural or multicultural world. They often raise their children in integrated neighborhoods or schools and the parents work in predominantly White job settings. This creates many levels of distress for Black families. In the cities of the Northeast, for example, Black families who move up the socioeconomic scale often find themselves living in predominantly White suburbs. Many of these families struggle to give their children a sense of their racial identity and yet prepare them to survive in a bicultural world. This can place an inordinate amount of stress on the family.

Sometimes the struggle to maintain middle-class status is so great that a family can be torn apart by it. Parents often work more than one shift or extra jobs and time with children is sometimes sacrificed. The following case illustrates this situation:

The Ross family came for treatment when their son Jeremy (aged 13) was referred by his school. The family consisted of Mr. and Mrs. Ross, Jeremy, and Melanie (aged 7). Mr. and Mrs. Ross had been married 14 years. Both were hard-working Black parents who had civil servant positions. Mr. Ross was a postman, Mrs. Ross a teacher. Mr. Ross worked long hours and often worked overtime, and Mrs. Ross was attending graduate school to get her masters in education. Jeremy's school reported that Jeremy, although an above-average student, was failing three of his subjects and was not working up to his potential in the others. His parents reported that he often did not obey them and would stay out long hours with his friends without telling the family.

The first key to the structural problems in this family came when the therapist tried to arrange a time for the first family session. It became clear that the parents were so busy that they were seldom available to each other or to the children. Time on a Saturday in which the whole family could be seen was finally arranged. In the first session, the parents very angrily told the therapist about their confrontations with their son. They explained that they were working very hard to give their children a better life but that their son was "ungrateful."

Many middle-class Black families, aware of the subtle forces of racism, put great pressure on their children to achieve. In more enmeshed families, this pressure can become intrusive. The Blackman family serves as an example:

The Blackman family was a middle-class Black family consisting of Mrs. Blackman (age 38), Mr. Blackman (49), and their chidren Karen (16) and John (9). They came for family therapy at the suggestion of their minister after Karen's grades became poor in high school and she became increasingly oppositional with her family. She had stopped attending Church, which in her family was a major issue.

Family sessions revealed that John was labeled the "good" child and Karen the "difficult" one. Her parents were first generation middle-class and had both worked hard at educational and career goals. Karen expressed a considerable amount of anger at her parents, which dated back to her earlier junior high school experience in which her parents had moved her from a local neighborhood school into what she called a "White private school." She had felt very isolated and had tried to express this to her parents but they had been so anxious for her to have a "good education" that they minimized her complaints. Finally in high school when her peers began dating, she felt even more socially isolated and resentful of her parents.

The therapist first joined with the parents in their well-intentioned struggle to find quality education for their child. She labeled their struggle as normal and typical of "good parents." She spoke of their struggle in the context of all Black parents to find the most well-balanced education for their children. She then helped Karen to express her concerns directly to her parents and to help them understand the social isolation she felt.

This process uncovered a basic disagreement between the parents in terms of their philosophy of education. Mr. Blackman reported that he felt strongly that Black kids should go to "the best schools." Mrs. Blackman argued for a school with other Black children. As the work with the family continued, it became clear that the Blackmans had basic disagreements on many life-style issues including where and how they should live. They were helped to renegotiate these issues and in turn to help their daughter find a school where she could feel less alone. Gradually, with her parents' understanding, Karen was able to improve her grades and by the time the transfer was made, she was passing all subjects.

The pressure exhibited by the Blackman family on their children grows out of a very real fear on the part of Black middle-class parents that the few gains that have been made in education and occupation will be "snatched away" from their children. The pressure to "make it" is great. Therapists are often unsympathetic to the parents in these situations and thus tend to overidentify with the child. This is a serious error. It is very important to these struggling Black parents to have their efforts recognized and appreciated.

RACIAL IDENTIFICATION ISSUES FOR BLACK MIDDLE-CLASS CHILDREN

The struggle to promote positive racial identification and self-esteem presents complications for upwardly mobile families who may live in all-White areas. Children often feel very isolated, particularly as they enter their preteen and adolescent years. At this point, social barriers often become more evident and a child who may have felt "accepted" at a younger age may now feel left out. Black parents, in an effort to address this dilemma, have begun "networking" with other Black parents and families in neighboring communities. Some have arranged informal groups and activities for their children. Others have used more formal social groups such as "Jack and Jill" clubs. Many families, feeling that these clubs were too "bourgie" or "stuck up," have started their own chapters or other clubs. Other families make a point of taking their children back to their former Black communities for their social life. As has been discussed in Chapter 5, Black churches have served an important social as well as spiritual function for many of these families. Black families will often travel a great distance in order to attend a Black church for the feeling of belonging and support.

In their efforts toward upward mobility some Black families have adopted a "color blind" attitude in which they deny the impact of racial differences. Unfortunately, it is often their children who bear the brunt of the cultural isolation. In recent years, I have seen an increasing number of Black adolescents and their families who are struggling with these dilemmas. One of the most important tasks for therapists working with these families is to help them open up communication between parents and children on these issues. The Carlton family was struggling with these issues:

Dwayne Carlton was a 15-year-old Black adolescent who was growing up in a suburban community in which Black people had always lived on the "other side of the tracks." His family was one of the first to move into the predominantly White section of town. Dwayne felt caught between White kids who saw him as different for racial reasons and Black kids who saw him as different in regards to class and as "stuck up." He was the only child of professional parents. His father, a banker, rigidly maintained that he had always operated in a color blind way and that he felt that his son should just "ignore" these issues. Ms. Carlton was a college professor who took a very passive role, attempting to placate her husband and her son. They often sent messages to each other through her. Mr. Carlton continued to "preach to" his son through his wife. This was quickly apparent in the first session. In subsequent sessions, the therapist worked with the father and son to open up communication about this issue and to help the son share his dilemma openly with his father. For a number of sessions the therapist had to block the father from "preaching" and help him to just hear his son's concerns. He was finally able to recognize his struggle and to help his son discuss ways in which he might find his own way in this difficult situation. Gradually Dwayne with his parents' support was able to find his own friends in school.

KINSHIP NETWORKS AND BLACK MIDDLE-CLASS FAMILIES

Mutual Aid

Unlike the isolation frequently observed in White middle-class families, Black middle-class families tend to maintain closer ties with their kinship networks. Mutually helpful involvement—both in economic and in emotional terms—with family members often provides the nuclear family with a sense of dependable support. McAdoo's (1978) study gives detailed descriptions of the kinds of help that upwardly mobile, middle-class Black families received from their kinship network. In 66% of the cases she studied, these families felt that they received a great deal of kinship help. Both financial and emotional aid from extended family was received by those subjects, comprising substantial outlays in these areas on the part of the network. This aid often continued to be given even after the subjects had achieved a level of financial security that exceeded that of their kin. McAdoo pinpoints family crises and major monetary outlays (e.g., the purchase of a home) as times when kin were most likely to be called upon for help. She further observes,

> Emotional support was an important element mentioned repeatedly by the parents. In times of stress, they turned to family members for help and felt confident that help would be available when needed. (p. 772)

Child care was another area in which these families gave and received help from this kinship network (McAdoo, 1978). There are many ways in which this exchange might occur: A grandmother may live in with her daughter and babysit for her while both parents work; on the other end of the exchange, a middle-class Black couple who are "doing well" may take in a nephew or niece so that they might attend a better school.

When Help Becomes a Burden

The close involvement that middle-class Black families often maintain with the extended family can sometimes be an issue for upwardly mobile families. In many Black families, the first person to attain a college degree represents the achievement of a major milestone and is a source of pride for the entire family. Often that person has been helped by extended family support or financial contributions. Once that person finishes school, it is expected that he or she will help others to get their education. Often this creates a financial burden for that young person, which is continued as he or she starts their own family.

Some Black professionals find themselves at the center or the hub of a complex extended family network, all of whom turn to them for emotional support, advice, and at times financial help. For many of these families, the issue becomes one of how to remain a part of their extended families without becoming overwhelmed by their demands. The following example illustrates this issue:

Marcia (age 26) was a young Black woman who worked as a teacher in a special education program. She sought treatment because she was feeling overwhelmed, anxious, and unable to sleep at night. Her parents had been divorced when she was 12, and she had been a parental child to her younger sisters. Marcia's family had been lower middle-class during her early years. They had struggled to send her to college, and she had worked her way through. Her current anxiety stemmed from a crisis concerning her younger sister (aged 19) who was in her second year of college. Her parents, who had been very hostile toward each other since their divorce, had become angry about payment and refused to pay for the sister's schooling. Marcia, in a typical gesture, had attempted to take on this burden. She became so overwhelmed with anxiety that she sought therapy. After some initial work with Marcia around her own need to control and take over, the therapist asked for a family session. Marcia's parents and both of her sisters agreed to attend. With the therapist's help, Marcia was able to share with her parents the burden that she felt for her sister's education. The therapist asked the parents if they had been aware that Marcia felt this pressure. They both reported that while they knew that Marcia was "helping" her sister, they had no idea of the strain this was causing on her. The therapist then asked the parents to discuss the ways in which they would handle this situation. They were able to work out a reasonable payment schedule.

In a follow-up session, the therapist instructed Marcia to ask her parents if they needed her to continue the job of "parenting" the family. They were rather surprised by this and emphatically told Marcia that they no longer needed her in that role. The therapist talked at length with the family about how divorced parents can still continue to function as a team on parental issues even if they don't choose to live together.

Marcia was helped to make clear "I" statements about her own needs in her family for the first time. She was able to make a small contribution to her sister's education without feeling obligated to take over the total responsibility.

EMOTIONAL CUTOFF FROM THE EXTENDED KINSHIP NETWORK

A number of authors have discussed the fact that for some middle-class Black families, "the achievement and maintenance of middle-class status may lead to an emotional cutoff from the family of origin" (Hines & Boyd-Franklin, 1982; McAdoo, 1978; Pinderhughes, 1982).

McQueen (1971) and Stack (1974) discuss this kind of dilemma for the Black middle-class professional, which McAdoo (1978) illustrates by discussing the case of a young Black professional whose extended family has sacrificed to help him achieve middle-class status. This dilemma is centered upon the expectation that the professional, now that he has achieved middle-class status, will in turn help his family. The expected aid necessitates that he limit his upward movement in order that his resources—financial, psychic, and physical—may remain available to his family. McAdoo summarizes his choices as follows:

> The mobile individual has two alternatives: (1) he must either continue his participation in the obligatory reciprocity stream, or (2) he must isolate himself and his family of procreation from his family of orientation. (p. 78)

This either/or choice for Black middle-class individuals and the psychological consequences of the isolation that can result from assuming the burden of responsibility should be an issue of concern for all therapists working with Black families. Often it seems that the Black individual who seeks upward mobility can do so only at the expense of close ties to his or her family of origin. While this may not mean the sacrifice of family holiday and ritual times, the break in day-to-day involvement with the family of origin can give rise to what are essentially class tensions (McAdoo, 1978). These tensions and the sense of disjunction they cause tend to make for even greater feelings of emotional cut-off:

> Probably one of the greatest dilemmas facing the upwardly mobile group is their relationship with blacks left behind. This isolation, while a crucial factor in coping with significant life changes that cause stress, increases the need for supportive therapy that must come from persons outside of the family sphere. Blacks newly arrived in the middle-class, or fighting to remain at working-class status, are often too vulnerable, economically and psychologically, to extend themselves for blacks who have been left behind. (p. 78)

The role of family therapy here is to help Black middle-class families achieve a balance of contact and involvement without drowning or cutoff. The stresses and strains on the Black middle-class family, as demonstrated by some of the case examples, can seriously impinge upon the family system as a whole. The toll these issues takes on the relationships of couples specifically is the focus of attention in the next chapter.

CHAPTER 13

Issues in the Treatment of Black Couples in Family Therapy*

One very important subsystem to be considered in the treatment of any family is that of the couple relationship. It is, in many ways, the nucleus of the family. This chapter explores the specific issues, problems, and needs that Black couples present in treatment. It addresses questions that have an impact on the therapeutic process, such as: What are the specific issues and concerns that bring a Black couple into treatment? Do traditional techniques in couples' therapy need to be modified in order to address successfully the problems presented by this population? A review of the literature on the topic of Black couple relationships reveals that research in this area has been sparse. Researchers have been enamored of the study of power dynamics in Black couples, much of it in reaction to Moynihan's (1965) assertion that Black families are matriarchal. A number of the researchers and authors have challenged Moynihan's interpretations and have found primarily egalitarian marital patterns in Black families (Billingsley, 1968; Hyman & Reed, 1969; Lewis & Looney, 1983; Mack, 1974; Middleton & Putney, 1970; Scanzoni, 1977; Willie & Greenblatt, 1978). A number of researchers studied marital intimacy as well as power. Lewis and Looney found differences between their Black and White populations on concepts such as marital expressiveness and satisfaction. There are, however, very few studies and little clinical material on Black couples in therapy. Clinicians who work with this population have emphasized the difficulty therapists encounter when trying to engage Black couples in therapy. However, the

*I would like to acknowledge the contribution of a number of colleagues to this chapter: Rozetta Wilmore-Schaeffer, A.C.S.W., Linwood Bullock, D.S.W., Anderson J. Franklin, Ph.D., and Charles E. Smith, Ed.D.

factors that directly or indirectly maintain the frequent wall of resistance—socialization issues of Black males and females, family of origin issues, the insidious effects of racism, socioeconomic realities as well as the dynamics of power—are often not articulated.

RESISTANCE OF BLACK COUPLES TO TREATMENT

As is discussed in the previous chapter, in many Black families from all economic strata who are working hard and who have upwardly mobile aspirations, there is an emphasis on "keeping up appearances." This is further complicated by the abundance of family "secrets" in many Black families. Because of these concerns, many Black couples and families will wait until a situation has reached crisis proportions before they seek help. In addition, they have often worked extremely hard to hide their problems from others. This can also be true of their approach to the therapist. The case of Susan and Joe illustrates this point:

Susan and Joe were a young Black couple in their early 30s. They had one child. Joe was a lawyer and Susan had been a teacher prior to the birth of their son. They came in following a crisis in which Joe had hit Susan. She had panicked and had taken their child to a friend's home. Susan reported that verbal abuse had been occurring for more than 3 years but that this was the first time Joe had hit her. Joe had finished law school 3 years earlier but had been unable to pass the bar exam. Each year as the time for the bar approached, he became angry and verbally abusive. Joe at first denied and attempted to minimize the problem. He threatened to withdraw from treatment. The therapist saw him alone for a session and joined with him around his feelings about the exam, the rage that this evoked in him, and his fears of failure. He was later able to share some of these feelings with his wife. He told her that he was afraid she would condemn him for his "failure." He had therefore begun to criticize her constantly about her own insecurities, particularly concerning her inability to find a job. Whenever she asserted herself, he would become enraged, accuse her of not caring about him, and threaten to hit her.

Both partners had hidden their difficulties from their extended families, their friends and neighbors. Susan expressed concerns that it might reflect on Joe professionally in their community. They continued to go to church every Sunday and pretend nothing was wrong. They kept up this facade at their parties and family gatherings as well.

The therapist worked with this couple for many months before they were finally able to stop minimizing their difficulties and could begin to face them openly. Only then were they able to share their insecurities and fears and begin to ask for support from each other.

INITIAL PRESENTATIONS OF BLACK COUPLES

Despite this resistance, however, more Black couples are seeking treatment than ever before. Thus, it is important to explore briefly the ways in which these couples may present. Although generalizations are difficult, the following categories summarize the different presenting constellations: (1) a couple that requests traditional marriage counseling; (2) an unmarried couple that has had a long-term, live-in or "common law" relationship; (3) premarital therapy—a couple that is considering marriage but who have concerns about their relationship; (4) a crisis couple that appears after a fight and then disappears for long periods of time; (5) divorce mediation; (6) a couple that initially presents a child as the problem.

From the above description, clearly the process of couples therapy with Black people is complicated and can appear in many forms. This is certainly true in the field of couples therapy in general and for members of other ethnic groups. Differences between ethnic groups do arise, however, around such issues as attitudes toward therapy and problem definitions. These and other issues are addressed in subsequent sections.

Although the request for traditional marriage counseling was certainly the most common 10 years ago, the marital scenario has changed radically and couples present with many different types of relationships. One of the most common is that of an unmarried couple who have a long-term, live-in or common law relationship. This situation can present in different forms depending on the generation of the couple. There are also socioeconomic issues involved: Among older Black couples, particularly those from low socioeconomic backgrounds, the practice of common law relationships is quite common. The couple may have a number of children together but may never have married either for financial reasons (i.e., fear of the loss of a welfare check) or because one or both parties have been married before and never officially divorced. In Black communities, there have always existed legal and nonlegal "marriages" in which the couple is treated within their community as if they were married. For some, the fact that they are not "legal" is a family secret. Often these couples enter treatment only when one member of the couple begins to put pressure on the other to "legalize" the relationship. These couples also tend to come to the attention of therapists when one member of the couple becomes dysfunctional. This could be for psychiatric reasons, alcoholism, drug dependency, or a medical crisis related to a terminal condition in one partner. This last situation can often threaten a relationship because the other partner may not be recognized as a "significant other" by the medical establishment and may discover that he or she has few legal rights.

The third example often involves young couples who may have lived together and are now escalating their commitment and considering marriage. Often, if there have been problems, these couples will appear for couple treatment for preventative purposes. This type of preventative measure is a relatively sophisticated use of couples therapy and is usually limited to young Black professionals.

The fifth example, divorce mediation, is now more common among Black couples for two reasons: (1) more lawyers tend to refer couples for therapy, and (2) often the cost of working out differences in a mediation process is far more effective than a long, drawn-out court battle.

The sixth example, the initial presentation of a child as the problem is still one of the most common ways in which many Black couples first enter treatment. Many Black families are very child focused and often enter treatment as a response to a problem that has developed in their child. Although these couples may genuinely believe the problem to relate to the child alone, this is a "safer" way in which to seek help. Most of these cases are school referred. The following example is typical of the course of treatment:

The James family is a Black family who appeared at their community mental health center with their three children, aged 9, 4, and 2. They had been referred by the school because their oldest child, Clarence, was acting out in school and was often oppositional to his teachers. The initial family sessions utilized the techniques of structural family therapy (Minuchin, 1974) to help restructure the family by putting the parents in charge and helping them to work together in their parenting of Clarence. In this process, it became very clear that the Jameses' marriage was in serious trouble. They often had angry arguments at home about their children, particularly Clarence, but they had never fully dealt with the difficulties between them.

As Clarence began to show improvement, the therapist raised with the James family the fact that his misbehavior had been a way of focusing their attention onto himself and away from their own difficulties. They were told that while their son had shown some improvement, his behavior would clearly become a problem again unless they dealt with their own issues as a couple. Although Mr. and Mrs. James would never have chosen couples therapy initially for themselves, they now had developed a trusting relationship with their therapist and were able to enter treatment as a couple.

The Role of Black Women in the Referral Process

The suspicion that is described above and the intimacy of the issues between couples are both factors in the resistance of Black couples to treatment. Negative attitudes toward therapy raise major issues for both

Black men and Black women but the full impact of this is clearly evident in the reaction of Black men to therapy in general, and to this modality in particular.

Referrals of Black couples are almost universally initiated by the woman in the relationship. While it is true for both Black and White populations that women seek therapy in greater numbers, in some White couples both parties mutually agree to seek treatment. This is exceedingly rare among Black people. When therapy is sought, Black women almost universally initiate the move to do so and the engagement of Black men in the treatment process is the first major treatment issue. Before exploring techniques that are useful in accomplishing this treatment goal, it would be helpful to explore two central issues: the characteristics of the process of socialization for Black men and women that make it difficult for them to seek help, particularly in the area of relationships; and the history of racial discrimination, which has a significant impact on these interpersonal processes.

GENDER DIFFERENTIATION AND THE SOCIALIZATION PROCESS

The Socialization of Black Women

For a Black woman, the area of male–female relationships becomes a very loaded issue early in her socialization experience. As with most processes of cultural assimilation, a great deal of the expectation that the Black female adolescent develops about women's roles is learned from observation of the female role models in her life. Many Black women report that since they saw their mothers, aunts, and grandmothers as extremely competent women who both raised children and worked, they have learned self-reliance and a belief based on the saying "God bless the child who's got her own." They were taught to get an education, a job, and to be able to provide for themselves.

Although there is, of course, a great deal of variability in male–female role models, the types of relationships that Black women in treatment have described as having observed in their mothers' relationships with men have fallen into one of the following six categories: (1) father absent, (2) weak or dysfunctional father, (3) transient male relationships, (4) traditional marriage, (5) strong or authoritarian father, (6) abusive male–female relationship. The type of male–female interaction pattern observed by the girl in her early socialization years clearly has an impact on her choice of men and her expectations for her own relationships. For example, Black women whose fathers were absent often reported one of two experiences. Either their mothers avoided male relationships and became very involved in childrearing, family, work, and church activities or they became involved in a series of transitory relationships with men over the early years of the young girl's life. Either situation might help convey to a young Black girl the sentiment that "Black men are no good" or that "They won't be there for you when you need them." Many Black women grow up with this expectation from an early age and have no experience of positive relational role models. Black women whom I have treated who have had this type of early experience frequently report that they do not know how to have a positive relationship with a man.

A variation on this theme is a situation in some Black families in which the man may be somewhat weak or dysfunctional. This is clearly a continuum and can include many different kinds of experiences. On one end of the continuum one might encounter a weak, "hen-pecked" Black man who brings home his paycheck every week to a domineering wife. At the other end, one may encounter a man with sincere dysfunctions such as alcoholism or drug abuse that contribute to his inability to provide for his family. Because of the "last hired, first fired" experience of many Black people, it is not uncommon for many Black men to face chronic unemployment problems. Since this places the burden of providing on the mother, her daughters learn from a very early age not to depend on a man for financial or emotional support.

Many Black women were raised in traditional two-parent homes in which their parents worked in an egalitarian pattern vis-à-vis each other, sharing power, decision making, and role responsibilities. These women often have a very realistic sense of the balance between communication, conflict resolution, and affection in a relationship. There are a number of variations on these roles, some of which are related to class differences. Most Black women who had grown up in poor, working-class or newly middle-class families had mothers who worked. Their role as breadwinners gave them an important position in the family. A smaller number of women had grown up in more middle-class homes and had mothers who raised the children and were primarily homemakers. Some of these women reported that their mothers were more dependent on their fathers. This type of relationship is often represented by the fifth category, that is, by a strong, authoritarian father. Many Black women raised in this situation identified with their fathers and became more aggressive and assertive. Others, however, clearly identified with their mothers and were often weak and submissive in their relationships with men. They expected domination and dismissed men who did not have this quality as "weak."

As in most ethnic populations, a number of Black women were raised in abusive homes in which there was a history of violent confrontations and physical and verbal abuse between parents and often toward the children. These women are at particular risk of recreating this pattern and becoming battered women as adults and/or becoming abusive toward their own children. Often these women will choose men who abuse them and their children.

It is extremely important to know what the socialization experience of each member of the couple has been because these patterns are often recreated within the couple dynamic.

The Socialization of Black Men

The legacy of racism and discrimination has had many effects on the socialization of Black men. Black mothers, acutely aware of this history, often attempt to protect their sons by giving them the message, "Be strong but not too strong." The lesson of a Malcolm X or a Martin Luther King can sometimes be interpreted to mean that if you are too much of a threat to the powers that be, you will be killed.

On the other hand, one can not underestimate the sociocultural impact of the Black "macho" role. This is particularly true in urban, inner-city environments. Young boys are taught that in order to survive and protect themselves on the streets, they cannot show "weakness." The message to "act bad even if you're scared" is a clear one. If a young Black man "acts weak," he will be ostracized by his peer group. It is not an uncommon experience in early childhood that if a young child falls down and mother runs to soothe him, his father and the older members of the family will stop her and say, "Come on, boy, get up, you're okay."

This becomes more complicated as a young boy enters adolescence and begins to establish his sexual identity. For many Black men who have been restricted from educational and occupational advancement, the sexual area becomes one of the few in which they can show their prowess and strength. Teenage boys are taught to conquer or "score" with women sexually. This concept, while it is certainly present in other ethnic groups, takes on a particular meaning for many young Black men because it is one of the few areas in which society allows them to score.

All of these issues—the impact of racial discrimination, the fear of showing weakness, and the need to demonstrate sexual prowess—have weighty implications for intimate couple relationships between Black men and women.

Many Black men and women today have to cope on a daily basis with the impact of discrimination on their lives. It may be felt in the reality of the substandard housing in which they live or in the survival pressure of constant financial burdens. Since many Black families are at the mercy of urban school systems, the fears that their children will get trapped in a similar cycle is overwhelming. Even Black men and women who have managed to escape the oppressive grip of poverty and enter the middle-class face subtle and overt forms of discrimination on their jobs and in their more integrated communities. These more subtle forms of racial bias can be just as deadly. Such cumulative pressures on the psyche of Black people take their toll on couple relationships. As is discussed in Chapter 12, many Black women and men experience a sense of powerlessness in their interactions with the world that is angrily acted out in their intimate relationships. Often a man or a woman who feels powerless in the outer world will make extreme attempts to control a loved one or spouse, making power and control issues major dynamics in many Black couple relationships. While these dynamics are often played out around concerns such as finances, decision making, and other control issues, the therapist treating such couples must be aware of the complexity of other underlying dynamics.

The socialization factors that prevent Black men from showing weakness have clear implications for intimate couple dynamics. For example, a Black man who has been taught from an early age to control hurt and pain will have a very difficult time expressing those emotions to his mate. A Black man who has been taught that he can never admit when he has failed will have a very difficult time asking for the support of his mate in sharing the pressures of the outside world.

In couple dynamics, this often presents in treatment as a "lack of communication." It is common in most ethnic groups for women to report in couples therapy that their men can't "talk about their feelings." However, this lack of communicational ability is an extremely loaded issue for many Black couples in particular because it runs directly counter to the often excessively defensive character of the socialization of many Black men. Black women use the support system of other women much more often and are socialized to share feelings about relationships at least with each other. Often there is no model for how this can be done in male–female relationships. This leads to tremendous conflicts as many Black women experience extreme frustration with this lack of expressiveness.

The impact on couple relationships of the Black male's need to demonstrate sexual prowess and power in relationships has many implications for the treatment of Black couples. It has implications for male–female relationships in general, particularly on the issue of fidelity. Many Black women have been socialized not to expect fidelity from a man, others only giving up after repeated experiences of infidelity.

The couple therapist, in exploring the meaning of fidelity in a relationship, needs to be aware that it may have many different levels of meaning for Black couples. For example, since many Black men feel beaten down by their experiences in the White world, sexual prowess becomes a way to reassert their manhood and regain their pride. These extramarital or extrarelational affairs may have more to do with these burdens and less to do with the failure of their primary relationship. In such situations, the ability of the therapist to open up channels of communication about such emotionally charged areas as pride, vulnerability, and the pressures and demands facing each person can have a significant impact on a man's ability to gain respect for his manhood from his partner.

Techniques for Engaging Black Men in Couples Therapy

Because of the resistance by Black men to the treatment process, the therapist must often make a decision early on as to whether to begin therapy with the woman alone. In the treatment of Black couples, the therapist often has no choice and must be more flexible in his or her approach if couples are to be engaged. All of the therapists interviewed for this paper were clearly in agreement on this issue. A number of strategies can prove helpful in using this approach.

First, the therapist must keep in his or her mind a clear understanding that he or she is working with a dyadic system. All interventions with the woman must be made with this in mind. When a Black woman first calls for couples treatment, therefore, it is important to find out the nature of the problem and to try to understand it from her viewpoint. In the initial session, her understanding of her partner's willingness to come in can be explored. If she acknowledges that he is reluctant, then a more general statement to the effect that most men feel threatened at first may help to normalize the partner's initial response.

Second, it is important to discuss carefully the nature of her partner's resistance and to help her figure out how to get him to come in. For example, although it is generally a good practice to avoid giving ultimatums, there are some situations in which a woman feels so victimized that she feels she must leave. When this is the case, it is often helpful for her to make very clear to her partner that if he does not go for treatment with her, she will leave. This kind of statement should be avoided if at all possible because it sets up a situation in which a Black man may feel forced to come, which in turn frequently engenders further oppositional feelings in the man since he is then robbed of the power to choose his own way of dealing with problems. Once again, this sense of lost autonomy is a particularly sensitive issue for the Black man who feels his choice to be inhibited by a racist society.

However, even if a male partner is forced to come, a therapist can establish a positive relationship with him and work through the initial reluctance.

Third, it is particularly helpful for the therapist to establish a time when he or she can talk to the man directly. Most men in general, and Black men in particular, resent the feeling of being "summoned" to come in. The woman should be asked, however, to tell her partner that the therapist will be calling. The therapist should call the man directly and not just use the woman as the messenger. During the initial phone conversation, it is important to establish first whether the man knows about the treatment. The therapist must be careful to clarify that she or he has spoken to his wife or mate wants to understand his point of view in order to try to help. The woman should be prepared in advance for the process of attempting to engage her partner in therapy. The therapist can explain that since she or he has had the opportunity to get to know her, it will be necessary to devote a considerable amount of energy to engaging her partner and joining with him in the initial session. This kind of preparation is important so that the woman does not feel threatened in this first joint session. This balancing process is a very delicate one, and the therapist will have to work hard to overcome the man's perception that the therapist is aligned with the woman.

Fourth, for Black men who are particularly resistant, the therapist may have to rely on the man's natural curiosity as things begin to change. In these situations, a woman may have to be seen individually for as long as 6 months before the man can be engaged. Lastly, if the therapist has been seeing a Black woman individually, it is crucial that the man be given at least one individual session and sometimes more before the partners are seen together. This is needed in order to balance the scales.

This question of alignment and coalition between the therapist and one spouse is a difficult one and must be addressed openly early in the process of couples therapy.

Alice and Charles, a Black couple in their 30s, entered treatment after living together for approximately 2 years. They had been involved with each other and had been dating for a total of 5 years. In the first session, it was clear that they were encountering serious communication difficulties and had very different values about male–female roles. For example, they would frequently argue about who should take the lead in their relationship. Charles would often become very angry with Alice whenever she walked ahead of him.

The therapist asked Charles and Alice to share with each other where they had learned what to expect in a couple relationship and who they had used as role models. Alice related that she had been raised by her mother in South Carolina. She was the oldest of three children. Her father had left the family at a very early age. She reported that she had never had a "real life" model for male–female relationships. Her mother did not date and her active involvement in her church was her only outlet. Her own concepts of male–female relationships had been formed from novels and movies. She had no clear ideas as to how fights could be handled or arguments resolved. Hers was a fairy tale conception of male–female dynamics.

Charles had been raised in Harlem. He was the youngest of four boys. His father, who had been actively involved in the Nation of Islam, had died when Charles was 5. His older brothers adhered to his father's tradition and continued many of his values. Charles's mother was a Baptist by religion and had never left her Christian faith. There was always some tension in the family about this divergence in tradition and values and in the area of male–female role expectations. His brothers had married in the Nation of Islam and their wives had taken roles very much in the background of the male relationships. His mother, although she remained Christian, allowed Charles to be raised in the Nation of Islam. The behavior of women he learned to expect was that of deferral to a man and taking the role of the follower of the man's lead to an extreme degree. He reported that he had not been a practicing Muslim since the death of the Honorable Elijah Muhammad (founder of the Nation of Islam) but many of these ideas were still very much a part of him.

The therapist was able to point out to this couple that they had had very different expectations of male–female relationships. This difference was reframed as "normal" in relation to their backgrounds and the issue was removed from the emotional charge of the label "good" or "bad" behavior. They could then discuss these differences and renegotiate their relationship.

SOME COMMON ISSUES IN THE TREATMENT OF BLACK COUPLES

Socioeconomic Issues and Differences in the Treatment of Black Couples

There are a number of socioeconomic issues that affect the treatment of Black couples. A large part of this is related to the impact of racism and discrimination. For example, when treating White couples of different socioeconomic levels, one often has a clear sense from the couple as to where they see their position in society. For many Black couples, this perception is contaminated by a number of factors. For example, as Black couples move up the socioeconomic ladder, they often find themselves caught betweeen two worlds. They are in an increasingly privileged position vis-à-vis the Black community, but they may have received relatively little acknowledgment in White society at large. For example, Black doctors and dentists tend to have a very privileged position in the Black community and in the past have had predominantly Black practices. It is not unusual, however, for them to find themselves cut off from acceptance by the mainstream of their professions.

This pattern is experienced by Black people at all socioeconomic levels and often leads to a feeling of dissatisfaction for many Black couples. In a similar vein, Black people without formal education frequently find themselves denied entry into the opportunity structure even though they have very fine talents. Discrimination can be deeply felt and can thus have a significant impact on the couple relationship.

There are also often socioeconomic differences within Black couple relationships that can be very problematic. It has been a common phenomenon for many generations in the Black community for women to have more formal education than men. There are a number of reasons for this. For Black families living in the South in previous generations, there was for the most part one type of work open to Black women, that is, household domestic work. The menial nature of this work tended to leave Black women in an extremely vulnerable position, open to many forms of employer abuse—including sexual harassment. Black families of previous generations often educated their daughters at Black teachers' colleges in the South in order to avoid this cycle, which created a situation in which a Black woman often had more formal education than her male partner. Because of the reported "shortage" of Black men today, many Black women are again choosing to marry across class lines. This can create a number of issues. The following couple illustrates this conflict:

Mary and Bill were a young Black couple in their early 30s. Mary was enrolled in professional school, and Bill had completed his high school education. Bill had a somewhat erratic job history and had many "dreams" that Mary became involved in fantasizing about. During her school years, Bill was very supportive. He worked in a factory and supported her. As her formal training was nearing completion, however, Bill became increasingly more agitated and angry with her. Mary withdrew from him and began to complain, for the first time, about the discrepancy in their careers and lives. Their work in couples therapy involved a number of levels. First, helping them to face their expectations of each other early in their relationship was given priority in the beginning of treatment. Mary was able to admit that she had never really accepted Bill for himself, but had married a dream of his "potential." Bill was able to acknowledge conflicting expectations regarding their relationship. On the one hand, he liked the idea that Mary would be able to contribute a great deal to the relationship; on the other hand, he had some very traditional expectations in terms of male–female interactions. He became very frightened as Mary approached achievement of her personal career goals. Bill's own fears of failure were confronted and he was able to ask her help in achieving his goals. They were able to renegotiate their relationship and the role expectations between them. Each person was helped to accept the other for what he or she was rather than as fantasy figures.

Multigenerational Transmission Issues in Black Couples

Bowen (1976) has identified a multigenerational transmission process that exists in all families (see also Chapter 3). By paying close attention to this process for Black couples the therapist can help them to clarify the ways in which they are repeating in their own relationships issues that were unresolved in their families of origin. In Black families, because of the frequency of "family secrets" that are highly toxic and never discussed, this becomes particularly important. For many Black couples, the knowledge that these repetitions are occurring together with careful "coaching" with their spouse and their therapist can lead to an ability to resolve the conflicts with their own extended family members and avoid the reenactment of these difficulties in their own relationships. The following example clarifies this pattern:

Art and Carol were a Black couple in their 40s. They had three children and had been together for about ten years. Theirs was a very volatile relationship that although not physically abusive, could quickly dissolve into loud angry verbal battles. Since they had never developed strategies for resolving conflicts, their antagonism persisted. Art, a businessman who made a reasonable salary, had not been able to fully support the family in the last 2 years because of a rather expensive cocaine habit.

The couple at first colluded to keep his drug dependency a secret from the therapist. Because of his erratic behavior, however, the therapist confronted the issue with the couple and thus opened it for discussion. Carol became very anxious during this session and was finally able to share that Art's behavior had frightened her because her father had been an alcoholic. This fact had been denied for many years by her family of origin. Her father had died approximately 2 years earlier at about the same time in which the couple's relationship began to deteriorate. She reported a sense of anger and helplessness at her mother for not challenging her father and at her father for being so verbally abusive toward her. As a result of these sessions, she finally confronted her mother with these issues and told her of her anger.

In subsequent sessions, she was able to confront Art, ultimately being able to state clearly that she would end the relationship if he did not enter a drug treatment program. Art was at first stunned by her assertiveness and became frightened at the thought of losing the relationship. He entered a program for his chemical dependency and managed to get himself off the drug. Carol learned that her codependent position had supported his drug habit by refusing to confront the issue. She was in fact an "enabler" of his addiction. This was very reminiscent of her mother's position vis-à-vis her father. They then began a long process of rebuilding their relationship on a healthier foundation.

Power Dynamics in Black Couple Relationships

Power dynamics are one of the few areas of Black couple relationships that have received some attention in the literature. Willie and Greenblatt

(1978), Mack (1974), and Middleton and Putney (1970) have all studied the power relationships between Black spouses of varying social classes. They have also compared these issues to those encountered in White families. Willie and Greenblatt (1978) found that, in general, Black families appear to be more egalitarian than White families. This was especially true of many middle-class Black families who were more egalitarian than any other family type. Mack (1974) found social class to be a more powerful factor than race, with working-class husbands of both races having more power than middle-class husbands.

Power is in some ways a complicated dynamic in Black families. Although the aforementioned study by Moynihan (1965) claimed that the power structure of Black families was matriarchal and thus deviant from the rest of American society, many of the studies also mentioned pointed to the frequent incidence of a more egalitarian structure in Black family life due at least in part to economic necessity. Although poor and working-class families of all ethnic groups clearly have to struggle with financial burdens, the socioeconomic stigma associated with being Black and poor is overwhelming for some families. Even as Black families approach a working-class or lower middle-class life-style, the feeling often remains of what Robert Hill has termed "one paycheck away from poverty." Survival has been such a major issue in many working-class Black families that cooperation around this issue has added an egalitarian character to many male–female relationships.

The issue of power in Black couple relationships is greatly affected by the influences of racism and discrimination, particularly in relation to the misuses and abuses of power in these relationships. This experience of racism cuts across all class and educational levels for Black people. Because of this issue, the impact of the pressures of racial discrimination plays a very significant role in the treatment of Black people. Often Black individuals, couples, and families feel powerless in the face of this racism. Therefore, the issue of empowerment is a very prominent one in the treatment process.

Communication Problems

Communication difficulties are one of the most common presenting issues in couple treatment in general, and this clearly is true of Black couples as well. For Black couples, however, communication is complicated by all of the factors discussed above—particularly those in such sensitive areas as suspicion and male role validation. Therapists who have worked with Black couples report that generally part of the difficulty lies in not knowing how to talk to one another. Because of many of the socialization issues previously discussed, it is often very difficult for Black people—especially Black men—to express their feelings directly. Because the expression of emotions is often seen as a sign of weakness, Black women often enter treatment with the complaint that their partners are emotionally unavailable. The therapist's first strategy in this type of situation is to join and connect with each person. Once a relationship of trust is established with both partners, the therapist can begin to explore what each member of the couple has brought to the relationship in terms of past experiences and expectations of each other. The therapist can then gradually begin to place emphasis on feelings. This process has to be handled especially delicately because many Black men may perceive this as the therapist's alignment with the woman. It is essential that the therapist avoid this pitfall, but he or she must do so without failing to help the man see that his wife or mate is truly unhappy. Once the partners' mutual caring can be tapped, their willingness to work on change can be elicited. If the therapist in any way suspects that the man may feel that an alliance is forming between the woman and the therapist, it is important to raise this question directly so that the issue can be addressed and discussed.

Techniques for Enhancing Communication in Black Male–Female Relationships

One of the most important techniques for improving communication in Black male–female relationships involves an educational component. The therapist will often have to use the sessions to help Black couples learn strategies for relating. This is extremely important because many Black people who come for therapy report that they have grown up without experiencing role models for positive male–female relationships. Some have been raised in single-parent homes without a model for this type of interaction. Others have grown up in situations in which they have witnessed angry, hostile, verbal, or physical exchanges as their only model of male–female interaction. Some Black men and women who have grown up in two-parent, intact families have initially reported a "good" relationship between their parents, but have later admitted that they had only a vague sense of their parents' "couple" interactions. Many older Black couples are very child focused and do not, in fact, have much of a couple relationship.

Within this context, couples therapy is often the first time that some Black couples have actually learned about the dynamics of positive intimate relationships. This educational component can be introduced by the therapist in a number of ways. The first concept is that if a relationship or a marriage is to be truly fulfilling for both partners, both must learn to talk about issues. It is important to stress that this includes positive and negative feelings. A very common statement from Black men and women is "Why should I tell her [him] I love her [him]. She [he]knows that." Helping a couple to express tender as well as angry emotions is an important first step. Because of the socialization issues related to the macho interpersonal style discussed above, many Black men want their partners to be more docile, particularly in the area of sexual interaction. Misconceptions about sexuality, particularly female sexual arousal, abound. Many Black men have been taught that sexual fulfillment for a woman comes only through intercourse. It is helpful to change this perception and begin to gradually introduce different ideas into the treatment process.

Many of the therapists interviewed have used this educational approach very successfully with Black couples. The therapist works with couples to help them learn how to listen to one another and truly hear what each partner is saying and feeling. The role of the therapist centers on aiding couples in understanding that they should never assume anything simply because they hear a particular statement from their partner. They should, rather, stop and ask each other, "What do you mean by that?" Couples often make assumptions about each other's feelings and participate in a process of "mind reading," in which each makes assumptions about the partner's feelings without first testing those assumptions by inquiring as to the partner's true feelings.

The same techniques are useful in the area of sexual interaction with Black couples. Both partner can be helped to learn to say, "That feels good," "I like that," or "Please do this" to each other. The therapist should work directly to address the process by which couples can themselves directly address problems in the relationship. Such statements as "I'm not happy about how our relationship has been going and I wonder if you have been feeling that way too" opens the floor for discussion rather than closing off communication by resorting to angry, accusatory statements. For many Black couples, this form of communication and directness in a relationship is very new and uncomfortable. It is, therefore, important to prepare both partners for the discomfort they may feel initially with adopting new patterns of communication. The therapist should state this early in the process but encourage the couple to try out these ideas even though they may initially seem foreign. Once they can push past the newness and their embarrassment aroused by these ways of communicating, they will often feel more at ease both with the process and with each other. Role playing and enactment in sessions have been found to be very useful in helping them try out new ways of relating in the safety and support of the therapeutic scenario.

By exploring the clinical and cultural issues that must be considered in the treatment of Black couples, family and couples therapists alike can gain a better understanding of effective strategies for engaging and working with these couples in therapy. The sociocultural factors in some of the resistance issues that have been introduced are of central importance to the successful implementation of these strategies, particularly as they relate to the socialization of young Black men and women. It is hoped that this perspective will help increase the effectiveness of therapists working with this group. As more Black couples reach out to the mental health community, more intensive research in this clinical area should be forthcoming.

IV

IMPLICATIONS FOR TRAINING AND FUTURE RESEARCH

CHAPTER 14

Implications for Training and Supervision*

Central to the issue of the treatment of Black families is the process of training therapists to do effective work with this population. This chapter will focus on a number of aspects of that training: (1) the role of graduate schools and training programs; (2) the role of formal didactic training on Black culture, family styles, and the broader issues of ethnicity; (3) the need for Black and other minority teachers and supervisors; (4) the concept of the empowerment of therapists through training; (5) the importance of helping therapists to examine their own culture, belief systems, and families; (6) taking trainees out into the community; (7) the concept of supervision and training as an antidote to staff burnout; and (8) the need for administrative support for training and for the implementation of the multisystems model.

THE ROLE OF GRADUATE SCHOOLS
AND TRAINING PROGRAMS

The training described in this book occurred in the field, within clinics and community mental health centers. However, this is extremely late in the process of training for this material to be presented to clinicians. With the possible exception of social workers, most health, mental health, and educational disciplines have relatively little exposure to multisystems issues and cultural and socioeconomic differences in their training programs. Many of the trainees whom I have taught over the years are learning about these issues for the first time in their residencies, internships, field placements, or practica. In the worst scenario,

---

*I would like to acknowledge the contributions of Rozetta Wilmore Schaeffer, A.C.S.W., Frank Dillon, A.C.S.W., Gloria Steiner, Ed.D., and Beth Hill, M.D., to this chapter.

this exposure does not take place until they have completed their training and are working in the field. Our training programs in psychiatry, psychology, medicine, social work, marriage and family therapy, nursing, and pastoral counseling must include this emphasis in their curricula from the outset. The multisystems approach is a viable treatment option and it must be given credibility at the training program level. The issues of ethnicity, including cultural, racial, and socioeconomic similarities and differences, must be included in these early training years. Without this exposure, clinicians arrive in our clinics and hospitals unprepared and unable to cope with the realities of service delivery to minority populations.

I began this book by stating that much of the literature described herein received only one printing and can now be obtained largely through libraries. Our university-based training programs are in a position to build their libraries around this topic and pull together a much-needed resource for their students.

FORMAL DIDACTIC TRAINING ON BLACK CULTURE AND ETHNICITY

In addition to the emphasis on broader training in family therapy and multisystems approaches, it is important that any program that trains therapists to work with families include formal instruction on cultural components. This should pertain to *all* courses and not just those with an ethnicity focus. This book and others like it can serve as texts for such programs and can be used to expose therapists to the diversity of family issues and presentations among Black families who come for treatment. Clearly such a program should discuss such vital areas as extended family systems, informal adoption, cultural and political values, and religious or spiritual orientation. It is also important that different socioeconomic groups among Black families be discussed—including poor families, two-parent and single-parent families, middle-class families, and upper-middle-class families. The issues are different in many cases and these differences should be taught. Most importantly, therapists should be encouraged to use this cultural material not to develop rigid stereotypes but to develop hypotheses and questions that they can test out with each new family. Only then can they truly allow Black people to "teach" them about their families.

There should also be an emphasis on the broader issues of ethnicity and a comparative course discussing differences and similarities between other cultural groups. There is also a need for formal seminars, grand rounds, colloquia, and so forth that can bring in experts on different cultural topics and groups into the training program on a regular basis.

THE NEED FOR BLACK AND OTHER MINORITY TEACHERS AND SUPERVISORS

In order for this training process to be both real and effective, schools of psychology and social work, family therapy training programs, clinical, school, child, and community psychology internships, social work practicum sites, psychiatry residency programs, and nursing training programs must include Black and other minority teachers and supervisors. These individuals can then serve as role models and bring a wealth of the kind of first-hand cultural material that is so valuable to those in training in this field. The more cultural diversity that can be established in the faculty, the more an openness about the discussion of these issues can be maintained.

There is a growing number of Black psychologists, social workers, psychiatrists, and nurses who can be tapped for their expertise. Community members can also be brought in as consultants on specific topics.

In addition, training programs can make a special effort to recruit Black and other minority trainees. This will help insure for the future a larger number of minority professionals specifically trained to work with inner-city populations. There must also be more of a cross-fertilization, with clinicians who have worked with Black and other minority populations being asked to teach in our university-based programs. By the same token, it would be very helpful for professors in the universities to visit these clinics, hospitals, and community mental health centers to be kept abreast of current needs and realities. The following sections on the supervisory process are relevant to university-based as well as on-site training programs.

EMPOWERMENT OF CLINICIANS THROUGH SUPERVISION AND TRAINING

Thus far, this book has focused on the process of empowering Black families through treatment. Just as empowerment is a concept of great import in treatment, it is a component essential to training programs for all family therapists and other mental health disciplines. Within this training context, empowerment takes the form of facilitating the development of the therapist's use of self via an understanding of his or her own culture, of cultures different from his or her own, and of his or her ability to serve as an agent of change. The central concept here is the belief that our work can make a difference for the families we treat.

The initial experience of clinicians of all disciplines who come to learn to work with Black families, particularly at many of our inner-city clinics, hospitals, mental health centers, and agencies is that of feeling overwhelmed, helpless, ineffective, and powerless to effect change. These families are definitely a challenge for the experienced therapist. For the novice, such common circumstances as initial resistance and suspicion, failure to keep appointments, and inability to follow through on issues can be exceedingly demoralizing and can create a feeling of inadequacy on the part of the therapist.

Many new clinicians (and some "old timers") frequently experience a sense of cognitive dissonance. They may have a great deal of knowledge and training to draw from their educational experiences as physicians, psychiatrists, psychologists, social workers, nurses, educators and school counselors, and pastoral counselors. They may not, however, have a conceptual framework that allows them to translate this knowledge into effective work with Black families and thus may quickly become overwhelmed. One cannot empower others if one feels powerless.

Within this context supervision and training serve a particular role. They provide a supportive environment in which the trainee can feel free to experiment, to acknowledge successes and failures, to risk, and to struggle with the complex tasks of treatment. The task of supervision and training is therefore a gradual empowerment of clinicians that is brought about by helping them to (1) feel more confident in their ability to treat; (2) understand their own culture, values, and familial background; (3) learn about the cultures of the families they treat; and (4) provide a theoretical multisystems framework within which they can view their work.

The key task of the supervisory process is the empowerment of clinicians via the mobilization of their feelings of confidence and competence in themselves and their work. The role of the therapist throughout this book has been described as a very active, supportive one. Not surprisingly, the role of the supervisor must also be a very active, supportive one. The role of the supervisor in the training process runs parallel in many areas to that of the therapist in working with families. One might visualize this supervisory role as the initial link in the chain of empowerment that is put into motion via the use of techniques similar in many areas to those the trainee will eventually apply in her or his work with Black families. For example, just as I have described in detail the need for the therapist to establish a personal, human connection with families in treatment, so too the supervisor must be willing to make use of her- or himself and her or his own experiences to establish a bond with the beginning therapist. This triggers and encourages the trainee's own use of self with families. Parallels to the multisystems approach to the treatment of Black families described in Chapter 8 include a similarity in structure: As in multisystems therapy with families, not only are there many different systems levels at which the training process occurs, but the process is cyclical rather than linear and training components are often employed simultaneously.

Thus, just as families who present for treatment often need help with their feelings of being overwhelmed and powerless to effect change, so too should trainees be advised of the universality of these feelings and of the support available during the training period. Supervision provides a life raft for the clinician in training. The supervisor may focus initially on the specific cases being handled by the trainee and provide directives and knowledge for the treatment of these cases. This is usually followed by a gradual shift to reviewing and exploring the trainee's own reactions to the family and his or her own understanding and development of active treatment plans. Videotapes and live supervision lend a hands-on experience to the process. This mobilizes therapists (just as it does families), putting them in charge of the process and empowering them with a growing sense of confidence that they can do this work. The instilling of this sense of capability is not an accidental byproduct of the process but is rather the very purpose of supervision. This approach to supervision therefore provides support, encouragement, and a step-by-step "what to do next" view of the therapeutic process, and a framework in which the clinician in training can begin to integrate a tremendous amount of knowledge.

It is important here to emphasize the central role of support and encouragement in this process, in particular because there is a definite multilevel relationship between the support that trainees receive from their supervisors and their ability to "be themselves" in the area of joining, so crucial to effective work with Black families. This support may take many forms. First, the supervisory situation should encourage trainees to feel free to take risks and to verbalize their own reactions to the treatment process and to the families they treat, including feelings of being frustrated and overwhelmed.

Second, just as I have talked throughout this book of the value of "reframing" a family's dynamics in a more positive way, it is important to normalize the process of training. Just as it may be helpful to an overwhelmed young single-parent mother to learn that all parents find the "terrible twos" difficult, it can be a great relief to trainees, who are very eager to learn and do well, to know that everyone struggles with this process.

Third, perhaps the most important contribution of the supervisory role is that of conveying to the trainee a sense of an active involvement and of a supportive presence. This involves having supervisors on the "front lines" in clinics and available to the training clinician on site or by phone when emergencies develop. This active form of supervision also involves "live" forms of supervision, which might take the form of demonstration interviews for a group of trainees, or clinical consultations with a trainee and a family that he or she is treating, allowing the trainee to learn by direct observation and modeling and taking the mystery out of the therapeutic process. Use of one-way mirrors and videotape can be very useful to trainees, provided that supervisors help new clinicians to normalize this for Black families who may be suspicious of these techniques.

Fourth, just as the problem-solving approach is very helpful to many Black families who are learning the treatment process, it is also a very effective training tool. A problem-solving approach can teach the therapist to use the process of problem assessment and solution as a "road map" for work with families. The supervisor can facilitate this process by constantly helping the new clinician to stay focused on problems to be solved and to identify the most important system levels at which interventions should be made. Initially, when learning this approach, therapists can easily drown in the details of the multisystems levels. The supervisory process allows the clinician an opportunity to constantly review the problems being addressed and to plan future strategies. It is very helpful for a supervisor to guide the new clinician in charting the progress of treatment and therapeutic change, an activity that can be an essential aid in working with Black families because progress may at times be painfully slow. This is particularly true when time is needed to engage resistant family members and/or cumbersome outside systems and bureaucracies.

The fifth aspect of this form of supervision involves an important aspect of empowerment: the development of the therapist's belief in his or her self and his or her own skills. This process involves an affirmation of developing skills and a conscious "weaning" from the step-by-step directive process that characterizes the earlier phases of supervision. Once again, this clearly parallels a process that has been described throughout this book vis-à-vis work with Black families, that is, establishing and giving positive feedback on a family's areas of strength. With new clinicians, this involves a continual process of acknowledgment of his or her own growth. Increasingly during this period, the trainee is encouraged and expected to take charge of the direction of the case with support from the supervisor. Gradually, as the trainee grows in confidence, this support takes the form more of a presence—a resource to be tapped when necessary—rather than of a step-by-step instruction.

In the completion phase of the training process, the emphasis in training is on filling in the gaps in learning and "fine tuning" the therapist as the instrument of change. More in-depth reading in family therapy and in cultural issues can be very useful at this phase. There is a shift once again in the use of supervision. The therapist and supervisor can now withdraw from a week-to-week monitoring of the treatment process and focus on reviewing and exploring failures and successes in treatment and learning from mistakes.

THE CULTURAL COMPONENT: THE THERAPIST'S OWN CULTURE AND FAMILY

A very important part of the process of training clinicians to work with Black families requires that they explore their own culture and family including beliefs, values, and biases (see also Chapter 6). Early in every training year, new trainees at our community mental health center are asked to collect material for and to construct their own genograms. It is requested that they seek out other family members and gain other perspectives on their family. For many new clinicians this is a very special and helpful part of the training process. A number have confided in me years later that it was an important catalyst in their own development as a clinician. The material gleaned from these genograms can be useful on many levels.

On a very personal level, it can help the therapists and their supervisors be aware of their particular areas of vulnerability when working with families and of their own countertransference. In group supervisory or training sessions it begins the process of using and sharing oneself with one's colleagues. The sharing of the therapists' own cultures is, in my experience, the most exciting and vibrant way to dispel stereotypes and to convey the notion of cultural diversity. As each trainee presents her or his own family, the concept that there is no such thing as *the* Black family, *the* Jewish, Irish, Italian, or Hispanic family becomes extremely clear. Again, this is an active, involved model of training. It is most effective if the supervisors or trainers begin by sharing their families and culture with their trainees.

As is explored at length in Chapter 6, this training model requires all of us to struggle actively with our own values, beliefs, and biases. In ethnicity training groups and seminars we have worked to help trainees struggle with the subjective nature of their own processes. Falicov (1988) has addressed the issue of helping clinicians to learn to think culturally in their family therapy training. McGoldrick, Pearce, and Giordarno (1982) have summarized a number of questions that are salient to this process:

> In training groups we often ask participants to (1) describe themselves ethnically, (2) describe who in their family experience influenced their sense of ethnic identity, (3) discuss which groups other than their own they think they understand best, (4) discuss which characteristics of their ethnic group they like most and which they like least, (5) discuss how they think their own family would react to having to go to family therapy and what kind of approach they would prefer. (p. 27)

This type of exploration takes the process of training to another level, that of the classification of values and biases that we have toward our own ethnic group and toward the ethnic groups of others. Because of the group discussion of these sensitive, personal issues, the therapist learns to treat these issues sensitively with client families. It also establishes group support for the exploration of the therapist's own countertransference to family members and his or her vulnerable areas as a therapist. If this is done supportively, it helps to foster cohesion in the training group and establishes a strong peer supervision network. This support is essential for working with family systems different from one's own.

THE USE OF VIDEOTAPES AND ONE-WAY MIRRORS

The family therapy field has pioneered the use of videotapes and one-way mirrors as training techniques. These models are consistent with the active model of supervision described above. They are particularly useful in developing cultural sensitivity because this often has a great deal to do with developing a personal style that can put families of many different cultures at ease and promote interaction. In addition to teaching family systems techniques, the use of videotapes and one-way mirrors can help to sensitize the clinician to how he or she is perceived by families and to maximize the therapist's use of self in the treatment process. As has been discussed, this is extremely important in work with Black families because they are seldom impressed by titles and require a personal connection and trust before they can open themselves up to a therapist and the treatment process.

Role Playing

Role playing is an invaluable tool for training therapists to work with Black families. This is particularly true if it is done as a training exercise with other staff or trainees and a supervisor. Different staff or trainees can be asked to play the parts of specific members of a Black family. It can be useful if they sometimes enact hypothetical cases. As training proceeds, it is particularly useful to enact actual case scenarios of families that staff or trainees are treating and that the group has viewed on videotape. The supervisor can then act out the responses that she recalls from watching the trainee conduct a session on videotape, so that the trainee can see clearly how Black families respond to her or him (Hunt, 1987). Sometimes the supervisor can enter the family and play the role of a particularly hesitant family member. A useful scenario regarding Black families is to help trainees deal with the anger of family members without becoming defensive, attacking, withdrawing, or chasing the family away from treatment.

The other useful practice in these role-playing training sessions is for the therapist to freeze the process periodically and ask the "family" or the "therapist," who are played by trainees, to share their reactions, feelings, conflicts, comfort, discomfort, and so on. Harry Aponte in live training sessions has demonstrated how this process can be used as a means for values clarification and as a way of uncovering and then getting past stereotypes. This is particularly useful in working with Black families where racial issues can considerably complicate this process.

BEYOND THE IVORY TOWER: TAKING TRAINEES OUT INTO THE COMMUNITY

One of the most important aspects of training clinicians to work in minority communities, particularly inner-city ones, is the need to expose them to these communities. This can be accomplished by taking them on a riding and walking tour of the city or community in which they will be working. Therapists should also be taken to eat at local restaurants and shop at local stores. It is important that new therapists, especially those from middle-class backgrounds who will be working with low-income families, be taken to visit and see where their clients live. A walk through an inner-city housing project may be a very new experience for a therapist. If this can be done in the summer when people are out on the streets it can truly be a learning experience.

Identifying individuals in the agency or clinic and in the community who can serve as resources can also be very helpful to trainees. Ministers and their church communities are important parts of such a resource network; if a relationship can be established with active ministers in the community, arrangements can often be made for therapists to visit churches.

The Need for Home Visits and Outreach

One of the most important aspects of treating Black families, particularly extended families, has to do with the willingness of therapists to make home visits. This is particularly important given the reluctance of key members of those families to enter clinics. Trainees need encouragement and active training in this technique; supervisors should be willing to accompany them initially and to help model the appropriate way to enter and respect a family's home. This is, of course, a very controversial point in the mental health field and one that generates a great deal of resistance from supervisors and trainees alike. In my experience, it is one of our most important therapeutic and training tools because it exposes trainees in a systematic fashion to the home life of Black families.

Trainees and supervisors often express fear of entering homes in inner-city neighborhoods that are perceived as dangerous. This perception can be accurate and needs to be discussed and respected. Precautions need to be taken for the therapist's safety, including a "buddy system" where another therapist or supervisor who knows the community well will go along.

Black families themselves are frequently very sensitive to the issue of a White therapist entering their home or community. When this is openly discussed with the family or family member before the home visit, arrangements can often be made for a family member to pick up or meet the therapist and serve as a guide in entering the community. Often this is the most positive approach and can quickly sensitize the therapist to the family's experience in their community.

FORMAL TRAINING IN THE MULTISYSTEMS MODEL

For many years in the mental health field, formal training in multisystems work with agencies and institutions has been limited to the field of social work. For family therapists of other disciplines to treat Black families effectively—particularly poor, inner-city families—this exposure must be incorporated formally into the training model and the didactic experience. A formal course series or lecture that focuses on key agencies within the community is essential. These might include welfare, child welfare, housing, courts, police, schools, special education and child study teams, hospitals, or other health and mental health services. The most useful way to present this material is through case vignettes and actual videotaped instruction.

Another extremely important component of the training involves again leaving the ivory tower of the clinic setting and visiting these agencies. The clinic director might make arrangements for the trainees to meet with the director or a supervisor at the child welfare agency, for example, to discuss the kinds of cases that they refer. A judge may be willing to have trainees sit in on a court session. A school principal at a school whose children are serviced by the clinic may be approached about introducing the trainees to his staff in order to facilitate future interventions. Our students also visit a major inpatient children's psychiatric hospital with whom we have a referral relationship, as well as a sexual abuse unit in a local hospital that frequently refers to our clinic. This process is an important way of establishing and maintaining good working relationships and openness of communication with other agencies. When family therapists are new to this type of outreach, it is very helpful for the supervisor to attend meetings with representatives of different agencies or to become a resource person for the clinician in the process of establishing contacts in other institutions.

THE MULTIDISCIPLINARY INTAKE TEAM AS A TRAINING MODEL

Cross-fertilization in the mental health field between different disciplines and approaches is an important aspect of the treatment of Black families. One way to accomplish this is by the use of multidisciplinary intake teams in which all new cases are presented and discussed by trainees, clinic staff, and supervisors of various disciplines—including psychiatrists, psychologists, social workers, nurses, teachers and educators, intake workers, mental health specialists, and paraprofessionals. This kind of exposure and input is invaluable as a training tool. It brings together the wealth and variety of experiences provided by these different disciplinary backgrounds, and often, cultural groups in the discussion of a particular case, thus allowing for more effective treatment planning. It is another opportunity for staff members and trainees in a training program to learn from each other and exchange strategies and ideas. It also provides an opportunity to incorporate other treatment approaches, including psychoanalytic and behavioral veiwpoints, with a family system model. This coalition approach also provides an excellent resource for the sharing of information about community supports that can aid particular families in crisis.

SUPERVISION, SUPPORT, AND TRAINING
AS AN ANTIDOTE TO STAFF BURNOUT

At many training programs within clinics, hospitals, medical schools, internships, residencies, and practicum sites, great emphasis is placed on educating trainees of various disciplines. Often, however, the staff who provide the backbone of an agency, hospital, or clinic are neglected in the training process.

Family therapy is a field in which a body of clinical knowledge and literature is just beginning to be written. The relative newness of family therapy as a field of research and practice makes it all the more essential that clinicians working in the field have access to ongoing support, supervision, learning, and exposure. Many clinicians discover that after rich in-depth training during their internships, practica, and residencies, they are left to "fend for themselves" as staff clinicians. This is not only unfortunate but also counterproductive because working with Black extended families and various other systems requires an active clinician who expends a great deal of energy in the process. The work can be overwhelmingly demanding and draining if the staff is not sufficiently supported. Staff burnout is a frequent complaint of staff members in inner-city clinics and community mental health centers.

There are many rewards for family therapists who work with Black families. Applying systems principles and producing change in complex family structures can be an exciting process. It is, however, a constantly evolving model and, as stated above, an extremely demanding one. Therefore, as an antidote to burnout, staff must also be "fed" by seminars and training opportunities that update their knowledge about cultural issues and family therapy and systems approaches. The ongoing process of clinical supervision is also an extremely important form of nurturing for staff and faculty as well as for trainees. It provides a support that is available in helping the therapist stand back from a complex family or system and analyze its structure.

The development of a peer support group among staff can also offer an essential support system for clinicians working with inner-city populations. Just as we need to encourage the development of support networks for the families that we see, we also need to develop them for ourselves as trainees and therapists. Staff members should recognize that they do not necessarily need outside "experts" to learn, but can learn and teach each other a great deal. Many agencies and clinicians have no regular group or forum for staff to meet and exchange their experience in working with Black and other minority families. There is a great need for this structure because of the sharing of these staff's cultural backgrounds and the experiences it allows. Hines (1988) recommends a team approach in which a small group of clinicians might work together with certain families:

> It is undoubtedly a rare therapist who has not faced moments of doubt about such work. Even when families are successfully engaged, they may leave treatment without termination interviews only to reemerge on the agency's rolls after another crisis. Therapists can be assisted by supervision to see this revolving-door phenomenon as an opportunity to help families to reach higher levels of functioning at various stages rather than as treatment failure. (p. 541)

Thus, the realization of empowerment that the supervision process facilitates in the therapist is particularly crucial for staff clinicians at all levels of experience. It continues to provide support and refueling in what can be a very demanding treatment process. In order for this to occur on a regular basis, there must be administrative support for training within clinics and mental health centers and for implementation of the multisystems approach.

ADMINISTRATIVE SUPPORT FOR STAFF TRAINING AND FOR THE IMPLEMENTATION OF THE MULTISYSTEMS MODEL

If training is to provide the antidote to burnout described above, it must occur on a regular basis with clear administrative support within the clinic setting. There is no doubt that it can keep a staff energized and highly productive in this work. To do this kind of work, however, clinicians require other types of administrative support. For example, the home visits, outreach, and multisystems involvement described in this book can take a very personal toll on staff clinicians. Hines (1988) recommends other ways in which administrative support can be used to counteract staff burnout. She suggests flexible administrative support that takes into account the hours a clinician devotes to a particular case rather than simply requiring that a number of cases be seen. There must also be administrative support for outreach. It is an indictment of the mental health system that dedicated clinicians must make home visits on their "lunch hours," early in the morning, or late in the evening because they do not have administrative support for doing this during work hours.

I was very surprised to discover that there are still clinics in this country which do not have evening hours so that families and extended families can be seen. This type of multisystems work requires a great deal of flexibility on the part of the clinician. By the same token, it requires administrative flexibility. It may necessitate a "comp time" program where a clinician who works a number of evenings per week is given time off for these services. I have seen good, competent, caring clinicians burn out because this administrative support was never provided.

The multisystems model has major implications for the ways in which we provide services to Black and many other minority populations. First, it requires a more flexible intake process. This process allows time for joining and connecting with families who are very new to and often suspicious of the treatment process. There must be administrative support for a new type of intake form which asks the "real questions" such as "who lives in the household?" and "what extended family members are involved?" There must also be support for training in this new approach. Clinicians often find themselves in conflict with their clinic administration if they postpone information gathering until the joining and problem solving stages have been addressed. There must be an understanding on the part of administrators that our intake forms may have informational gaps until trust has been established with a family. We lose a large number of Black families, particularly in inner-city mental health centers, because of the rigidity of our intake policies.

There must also be administrative support for the hiring of Black and other minority clinicians to work in agencies and clinics which serve this population. This commitment gives a very clear message to the communities we serve.

In order to establish outreach to other social service agencies, schools, churches, parent and community groups, administrative support is also necessary. These contacts should be made at the clinic or hospital or mental health center level. In some clinics, there are positions of community liaisons whose function it is to build these bridges and create a central resource file. This would greatly enhance the work of individual clinicians and improve service delivery to Black and other populations. Each individual clinician would not have to reinvent these contacts but could quickly help the family to address a system problem more directly.

EMPOWERMENT THROUGH SELF-DETERMINATION

Clinicians, in my experience, often become overwhelmed and discouraged when we discuss the need for administrative interventions and reorientation in university-based and on-site training programs. The focus must be kept on the obligation of these programs to provide training and support. However, it is important to remember that you do not have to wait for this training to "trickle down" from the top.

Empowerment begins with you. The training process described herein grew out of the efforts of a number of supervisors, staff, and trainees. We tried new ideas, acknowledged our successes and failures, learned from our mistakes, and sought to support each other through this process. We went to conferences and learned and shared our ideas. Do not wait to be given this training, create it. Find a support system of other peers and begin working on change. Try out this approach with the Black families you treat and test its relevance with other ethnic groups.

This book is intended as a beginning. It summarizes my own clinical experiences and those of clinicians whom I have supervised. To the degree that it gives each of you the right to insist upon and to create your own training process, to develop your own intervention strategies, to network with clinicians at other agencies, to explore your own theories, and to follow your own cultural hunches, it has more than accomplished its task.

CHAPTER 15

Conclusion and Implications for Future Clinical Work and Research

This book has presented a number of challenging concepts that can increase our effectiveness in working with Black families. Here I wish to review and summarize the important issues raised and point to directions for future work in this area.

The most central underlying theme of this book is the concept of empowerment. It has been presented here in two ways: (1) the empowerment of Black families through a multisystems treatment approach to produce change in their lives and (2) the empowerment of clinicians by providing them with the tools to work effectively with these families. This concept is one of the most important contributions that this book can make.

Over the years, when I have made presentations at conferences, I have met many well-meaning clinicians and practitioners of all disciplines—including family therapists, psychiatrists, psychologists, social workers, nurses, physicians, teachers, educators and pastoral counselors—who desperately wanted to learn to treat Black families effectively. Many felt, however, that they did not have the tools to do so. A large number of these clinicians were burdened by heavy caseloads and lack of training and were prime candidates for burn out. I have written this book for you—the dedicated service providers—who need tools with which to accomplish a much needed job. It is intended as a curriculum resource for training programs in all mental health and educational disciplines and as a tool for teachers of family therapy. It is also a handbook for those on the "front line" of service delivery to all Black families. With this in mind, I have stressed clinical case examples and the need to conceptualize treatment as a multisystems approach. In my own personal experience, it is these skills that are most needed by and useful to those directly involved in this work. This book, therefore, is a clinical and not a research text. It is my hope, however, that it will generate theoretical and research questions for years to come. There is definitely a need for more studies that demonstrate empirical rigor in the clinical and family therapy field, particularly relating to Black and other minority families. It would also be especially gratifying if graduate students interested in those issues were to find meaningful dissertation and thesis projects from the material presented here. This book is intended as a summary of what we currently know about the treatment of Black families. It is my hope that it is only a starting point that will inspire more discussion and debate in the clinical field.

I have also written this book for and dedicated its analyses to the many different Black families who need our services. This work has provided a conceptual understanding of their needs and has captured the similarities as well as the diversity that exists among Black families. Above all, it has been about identifying the strengths in these families and utilizing them in therapy. Within this context, the cultural strengths and survival skills presented here are a lens through which we can assess functional as well as dysfunctional patterns in Black families. It provides a model of the changes toward which we are working in the therapeutic process. If we know what well-functioning Black extended families or single-parent families are like, we shall have a clearer picture of how to produce that change and accomplish our treatment goals.

Related to this issue, many times when I have spoken to predominantly Black audiences, individuals have approached me at the end of a presentation and shared how validated they felt to hear their own family patterns such as extended families, informal adoptions, and church families described in terms of their strengths. This book will continue to provide that validation to a wider audience of Black people.

Another issue that has been repeatedly addressed is that of racism and the impact of socioeconomic realities. If we are to work effectively with Black families, we must confront the issues of racism as well as the crippling poverty of many Black people. We cannot pretend that these racial issues are not part of the treatment process or that they disappear as a Black family moves up the socioeconomic ladder. We cannot take refuge in a class not race approach. We must recognize both. It is important to remember that even if the therapist does not perceive race or racism as an issue, it is certainly an ever-present reality for many Black families. Our acknowledgement that racism and class issues still exist in spite of the tremendous gains of the last 20 years allows us to empower ourselves and the Black families we treat to fight against them and to counteract their effects.

Another important theme that this book has stressed is that "there is no such thing as *the* Black family." Far more work needs to be done to document the diversity among Black families and the range of attitudes, behaviors, and cultural values. More work needs to be done to clarify geographic and cultural differences. As mentioned in Chapter 1, the case examples in this book are drawn primarily from a Northern urban sample of both inner city and middle-class Black families. Further discussion of urban versus rural differences and Northern versus Western versus Southern distinctions by the therapists from other parts of the country would be useful. In addition, West Indian families are a group of Black families that have settled in large numbers in the northeast United States, particularly New York, Miami, and Canada and who have received very little attention in the clinical and research literature. Although they share some similarities with Black Afro-American families, it would be a serious error to assume that all the issues presented in this book apply to a West Indian family as well. There is also a great deal of cultural diversity among these families, many of whom originated from different Caribbean islands in the West Indies. African families who have immigrated to this country since World War II constitute another group of Black families which have been virtually ignored in the literature.

Throughout this process, I have reiterated my concern that the cultural and clinical material presented here not be taken as a set of stereotypes that must be rigidly applied to all Black families. I am acutely aware that this material can be misinterpreted or misused in this way. Rather, as I have stated throughout, it is my sincere hope that therapists will view this book as presenting a set of hypotheses that can be accepted or rejected by each therapist with each new Black family in treatment. This is in fact the strength of this model, providing as it does a new beginning point for each new therapeutic encounter. It can therefore be useful to the beginning therapist, while also providing a thoughtful, comprehensive summary for the experienced clinician.

There are those in the mental health field who may feel that a book such as this—and ethnicity work in general—is rife with generalizations and that it oversimplifies complex issues. There is no question that this occurs to some degree. When one attempts to delve into areas as complex as culture and race with its differences in terms of social class, geography, and gender, it is indeed very difficult to fully capture the breadth of diversity. It is inevitably necessary to simplify or separate out complex concepts in order to clarify them. In my view, the benefits of this approach far outweigh the disadvantages, provided we are each committed to being vigilant about the dangers of stereotyping. I would wish this book to initiate discussion among clinicians, practitioners, researchers, and Black families, discussion that will sharpen perceptions and force each of us to clarify them further.

The course of writing this book has forced me to examine these issues at a very deep, personal level and to take full ownership of my own beliefs. I truly hope that it will enable others to begin this process for themselves, for it is only then that we can really provide effective service to Black people and to all of the families we treat. This aspect of exploring our own core beliefs, values, stereotypes, and family experiences as a prerequisite to our work with Black families is a very important contribution of this book. These were some of the most difficult sections to write and required a very special level of "soul searching" on my part. I recommend that process highly. It is liberating; it opens up the many parts of ourselves that we need to be able to tap in order to be clinically effective. This liberation allows us to listen freely, use ourselves differently, and interact with others more openly and effectively.

Some readers, after completing this book, will wish for more comparisons with other ethnic groups. The process of clarifying the cultural and clinical issues for Black families was an enormous task. It was never my intent to provide this comparison and it is clearly beyond the scope of this book. McGoldrick, Pearce, and Giordano (1982) have provided some of these comparisons. However, there is a need for far more literature and research exploring similarities and differences between ethnic groups. This will further our understanding of the ways in which we are different and the things that we all share in common.

I have presented the multisystems approach as the treatment model that I have found most effective in providing service delivery to Black families. For years, therapists in the family therapy field have struggled with integrating their family systems work with their original training in individual therapy and the need to interface with other systems and agencies. The multisystems approach provides a conceptual framework for integrating these different levels. It also allows us to broaden our definition of "family" and include the extended family members who are so significant in many Black families. Perhaps most importantly, the multisystems approach allows the therapist to generate options and creates the context in which empowerment can occur. The multisystems approach also has a broad-based relevancy to many other ethnic groups and many other complex treatment situations. Readers of this book must now test its applicability with other cultural and socioeconomic groups. It would benefit the entire field if they would publish their experiences so that we can add to the body of expanding material on this topic.

The multisystems approach also has major implications in terms of planning for ethnically diverse populations and the development and implementation of public policy. It speaks to a clear approach to service delivery for Black and other minority populations and argues for a re-allocation of resources in the direction of creating more agencies and reordering the priorities of existing ones in order to address these culture-specific needs. To the degree that funding is provided, agencies will be able to implement a multisystems approach. When this model is presented, those at the public policy level ultimately raise the question of cost effectiveness. It has been my experience that there is presently a tremendous amount of duplication of services, which is unnecessarily wasteful. For example, in the child guidance model of treatment, a family with five acting-out children might be assigned to five different therapists each of whom might be relating to the parents separately. This is redundant, expensive, and often confuses both the therapist and the family. The validity of these approaches must be with careful comparative research.

The kind of interaction described herein between social service agencies, community service agencies, courts, police, schools, hospitals, and mental health clinics occurred on the micro level because clinicians, supervisors, and clinic administrators worked to create it. This level of cooperation must be mandated on a macro, public policy level so that these various agencies can more effectively provide these services to families. This is necessary if we are to avoid the problem of agencies working at cross purposes.

It is clear that public policy considerations must refocus on the mental health needs of poor, Black, and other minority populations and develop governmental strategies for changing our training and service delivery approaches. There must also be further exploration of the needs of Black families who are not at the poverty level but at other class levels. Although a more extensive exploration of this is beyond the scope of this book, it is urgently needed if change is to occur.

Finally, as I have stressed throughout, it is imperative that the area of ethnicity and the treatment of Black families become an integral part of the curriculum of every training program in family therapy and in every other health, education, and mental health discipline. In the past I have described the work on ethnicity as a pendulum within this field. As recently as 20 years ago it was not viewed as a relevant area of study. This book illustrates the swing of the pendulum to a very specific focus on a neglected ethnic group. It is my hope that the areas presented here will assume a central focus in training and receive full acceptance as a major part of our training approaches. The pendulum will then reach its center and our view of families will be more complete.

References

Adams, C. (1977). The Black family: Implications for social work, education and practice. *Dissertation Abstracts International* (No. 78-03862).

Allen, B. (1982, July). It ain't easy being pinky. *Essence*, 67, 128.

Allen, W. R. (1978, February). The search for applicable theories of black family life. *Journal of Marriage and the Family*, 117–129.

Aponte, H. (1974). Organizing treatment around the family's problems and their structural biases. *Psychiatric Quarterly*, 48, 8–12.

Aponte, H. (1976a). The family-school interview: An ecostructural approach. *Family Process*, 15(3), 303–311.

Aponte, H. (1976b). Underorganization in the poor family. In P. J. Guerin (Ed.), *Family therapy: Theory and practice*. New York: Gardner Press.

Aponte, H. (1978). Diagnosis in family therapy. In C. B. Germain (Ed.), *Social work practice: People and environments*. New York: Columbia University Press.

Aponte, H. (1980). Videotape of a black family in Newark. Prepared during continuing education program on Structural Family Therapy at University of Medicine and Dentistry, New Jersey Medical School, Newark campus.

Aponte, H. (1985). The negotiation of values in therapy. *Family Process*, 24(3), 323–338.

Aponte, H. (1986). If I don't get simple, I cry. *Family Process*, 25(4), 531–548.

Aponte, H., & Van Deusen, J. (1981). Structural family therapy. In A. Gurman & D. Kniskern (Eds.), *Handbook of family therapy*. New York: Brunner/Mazel.

Auerswald, E. (1968). Interdisciplinary versus ecological approach. *Family Process*, 7, 204.

Bagarozzi, D. A. (1980). Family therapy and the black middle class: A neglected area of study. *Journal of Marital and Family Therapy*, 6(2), 159–166.

Bernard, J. (1966). *Marriage and family among Negroes*. Englewood Cliffs, NJ: Prentice Hall.

Billingsley, A. (1968). *Black families in white America*. Englewood Cliffs, NJ: Prentice Hall.

Billingsley, A., & Giovannoni, J. M. (1970). *Children of the storm: Black children and American child welfare*. New York: Harcourt Brace Jovanovich.

Birdwhistell, R. L. (1970). *Kinesis and context: Essays on body motion communication*. Philadelphia: University of Pennsylvania Press.

Blassingame, J. W. (1972). *The slave community: Plantation life in antebellum South*. New York: Oxford Press.

Blood, R., & Wolfe, D. (1969). Negro–white differences in blue collar marriages in a Northern metropolis. *Social Forces, 48*, 59–64.

Bohannan, P. (1964). *Africa and Africans*. New York: American Museum of Science Books.

Bowen, M. (1976). Theory in the practice of psychotherapy. In P. J. Guerin (Ed.), *Family therapy: Theory and practice*. New York: Gardner Press.

Bowen, M. (1978). *Family therapy in clinical practice*. New York: Jason Aronson.

Boyd, N. (1977). *Clinicians' perceptions of Black families in therapy*. Unpublished doctoral dissertation, Teachers College, Columbia University, New York.

Boyd-Franklin, N. (1983). Black family life styles: A lesson in survival. In A. Swerdlow & H. Lessinger, *Class, race, and sex: The dynamics of control*. Boston, MA: G. K. Hall (with Barnard College Women's Center).

Boyd-Franklin, N. (1987). The contribution of family therapy models to the treatment of Black families. *Psychotherapy, 24*(35), 621–629.

Brice, J. (1982). West Indian families. In M. McGoldrick, J. K. Pearce, & J. Giordano (Eds.), *Ethnicity and family therapy* (pp. 123–133). New York: Guilford.

Brisbane, F. L., & Womble, M. (1985–86). Treatment of Black alcoholics. *Alcoholism Treatment Quarterly, 2*, (3/4).

Bronfenbrenner, V. (1977). Toward an experimental ecology of human development. *American Psychologist, 45*, 513–530.

Carter, E. A., & McGoldrick, M. (Eds.). (1980). *The family life cycle: A framework for family therapy*. New York: Gardner Press

Carter, E., & Orfandis-McGoldrick, M. (1976). Family therapy with one person and the family therapist's own family. In P. J. Guerin (Ed.), *Family therapy: Theory and practice*. New York: Gardner.

Cazenave, N. (1979, November). Middle income Black families: An analysis of the provider's role. *Family Coordinator, 28*.

Cedrik X (Clark). (1973). The role of the white researcher in black society: A futuristic look. *Journal of Social Issues, 29*(1), 109–118.

Clark, K., & Clark, M. (1939). The development of self and the emergence of racial identification in Negro preschool children. *Journal of Social Psychology, 10*, 591–599.

Colon, F. (1980). In E. A. Carter & M. McGoldrick (Eds.), *The family life cycle: A framework for family therapy*. New York: Gardner.

Comer, J., & Poussaint, A. (1975). *Black child care*. New York: Simon & Schuster.

Comstock, G. W., & Partridge, K. B. (1980). Church attendance and health. *Journal of Chronic Disease, 25*, 665–672.

Davis, G., & Watson, G. (1983). *Blacks in corporate America*. Garden City, NY: Doubleday.

Deitrich, K. T. (1975). A re-examination of the myth of black matriarchy. *Journal of Marriage and the Family, 37*, 367–374.

Deutsch, M., & Brown, B. (1964). Social influences in Negro–white intellectual differences. *Social Issues*, 27–36.

De Veaux, A. (1982, July). Loving the dark in me. *Essence*, pp. 67, 128.

Du Bois, W. E. B. (1903). *The souls of Black folk.* Chicago: McClurg.

Edwards, H. (1968). Black Muslim and Negro Christian family relationships. *Journal of Marriage and the Family, 30,* 604–611.

Ernst, R., & Hugg, L. (1976). *Black America: Geographic perspectives.* New York: Anchor Books.

Falicov, C. (1988). Learning to think culturally in family therapy training. In H. Little, D. Breunlin, & D. Schwartz (Eds.), *Handbook of family therapy training and supervision,* (pp. 335–357). New York: Guilford.

Franklin, A. J. (1988, February). *Therapeutic support groups for Black men.* Paper presented at the conference of the American Group Psychotherapy Association, New York, NY.

Frazier, E. F. (1950, Summer). Problems and needs of Negro children and youth resulting from family disorganization. *Journal of Negro Education, 276–277.*

Frazier, E. F. (1963). *The Negro church in America.* New York: Schocken.

Frazier, E. F. (1966). *The Negro family in the United States.* Chicago: University of Chicago Press.

Foley, V. (1975). Family therapy with black disadvantaged families: Some observations on roles, communication and technique. *Journal of Marriage and Family Counseling, 1,* 29–38.

Gary, L. (Ed.). (1981). *Black men.* Beverly Hills, CA: Sage.

Gary, L., Beatty, L., Berry, G., & Price, M. (1983, December). *Stable Black families final report.* Report submitted to United Church of Christ Commission for Racial Justice.

Giddings, P. (1983). *When and where I enter.* New York: William Morrow.

Goodman, M. E., & Berman, A. (1970). Tract town children. In C. Willie (Ed). *The family life of Black people* (pp. 203–215). Columbus, OH: Merrill.

Grier, W., & Cobbs, P. (1968). *Black rage.* New York: Basic Books.

Griffith, E. H., English, T., & Mayfield, V. (1980). Possession, prayer and testimony: Therapeutic aspects of the Wednesday night meeting in a black church. *Psychiatry, 43,* 120–128.

Guerin, P. (Ed.). (1976). *Family therapy: Theory and practice.* New York: Gardner.

Guerin, P., & Pendagast, E. (1976). Evaluation of family system and the genogram. In P. Guerin (Ed.), *Family therapy: Theory and practice.* New York: Gardner Press.

Haley, A. (1977). *Roots: The saga of an American family.* New York: Doubleday.

Haley, J. (1973). *Uncommon therapy: The psychiatric techniques of Milton H. Erickson.* New York: W. W. Norton.

Haley, J. (1976). *Problem-solving therapy.* San Francisco: Jossey-Bass.

Hartman, A. (1978). Diagrammatic assessment of family relationships. *Social Casework, 59,* 465–476.

Hartman, A., & Laird, J. (1983). *Family-centered social work practice.* New York: The Free Press.

Henggler, S. W., & Tanormina, J. B. (1980). Social class and race differences in family interaction: Pathological, normative or confounding methodological factors? *Journal of Genetic Psychology, 137,* 211–222.

Herskovits, M. J. (1958). *The myth of the Negro past.* Boston: Beacon Press.

Hill, R. (1972). *The strengths of black families.* New York: Emerson–Hall.

Hill, R. (1977). *Informal adoption among Black families.* Washington, DC: National Urban League Research Department.

Hines, P. M., & Boyd-Franklin, N. (1982). Black families. In M. McGoldrick, J. K. Pearce, & J. Giordano (Eds.), *Ethnicity and family therapy* (pp. 84–107). New York: Guilford.

Hines, P. (1988). The family life cycle of poor Black families. In B. Carter & M. McGoldrick (Eds.), *The changing family cycle: A framework for family therapy* (2nd ed.). New York: Gardner Press.

Hines, P. (personal communication, January 8, 1987).

Hollingshead, A., & Redlich, F. (1958). *Social class and mental illness: A community study.* New York: Wiley.

Holman, A. (1983). *Family assessment: Tools for understanding and intervention.* Beverly Hills, CA: Sage.

Hunt, P. (1987). Black clients: Implications for supervision of trainees. *Psychotherapy, 24*(1), 114–119.

Hyman, H. H., & Reed, J. S. (1969). Black matriarchy reconsidered: Evidence from secondary analysis of sample surveys. *Public Opinion Quarterly, 33,* 346–354.

Jackson, L. B. (1975). The attitudes of black females towards upper- and lower-class black males. *Journal of Black Psychology, 1,* 53–64.

Jahn, J. (1961). *Muntu.* New York: Grove Press.

Jackson, G. (1980). The emergence of a Black perspective in counseling. In R. Jones (Ed.), *Black psychology* (2nd ed.). (pp. 294–313). New York: Harper & Row.

Jensen, A. (1969). How much can we boost IQ and school achievement? *Harvard Educational Review, 39,* 1–123.

Johnson, C. S. (1967). *Growing up in the black belt.* New York: Schocken.

Jones, R. (Ed.) (1980). *Black psychology* (2nd ed.). New York: Harper & Row.

Kardiner, A., & Ovesey, L. (1951). *The mark of oppression.* Cleveland: World Publishing.

King, A. (1969, November). Adolescent perception of power structure in the Negro family. *Journal of Marrige and the Family,* 751–756.

Kinney, E. (1971). Africanisms in the music and dance of the Americas. In R. Goldstein (Ed.), *Black life and culture in the United States.* New York: Crowell.

Kliman, J., & Trimble, D. (1983). Network therapy. In B. Wolman & G. Stricker (Eds.), *Handbook of family and marital therapy.* New York: Plenum.

Knox, D. H. (1985). Spirituality: A tool in the assessment and treatment of Black alcoholics and their families. *Alcoholism Treatment Quarterly, 2*(3/4), 31–44.

Ladner, J. (1971). *Tomorrow's tomorrow: The Black woman.* Garden City, NY: Doubleday.

Lewis, D. K. (1975). The Black family: Socialization and sex roles. *Phylon, 36,* 221–237.

Lewis, J., & Looney, J. (1983). *The long struggle: Well-functioning working-class Black families.* New York: Brunner/Mazel.

Lindblad-Goldberg, M., & Dukes, J. (1985). Social support in black, low-income, single-parent families: Normative and dysfunctional patterns. *American Journal of Orthopsychiatry, 55,* 42–58.

Lindblad-Goldberg, M., Dukes, J., & Lasley, J. (1988). Stress in Black, low-income, single-parent families: Normative and dysfunctional patterns. *American Journal of Orthopsychiatry, 58*(1), 104–120.

Mack, D. (1974). The power relationship in black families and white families. *Journal of Personality and Social Psychology, 39*(3), 409–413.

Madanes, C. (1981). *Strategic family therapy.* San Francisco: Jossey-Bass.

Mathis, A. (1978, November). Contrasting approaches to the study of black families. *Journal of Marriage and the Family,* 667–676.

Mayfield, W. (1972). Mental health in the black community. *Social Work, 17,* 106–110.

Mbiti, J. S. (1969). *African religions and philosophies.* Garden City, NY: Anchor Books.

McAdoo, H. P. (1978). Factors related to stability in upwardly mobile black families. *Journal of Marriage and the Family, 40*(4), 761–776.

McAdoo, H. P. (Ed.). (1981). *Black families.* Beverly Hills, CA: Sage.

McAdoo, H. P., & McAdoo, J. L. (Eds.). (1985). *Black children: Social, educational and parental environments.* Beverly Hills, CA: Sage.

McGoldrick, M. (1982). Normal families: An ethnic perspective. In F. Walsh (Ed.), *Normal family processes* (pp. 399–424). New York: Guilford.

McGoldrick, M., & Gerson, R. (1985). *Genograms in family assessment.* New York: W. W. Norton.

McGoldrick, M., Pearce, J., & Giordano, J. (Eds.). (1982). *Ethnicity and family therapy.* New York: Guilford.

McQueen, A. (1971, Spring). *Incipient, social mobility among poor Black urban families.* Paper presented at Howard University Research Seminar, Washington, DC.

Merton, R. K. (1972). Insiders and outsiders: A chapter in the sociology of knowledge. *American Journal of Sociology, 78,* 9–48.

Middleton, R., & Putney, S. (1970). Dominance in decisions in the family: Race and class differences. In C. V. Willie (Ed.), *The family life of black people* (pp. 16–22). Columbus, OH: Charles E. Merrill.

Minuchin, S., Montalvo, B., Guerney, B. G., Jr., Rosman, B. L., & Schumer, F. (1967). *Families of the slums.* New York: Basic Books.

Minuchin, S. (1974). *Families and family therapy.* Cambridge, MA: Harvard University Press.

Minuchin, S., & Fishman, C. (1981). *Family therapy techniques.* Cambridge, MA: Harvard University Press.

Mitchell, H., & Lewter, N. (1986). *Soul theology: The heart of American Black culture.* San Francisco: Harper & Row.

Moynihan, D. P. (1965). *The Negro family: The case for national action.* Washington, DC: U.S. Department of Labor.

Nobles, W. W. (1974). Africanity: Its role in black families. *The Black Scholar, 5,* 10–17.

Nobles, W. W. (1978). Toward an empirical and theoretical framework for defining black families. *Journal of Marriage and the Family,* 679–688.

Nobles, W. (1980). African philosophy: Foundations for Black psychology. In R. Jones (Ed.), *Black psychology* (2nd ed.) (pp. 23–36). New York: Harper & Row.

Papp, P. (1981). Paradoxes. In S. Minuchin, & C. Fishman (Eds.), *Family therapy techniques*. Cambridge, MA: Harvard University Press.

Parker, S., & Kleiner, R. (1966). Characteristics of Negro mothers and single-headed households. *Journal of Marriage and the Family, 28,* 507–513.

Parnell, M., & Vanderkloot, J. (1989). Ghetto children. In L. Combrinck-Graham (Ed.), *Children in family contexts: Perspectives on treatment*. New York: Guilford.

Pattison, E. M. (1977). A theoretical-empirical base for social system therapy. In E. F. Foulks et al. (Eds.), *Current perspectives in cultural psychiatry*. New York: Spectrum.

Peters, M. F. (1981). Parenting in Black families with young children: A historical perspective. In H. McAdoo (Ed.), *Black families* (pp. 211–224). Beverly Hills, CA: Sage.

Peters, M., & Massey, G. (1983). Mundane extreme environmental stress in family stress theories: The case of black families in white America. *Marriage and Family Review, 6,* 193–218.

Pettigrew, T. (1964). *A profile of the Negro American*. Princeton, NJ: Van Nostrand.

Pinderhughes, E. (1982). Afro-American families and the victim system. In M. McGoldrick, J. K. Pearce, & J. Giordano (Eds.), *Ethnicity and family therapy* (pp. 108–122). New York: Guilford.

Pinkney, A. (1975). *Black Americans*. Englewood Cliffs, NJ: Prentice-Hall.

Pipes, W. H. (1981). Old-time religion: Benches can't say "Amen." In H. McAdoo (Ed.), *Black families* (pp. 54–76). Beverly Hills, CA: Sage.

Rainwater, L. (1965). Crucible of identity: The Negro lower-class family. In T. Parsons & K. B. Clark (Eds.), *The Negro American* (pp. 160–204). Boston: Beacon Press.

Rainwater, L. (1966). Crucible of identity: The Negro lower-class family. *Daedalus, 95,* 172–216.

Riessman, F., Cohen, J., & Pearl, A. (1964). *Mental health of the poor*. Glencoe, IL: Free Press.

Rodgers-Rose, L. (1980). *The Black woman*. Beverly Hills, CA: Sage.

Rose, W. L. (1982). *Slavery and freedom*. New York: Oxford University Press.

Royse, D., & Turner, G. (1980). Strengths of Black families: A Black community's perspective. *Social Work, 25*(5), 407–409.

Sager, C., & Brayboy, T. (1970). *Black ghetto family in therapy. A laboratory experience*. New York: Grove Press.

Sawyer, E. (1973). Methodological problems in studying so-called "deviant" communities. In J. A. Ladner, *Death of white sociology*. Westminster, MD: Random House.

Scanzoni, J. (1971). *The Black family in modern society*. Boston: Allyn and Bacon.

Scheflen, A. E. (1973). *Communicational structure: Analysis of a psychotherapy transaction*. Bloomington, IN: Indiana University Press.

Selvini-Palazzoli, M., Boscolo, L., Cecchin, G., & Prata, G. (1978). *Paradox and counterparadox*. New York: Jason Aronson.

Solomon, B. (1976). *Black empowerment: Social work in oppressed communities*. New York: Columbia University Press.

Speck, R., & Attneave, C. (1973). *Family networks*. New York: Vintage.

Stack, C. (1974). *All our kin: Strategies for survival in a black community.* Copyright © 1974 by Carol B. Stack. Reprinted by Harper & Row, Publishers, Inc.

Staples, R. (1971, February). Toward a sociology of the black family: A theoretical and methodological assessment. *Journal of Marriage and the Family,* 119–138.

Staples, R., & Mirande, A. (1980, November). Racial and cultural variations among American families: A dicennial review of the literature on minority families. *Journal of Marriage and the Family,* 887–903.

Thomas, M., & Hughes, M. (1986). The continuing significance of race: A study of race, class and quality of life in America, 1972–1985. *American Sociological Review, 51,* 830–841.

Thomas, A., & Sillen, S. (1974). *Racism and psychiatry.* Secaucus, NJ: Citadel.

Thompson, C. (1987). Racism or neuroticism: An entangled dilemma for the Black middle-class patient. *Journal of the American Academy of Psychoanalysis,* 15(3), 395–405.

U.S. Bureau of Census. (1985). *Household and family characteristics, March 1970/ 1978/1984.* Current Population Reports (Series P-20, Report Nos. 218, 340, 398). Washington, DC: Government Printing Office.

Walker, A. (1982, July). Embracing the dark and the light. *Essence,* pp. 67, 128 (Reprinted from *Black Scholar,* March–April, 1973).

Weaver, D. (1982). Empowering treatment skills for helping black families. *Social Casework, 6,* 100–105.

White, J. (1972). Towards a black psychology. In R. Jones (Ed.), *Black psychology.* New York: Harper & Row.

White, J. (1984). *The psychology of blacks: An Afro-American perspective.* Englewood Cliffs, NJ: Prentice-Hall.

Williams, L. (1987, July 14). For the black professional: The obstacles remain. *New York Times,* p. A16.

Willie, C. V. (Ed.). (1970). *The family life of black people.* Columbus, OH: Charles E. Merrill.

Willie, C. V. (1974, January). The black family and social class. *American Journal of Orthopsychiatry, 44,* 50–60.

Willie, C. V. & Greenblatt, S. L. (1978). Four classic studies of power relationships in Black families: A review and look to the future. *Journal of Marriage and the Family,* 40(4), 691–696.

Wilmore, G. (1973). *Black religion and Black radicalism.* Maryknoll, New York: Orbis.

Wilson, W. (1980). *The declining significance of race* (2nd ed.). Chicago: The University of Chicago Press.

Wilson, W. (1987). *The truly disadvantaged: The inner city, the underclass and public policy.* Chicago: The University of Chicago Press.

Yearwood, L. (Ed.). (1980). *Black organizations: Issues on survival techniques.* Lanham, MD: University Press of America.

Index